ANZAC'S DIRTY DOZEN

ANZAC'S DIRTY DOZEN

12 MYTHS OF AUSTRALIAN MILITARY HISTORY

EDITED BY
CRAIG STOCKINGS

NEWSOUTH

A NewSouth book

Published by
NewSouth Publishing
University of New South Wales Press Ltd
University of New South Wales
Sydney NSW 2052
AUSTRALIA
newsouthpublishing.com
#anzacdirty12

© in this edition Craig Stockings 2012
© in individual chapters is retained by the chapter authors
First published 2012

10 9 8 7 6 5 4 3 2 1

This book is copyright. Apart from any fair dealing for the purpose of private study, research, criticism or review, as permitted under the Copyright Act, no part may be reproduced by any process without written permission. Inquiries should be addressed to the publisher.

National Library of Australia Cataloguing-in-Publication entry
   Title: Anzac's dirty dozen: 12 myths of Australian military history/edited by Craig Stockings.
   ISBN: 978 174223 288 1 (pbk.)
   Subjects: Australia – History, Military.
   Australia – Armed Forces – History.
   Other Authors/Contributors: Stockings, Craig, 1974–
   Dewey Number: 355.00994

Design Josephine Pajor-Markus
Cover Design by Committee
Cover images Figure on left: © Photo: IWM (IWM PST8244); figures on right: Mitchell Library, State Library of NSW (Posters/World War 1939–1945/6)

CONTENTS

Acknowledgments *vii*

Contributors *viii*

Introduction: Myths and Australian Military History *1*

1 Australian military history doesn't begin on Gallipoli *11*
   Craig Wilcox

2 The 'superior', all-volunteer AIF *35*
   John Connor

3 What about New Zealand? The problematic history of the Anzac connection *51*
   Chris Clark

4 Other people's wars *73*
   Craig Stockings

5 'They also served': Exaggerating women's role in Australia's wars *100*
   Eleanor Hancock

6 The nonsense of universal Australian 'fair play' in war *112*
   Dale Blair

7 The unnecessary waste: Australians in the late Pacific campaigns *138*
   Karl James

8 Lost at sea: Missing out on Australia's naval history   *165*
    Alastair Cooper

9 'Landmark' battles and the myths of Vietnam   *186*
    Bob Hall and Andrew Ross

10 The myth that Australia 'punches above its weight'   *210*
    Albert Palazzo

11 Critical reflections on the Australia–US alliance   *235*
    Michael McKinley

12 Monumental mistake: Is war the most important thing in Australian history?   *260*
    Peter Stanley

Epilogue   *287*

Notes   *293*

Index   *323*

ACKNOWLEDGMENTS

First and foremost I must acknowledge the authors of the various chapters of this book. The quality of their scholarship was matched by a spirit of co-operation which made the job of editing – without exaggeration – a pleasure. As readers familiar with Australian military historiography will be aware, the list of contributors to this book represents a large portion of the leading edge of scholarship in this field. I am personally and professionally indebted to a number of them. Thank you for being part of this project.

I would also like to express my gratitude once again to Phillipa McGuinness and the team at NewSouth Publishing. After having completed a number of projects with this publisher, I was, this time, unsurprised by the continuing vision, expertise, skilled and friendly support provided.

Further thanks to the long list of others who have assisted in any way in this project. I trust the product matches your faith and expectations.

Craig Stockings

CONTRIBUTORS

Dr Dale Blair is a freelance historian currently teaching at Deakin University, Burwood campus. His areas of academic interest include Australia's involvement in World War I at home and abroad. His most recent publication is a battle narrative and analysis, *The Battle of Bellicourt Tunnel: Tommies, Diggers and Doughboys on the Hindenburg Line, 1918* (2011). Other publications include his study of the 1st Battalion, AIF, *Dinkum Diggers* (2001), and his study of illegitimate killing in World War I entitled *No Quarter* (2005).

Dr Chris Clark is head of the Office of Air Force History for the Royal Australian Air Force and a visiting fellow at the University of New South Wales, Australian Defence Force Academy. Although his interest since 2004 has been primarily on the history of air power, he has written extensively on broader aspects of Australian defence over many years. His *Encyclopaedia of Australia's Battles* (3rd edition 2010) continues to be a standard reference.

Dr John Connor lectured in history at the Menzies Centre for Australian Studies, King's College, London, before taking up his current position as a senior lecturer in History at the University of New South Wales, Australian Defence Force Academy. His first book, *The Australian Frontier Wars 1788–1838* (2002), was shortlisted for the Royal United Services Institute's Westminster

Medal for Military Literature. His most recent book, *Anzac and Empire: George Foster Pearce and the Foundations of Australian Defence* (2011), is a biography of the Australian defence minister during World War I.

ALASTAIR COOPER is a public servant and Navy Reserve officer with an abiding interest in Australian naval and military history. He was a contributing author to *The Royal Australian Navy*, the centenary history of the RAN, and is currently an interviewer for the RAN Oral History Collection.

DR BOB HALL is a visiting fellow at the University of New South Wales, Australian Defence Force Academy. He is a Vietnam veteran and author of *Combat Battalion: The Eighth Battalion in Vietnam* (2000). Together with Dr Andrew Ross he is working on an Australian Research Council funded study of the combat performance of the 1st Australian Task Force in Vietnam.

DR ELEANOR HANCOCK is an associate professor of History at the University of New South Wales, Australian Defence Force Academy. She has published on the history of the German war effort in World War II and on issues relating to women in the armed forces. She is the author of *The National Socialist Leadership and Total War 1941–1945* (1991); and *Ernst Röhm: Hitler's SA Chief of Staff* (2008).

DR KARL JAMES has been a historian at the Australian War Memorial, Canberra, since 2006, where he has specialised in Australia's involvement in World War II. In 2011, he curated the memorial's special seventieth anniversary exhibition: 'The Rats of Tobruk, 1941'. Karl completed his doctoral thesis on the Bougainville campaign of 1944–1945, at the University of Wollongong.

Dr Michael McKinley is senior lecturer in International Relations and Strategy in the School of Politics and International Relations at the Australian National University. He has recently published *Economic Globalisation as Religious War: Tragic Convergence* (2007). His current major research projects comprise an analysis of the grand strategic decline of the United States by way of an historical comparison with the pre-Reformation Church, the problems of the neo-liberal university in teaching the subject of terrorism and counter-terrorism, and a comprehensive critique of the Australia–US alliance based on previously excluded historical evidence.

Dr Albert Palazzo is a senior research fellow at the Australian Army's Directorate of Research and Analysis in Canberra. He has written widely on warfare in the modern age and on the Australian Army in particular. His many publications include: *Seeking Victory on The Western Front: The British Army & Chemical Warfare in World War I* (2000); *The Australian Army: A History of its Organisation 1901–2001* (2001); *Defenders of Australia* (2002); *The Third Australian Division; Battle of Crete* (2005); *The Royal Australian Corps of Transport: Australian Military Operations in Vietnam* (2006); and *Moltke to bin Laden: The Relevance of Doctrine in Contemporary Military Environment* (2008). His current project is a book on the Australian Army and the war in Iraq.

Dr Andrew Ross is a visiting fellow at the University of New South Wales, Australian Defence Force Academy. He is a former analyst with Central Studies Establishment, Defence Science and Technology Organisation. He is the author of *Armed and Ready: The Industrial Development and Defence of Australia 1900–1945* (1995). Together with Dr Bob Hall he is working on an Australian Research Council funded study of the combat performance of the 1st Australian Task Force in Vietnam.

Contributors

DR PETER STANLEY heads the Centre for Historical Research at the National Museum of Australia. Formerly principal historian at the Australian War Memorial, he is an adjunct professor at the Australian National University and a visiting associate professor at the Australian Defence Force Academy. He has written 23 books, mainly in Australian and British military social history, including *Quinn's Post, Anzac, Gallipoli* (2005); *Invading Australia* (2008); *A Stout Pair of Boots* (2008); *Men of Mont St Quentin* (2009); *Bad Characters: Sex, Crime, Mutiny, Murder and the Australian Imperial Force* (2010); the children's novel *Simpson's Donkey* (2011); and most recently *Digger Smith and Australia's Great War* (2011).

DR CRAIG STOCKINGS is a senior lecturer in History at the University of New South Wales, Australian Defence Force Academy. His areas of academic interest concern general and Australian military history and operational analysis. He has recently published a history of the army cadet movement in Australia, *The Torch and the Sword* (2007); and *Bardia: Myth, Reality and the Heirs of Anzac* (2009), a study of the First Libyan Campaign in North Africa 1940–1941.

DR CRAIG WILCOX is a historian who lives in Sydney. His publications include: *For Hearths and Homes: Citizen Soldiering in Australia 1854–1945* (1998); *Australia's Boer War: The War in South Africa 1899–1902* (2002); and *Red Coat Dreaming* (2009), a study of colonial Australia's fascination with the British army. His current projects include an entry on Paul Brickhill for the Australian Dictionary of Biography.

[INTRODUCTION]

MYTHS AND AUSTRALIAN MILITARY HISTORY

Be warned at the very outset that this book may disturb, or even offend. It is, quite purposefully, a challenging collection of essays that, in debunking some of our most resilient misconceptions, goes beyond the controversial *Zombie Myths of Australian Military History*, published in 2010. Both books might be read together in a complementary manner, yet they stand alone in their own right. While they share similarities in style and presentation, *Anzac's Dirty Dozen* is fundamentally different. Where the original *Zombie Myths* chose to examine a number of specific incidents in Australian military history – including Kokoda, the sinking of HMAS *Sydney* II, and Australian involvement in East Timor – this collection of essays takes a bolder thematic approach. This time around we are not so much concerned with laying to rest individual myths. In these twelve chapters we take aim at whole tribes and traditions. The stakes are higher.

Some explanations may be in order for those who have no idea of the kinds of myths we are talking about. The published and public spheres of Australian military history – official publications, popular books and novels, the speeches of Anzac Day and its associated political rhetoric, and the language of public commemoration, for example – are landscapes of legends. But they are also minefields of misconception. Rather than the pursuit of what we might call historical truths, across the length and breadth of Australia's military heritage, from before first European contact to the present day, accuracy and objectivity are often subordinated to a narrative bent on commemoration, veneration, and capturing the essence of idealised 'Australian' virtues. The driving needs to celebrate the deeds of past servicemen and promote conceptions of national identity wrapped in the imagery of war have come to dominate our public discourse. The overarching social and emotional rhetoric of 'Anzac' and the 'digger' are paramount in this regard.

From this foundation myth a whole host of historical misunderstandings has spawned – and they are surprisingly resilient. Many of the myths in question, including those discussed at length within this book (and the original *Zombie Myths* for that matter) share a common set of characteristics. They lack vitality and 'freshness'. They are empowered by misdirected and unquantifiable energies. They appeal to instinct and sentiment more than reason. They shun critique or critical inquiry (as their champions and advocates shun those who attempt it). Although perhaps based on kernels of truth, the myths that permeate our understanding of Australia's military past are for the most part divorced from any sort of rational accuracy or precision. At the same time, the considerable – if slow-witted – inertia of such myths seems to give them a life of their own. Many of the misconceptions of Australian military history have survived the blows landed by academics and historians for decades. Each time an individual 'story' might lurch or stumble for a short time, but then it seems to grow back undiminished. And it's getting worse, because these myths are now aided as never before by blogs, Wikipedia, Anzac supplements in the weekend papers, and bestselling popular histories not always based on archival research.

This is not a harmless phenomenon. The persistent misunderstanding and misrepresentation enshrined in the myths of Australian military history skew proper understandings and interpretations of this nation's military heritage. They warp and twist our perceptions of war. They shape our picture of ourselves in obscuring and inaccurate ways. Moreover, they situate our attitudes to the past falsely, distort our reading of the present and our expectations for the future. They are monsters of the mind.

But do not despair, for there is yet hope. This book is an extended attempt to target some of these cherished myths and to expose them to the light of genuine, analytical scholarship. Reasoned arguments, thorough analysis and critical rigour form the toolbox used by the historians and professional researchers who have written the chapters that follow. As long-lived and resilient as these manifold misconceptions have proven to be, myths are still myths. By exposing them to careful research and analysis, it is possible to separate them from what might be called 'real' Australian military history. This is our hope.

In line with this aim, *Anzac's Dirty Dozen* opens by looking at what is often quite erroneously thought of as the 'beginning': that is, the mistaken notion that the nation's military history began at Gallipoli in 1915. On an intellectual level, most Australians are aware – in the background of their memories – that Australia does have a military past that pre-dates the invasion of Turkey in 1915. On an emotional or sentimental level, however, the story starts at Gallipoli. This mistaken representation, as Craig Wilcox shows in Chapter 1, excludes the fact that for a very substantial period the British Army was the 'Australian' Army. Any notion that it all began at Gallipoli diverts attention for the mass engagement in citizen soldiering in Australia that pre-dated World War I.

Even those with only a passing knowledge or interest in Australia's involvement in the war of 1914–1918 will be certain of one key aspect: the Australian Imperial Force (AIF) was the only all-volunteer army in that war. This presumption is not by chance, as the message has been consistently passed on for generations. General Sir John Monash, commander of the Australian Corps on the Western Front, first made the claim in his 1920 book *The Australian Victories in France*, and it has been an assertion maintained by countless authors, and more recently websites, ever since. The only problem with this important and well-known fact is that it is totally false. As John Connor argues in Chapter 2, the AIF was not the only all-volunteer army in World War I. Importantly, another and perhaps even more insidious myth has developed out of this basic factual error: that the volunteer status of Australian troops in World War I made them inherently superior to their conscript counterparts. This notion too is ready to be put to rest.

One key misinterpretation that grew from Australia's involvement in World War I, and especially the bloodshed of Gallipoli and the Western Front, was the birth of the idea that 'Anzac' exemplifies Australia's bond with our natural brothers-in-arms across the Tasman Sea. In truth, as Chris Clark explains in Chapter 3, this was not at all how the relationship was initially conceived. Before and after Gallipoli, the New Zealanders thought themselves far superior soldiers to the Australians, and they fought very hard to keep their identity separate and distinct from the Australian-dominated Anzac image.

Another popular misconception, cutting across the colonial era and extending right through the twentieth century and beyond, is that Australia has generally been involved in 'other people's wars'. As unnecessary as these wars have been costly, this myth would have it that we have done so either out of unthinking fidelity to great power protectors — Britain or more recently the United States — or as a consequence of being duped or manipulated by these 'big brother' allies. Many authors and commentators have chosen specific wars and sought to demonstrate Australia's mistaken choice to become involved, arguing that decisions were made for the wrong reasons, with incomplete knowledge of circumstances, or under external coercion. Collectively, such sentiments capture perhaps the most widespread misconception of Australian military history. As Craig Stockings demonstrates in Chapter 4, such ideas are fundamentally mistaken.

While it seems Anzac Day is becoming Australia's *de facto* national day, and that Anzac is constructed as our national story, one might think that the greatest apparent problem for such a mythology is its exclusion of half of Australia's population – women. But by twist of perception this is not the case. Somehow, women have managed to be included within the contemporary Anzac paradigm. The idea that Australian women, despite being excluded from almost all aspects of direct experience in twentieth-century conflict, still managed to make an important contribution to the Australian war effort – especially in the two World Wars – has grown dramatically. As appealing as this exaggerated truth might appear, and as useful as it might be to avoid Anzac friction along gendered lines, it is nonetheless an emerging and powerful myth that Eleanor Hancock sets out to challenge and expose it for what it is in Chapter 5.

Dale Blair, in Chapter 6, addresses the equally mistaken notion of Australian ethical or moral exceptionalism in war. 'Australian soldiers are nothing if not sportsmen, and no case ever came under my notice of brutality or inhumanity to prisoners', wrote General Sir John Monash after World War I. There is no doubt a great many Australian servicemen in this and other conflicts have indeed attempted to uphold such chivalrous and sporting notions, and to act fairly and within the bounds of existing conventions or rules of war when called to the service of their country. That this idea applied universally, however, and the suggestion that somehow Australian troops are unique and have unwaveringly applied their 'digger-ethic' of fair play on every battlefield, is simply untrue. Regardless of how uncomfortable an acceptance of Australian atrocities in war might be, or how awkwardly it might sit within the contemporary public's unquestioning veneration of the deeds of past servicemen, it is a part of this nation's military past.

Australia's record in World War II up to 1943 was a proud one. Australian sailors and airmen had fought all over the world, and while its soldiers had endured bitter retreats in Greece and Crete, they had won glory at Tobruk and spearheaded Allied troops at El Alamein. In Papua, Australians fought in some of the worst conditions of the war to wrestle Kokoda, Buna, Gona and Sanananda from the Japanese. During the later phases of the Pacific War, however, the army was left behind, excluded from the Allied recapture of the Philippines and restricted to 'mopping-up' in New Guinea, Bougainville and Borneo. This was a period of disagreement and disappointment – and it has remained so ever since. Time and again veterans, journalists and writers have repeated the notion, almost as a mantra, that Australia's final campaigns in the Pacific were an 'unnecessary war' where lives were wasted needlessly for nothing other than political reasons and in campaigns that did nothing to bring about Japan's surrender any sooner. As Karl James demonstrates in Chapter 7, however, this orthodoxy, which has been such a consistent complaint over time, does not make it true. The idea of an 'unnecessary waste' is an inaccurate and misleading interpretation.

It is certainly unusual, notes Alastair Cooper in Chapter 8, that an island continent like Australia – where the overwhelming majority live on the coastal margins, whose modern incarnation was founded by a navy, and which is as deeply dependent on maritime trade and industry – should have so little naval history. He examines the dearth of naval history in this country, investigates some of the key reasons why such a situation has come about, and offers some subject matter within the limited existing genre of Australian naval history that calls for much greater attention. Australia is missing out on its naval history, Cooper suggests, and it is time for a change.

In Chapter 9, Bob Hall and Andrew Ross set out to correct a set of pervasive and influential myths concerning the experience of Australian soldiers in the Vietnam War. Contrary to dominant popular public conceptions of that war, influenced to their core by Hollywood imagery and imported American representations, Australia's war in Phuoc Tuy Province was never about large-scale 'landmark' battles such as Long Tan. These were aberrations and of little relevance when compared to the more common and significant 'contacts' which characterised the face of battle for the men of the Australian Task Force in Vietnam. In addition, prevailing ideas of how conclusively such battles were 'won' by Australian troops need to be rethought in their fuller political context. Nor do enduring ideas of their adversary's 'owning' the jungle or 'owning' the night have any real resonance or relevance for the Australians in Vietnam; quite the converse. Australia's Vietnam combat experience was not the same as that of the South Vietnamese or the Americans. Nor in many ways was it the war of the silver screen or dominant public memory. It is time to see it and accept it on its own terms.

In Chapter 10, by closely examining Australian involvement in East Timor, Iraq and Afghanistan, Albert Palazzo challenges the recent but misguided claim that Australian servicemen 'punch above their weight'. This institutionalised myth is built on a thin veneer of self-perception and a reputation won by the few rather than by the many. Moreover, it is a dangerous delusion that obscures more than it reveals, and prevents honest internal or external assessment of the Australian Defence Force's true capabilities and weaknesses. It is a tempting cure-all to politicians and policy-makers who seek the comfort and convenience of a force that can be deployed in support of allied operations overseas without having to pay for it. This is not a critique of the training, professionalism and commitment of individual servicemen and women, but rather a critical analysis, at an institutional level, of a myth without any basis in reality.

There runs throughout the history of Australian political, diplomatic, military and public discourse, a long and continuing tradition of frequent and heartfelt professions of faith in the Australian–US alliance. Such faith, such unquestioning and uncritical certainty in the absolute and indispensible nature of the relationship lumbers along, no matter what contrary evidence the historical record might contain. In Chapter 11, Mike McKinley provocatively asks and answers two key questions: why is the Australian–US alliance so privileged and unchallenged in academic and general discussions about Australian security and strategy? And what should we make of the grand claims made in support of the alliance? The first admits no easy answer, because ultimately the defenders of the alliance possess a temperament of conviction in things that can only be believed with their eyes and ears closed. Faith, not rationality, is the currency here. The second part is easier. The overblown claims are at best the repetition of myth; at worst they are fiction. Both misconceptions reign nevertheless, standing reminders that a myth can be killed again and again, but never really die.

To conclude, in Chapter 12 Peter Stanley confronts perhaps the most persistent myth of all: that war is central to Australia's history, the biggest thing in it. This one single aspect of the Australian historical experience is given an increasingly privileged position. It crowds out and overwhelms the many other parts of Australia's history that are worthy of attention and empathy. In many ways, Australian military history's gazumping of everything

Introduction

else stems from the familiar idea that the landing on Gallipoli represented 'the birth of a nation', and seems to entrench itself further and further in the national psyche on Anzac Day each year. Stanley examines this issue in three ways. First, he looks at recent arguments that criticise the centrality of Anzac Day in unduly skewing Australian history towards war. Second, he considers other aspects of Australian historical experience that could be used to complement the attention accorded to war in justifiable and proportional ways. Last, as a way of evaluating whether or not war justifies its supposed centrality in Australia's history, he considers the passionate public debates about the war memorials proposed for the shore of Canberra's Lake Burley Griffin.

This collection is unified by a single intention: the need to acknowledge and confront the persistent and general misconceptions of our military past, and to understand what really happened. Our destruction of myths isn't for its own sake, as an end in itself, but because good history demands it. Let us re-affirm before turning another page that at the heart of any mantra-like myth is an absence of critical cognition, even of rational inquiry. Myths thrive when there is little curiosity, no drive for insight and no intellectual reflection. Many of Australia's military myths live on through belief rather than knowledge, on conformity rather than inquiry, and on sentiment rather than facts. These characteristics are the enemies of free rational thought and reason, the very goals towards which most teachers, academics and historians strive. Readers deserve better history, not to mention those who have risked their lives in the armed forces. This is why we have written this book.

Some readers may not like what follows. The authors themselves understand that no one likes to have their closely held beliefs challenged. We are well aware of the danger of interfering with the forces that animate our myths, particularly aspects of the Anzac legend and the powerful sentiments of nationalism and identity associated with it. By the end of this book, perhaps a number of your more comfortable beliefs might be challenged, calm preconceptions disturbed, and safe stereotypes swept away. But our goal is worth the risk. In the end, a rattled reality is surely preferable to a zombie-like stare.

[1]

AUSTRALIAN MILITARY HISTORY DOESN'T BEGIN ON GALLIPOLI

Craig Wilcox

'There will be two volumes', Grace Hendy Pooley told colleagues and publishers as she wrote the first full-length military history of Australia, and neither would be brief.[1] She would have to cover New Zealand, of course, with its history so closely linked to Australia's. But even if New Zealand were ignored, how could she possibly squeeze such an abundance of life-changing, nation-shaping events into a single binding?

And that was without a single page on conscription or soldier settlement as we know them, and without a word on Kokoda, Long Tan or Gallipoli. These were in the unimaginable future in 1912 when Pooley was pitching her work-in-progress. Struggling to find a path down her mountain of notes, she seems not to have submitted a finished manuscript – at least not before a new war stole the attention of readers and booksellers. Had she been a tougher thinker, a nimbler writer and a cannier publicist – and, perhaps, had she been a man – her *History of the Military in Australia and New Zealand* might have reached the bookshops before World War I, making it harder for Australians today to assume they have no martial story worth speaking of before the landing at Anzac Cove on 25 April 1915.

Not that many people believe Australian military history began that day on the Gallipoli peninsula. Anyone so misinformed can be immediately set straight by a dozen good books and reputable websites. Jeffrey Grey's *Military History of Australia*, a volume rich in the hard-headed pithiness that Pooley so badly needed, gives a generous four out of eleven chapters to the thirteen decades from the First Fleet to World War I. The Australian War Memorial's website spends four of its thirteen 'Australians at war' pages in the same way. You could even say that awareness of those pre-Anzac decades is growing. There is a push to build a national Boer War memorial, and even the pugnacious scepticism of Keith Windschuttle hasn't halted the re-labelling of clashes between colonial settlers and Indigenous Australians as a species of conquest.[2]

But that's history with a capital H, something for pundits and pupils to ponder, a matter for heads rather than hearts. The national military story is different again, more emotional and more important. It's a public interpretation – a civic sermon as historian Ken Inglis might say[3] – lovingly crafted from cruel and confusing realities about the pit of human suffering to make a morally and socially improving tale, one which harnesses selected facts and downright exaggerations to the vital job of nation-building.

This national military story almost always begins on Gallipoli, and the anniversary of the landing remains the official moment for its telling and re-telling. It is a saga of great battles, great slaughter, great suffering, and the noble endurance of it all. The war in which the Gallipoli campaign was fought becomes 'Australia's greatest tragedy', to quote another good book on Australian military history.[4] It was full of supposed firsts for a people who had left their colonial infancy behind only a dozen or so years earlier

– their first mass military mobilisation, their first debates over conscription, their first soldier settlement program, and the first appearance of a unique Australian character. The lean and stoic 'diggers' who fought and died at Anzac Cove and in the war's later battles 'got you a tradition', as South Australia's governor lectured his citizens soon after the war ended,[5] and it helped the emerging nation through the collapse of the British empire that had nurtured it. Today the saga serves as a rallying point amid the flux of a multicultural society. As immigration obscures the monotone pink face of an older Australia , the saga seems to become ever more urgent. 'The re-energising of Anzac', Paul Kelly observed a year ago, 'has become the central organising principle of Australia's past and how the nation interprets its future'.[6]

The national military story looks forward from 1915, as the prime minister said recently, to chart how 'the tide of history has taken Australians to war on three continents over more than a century'.[7] However different in their scale and meaning and experience, these subsequent wars become re-enactments of Gallipoli in official memory and public reflection, with the same suffering and quiet nobility, the same Australian character on display, the same strangely comforting sense that our troops are always among war's victims rather than its perpetrators. Vietnam wasn't easy to squeeze into this mould, but eventually the tale of Long Tan became a re-run of Anzac Cove, and all was well.

While the national military story looks forward from 1915, with this heartfelt but selective gaze, it rarely looks backward at all. It ignores most of what could fall into view from our earlier martial history as irrelevant, quaint, sometimes even disturbing. The clashes that punctuated the advance of the colonial frontier still seem too sparse, too shabby, and perhaps too shameful to count as real war for many Australians today. The British redcoats who garrisoned Australia from 1788 to 1870 seem colourful enough, but they represent a foreign presence, variously bumbling and tyrannical as they stand over convicts, shoot down Aborigines, overthrow a governor and slaughter innocent goldminers at Eureka Stockade. The military activity of the colonists themselves – all those volunteer corps with their strange uniforms, and those charming sandstone forts whose guns never fired in anger – seems fledgling and feeble, amounting to nothing but a walk-on part on the sideshow that was the Sudan War of 1885. The greater supporting role played by Australians in the Boer War, fought in South Africa from 1899 to 1902, stirs a little pride – but at the expense of real knowledge about this brutal conflict and popular support at the time for that brutality.

Anyway, the whole vista from the First Fleet to Federation was pre-national and so pretty pointless, wasn't it? The Australian War Memorial might display military relics predating World War I, but only in two tiny galleries safely tucked away at basement level, and it defensively shies away from remembering any fighting on the frontier.[8] If a few antique military episodes survive on the edge of popular memory, they do so only as preambles before the sermon. The lacklustre defence of Elands River Post during the Boer War prefigures Gallipoli just as surely as Long Tan repeats it.[9] Harry 'Breaker' Morant and his comrades are not opportunistic killers of unarmed Boers, but brave diggers punished unfairly by the same dastardly Brits who went on to bungle things at Gallipoli and on the Western Front.[10] About to be similarly conscripted into the story, and similarly distorted, is Aboriginal resistance to colonial settlers. Until recently, proud accounts of eighteenth and nineteenth-century Aboriginal ingenuity and bravery were exercises in lifting the spirits of Indigenous Australians today, and were therefore indifferent or even hostile to the national military story.[11] A new, subtler but no less romantic and unhistorical effort now claims Aboriginal resistance as a heritage for everyone.¹² Surely it will one day become the national military story's prologue.

Building a nation probably demands a saga as simple and selective and inspiring as this. If the price is a cramped view of history in the minds of politicians, journalists and the public, and sometimes even museum curators, teachers and historians, then it might be a price worth paying. But a sense of the past that follows a few threads bound to a single moment ignores the vastness and confusion of life in every age. Worse, it tidies it all up and packs it away forever inside a box that's labelled neatly, indelibly – and falsely. Historians' understanding of what a colonial past can mean has been revolutionised over the past few decades, with the old focus on a sunlit path to nationhood giving way to something richer and more riotous.¹³ Crafting a complex and politically useless vision that sometimes anticipates, sometimes contradicts and sometimes subverts our national military story has been a small part of that revolution,¹⁴ but it could be a larger one, and it ought to be better known. We need to glimpse it as Grace Hendy Pooley tried to see it, as taking place more in Australia than in the uniformed ranks of our expeditions overseas, more in wider military activity than in brief moments of conflict, and more as a tapestry in itself than a few threads leading straight to a national future.

The view extends back further than Pooley might have guessed. Organised conflict among the Aboriginal societies that possessed Australia for millennia was normally confined to individual punishment and petty raids, but it seems to have regularly peaked in dangerous clashes – what the Yolngu people of Arnhem Land called *ganygarr*, 'the spear fight to end all spear fights'¹⁵ – between groups of men who might paint their bodies in shades weirdly prefiguring the British army uniforms their descendants would come to know so well. 'On the morning on which we were to fight', a Gippsland Aborigine said of one clash, 'we were all ready, and were painted in pipeclay because we were very angry at our men being killed' in previous fights, 'and also to frighten our enemies' who had painted themselves in red ochre to show they had already drawn blood. 'They are not many of you', one of them mocked. 'Never mind, we will see', came the laconic reply. 'Then we fought', and soon ochre was fleeing from pipeclay. 'By and by I shot one man, and others were speared. Several women were caught ... this was how I got my first wife.'[16]

A nineteenth-century German artist depicted a *ganygarr* in the same way he might have drawn a skirmish between volunteer *jaeger* companies on his local heath.[17] But casualties were few. The aim was to minimise death while asserting bravery and settling disputes, maybe also to prevent war evolving too far beyond a branch of ritual. Among the Yolngu, at least, a man who sparked too much fighting might be judged a menace to his own people and killed. But for all its choreography and restraint, *ganygarr* was war as it was fought before notions of standing and fighting to the death, of bitter defeat and triumphant victory. It drew in many men and some women too – which seems a lame statement until we reflect that only one in ten white Australians put on uniform during World War II. Aboriginal Australia wasn't military in the modern sense, but it was periodically martial. Only its ignorance of writing has denied us sagas of home-grown Hectors and Hercules.

Waging *ganygarr* against British colonists from 1788 to the 1920s was more spectacular but less effective, and so less common than the smaller raids and ambushes described by John Connor in *Zombie Myths of Australian Military History* and elsewhere.[18] But, as Connor reminds us, the raids and ambushes also had a warlike character. After eight years of accommodation with the white advance, the Wiradjuri around Bathurst resisted the tide for a year or more in a conflict that surely edged aside most peaceful pursuits. Over just two days in May 1824 they attacked three stations, and they spent much of September fleeing from an official expedition of 40 soldiers and other unofficial avengers. The Wiradjuri may have lost dozens of dead by the end of the year, along with their way of life. The only sustained military attack on white Australia – the Japanese air raids on Darwin twelve decades later – killed 300 people, but it had nothing like these consequences for its survivors.

If the frontier struggle could be disastrous for the losers, it could be at least harrowing for the victors. The first white settlers of Victoria fought off a long Aboriginal assault during the 1830s. One man seemed to count it hardly worth mentioning 'having had a servant killed, others attacked, and sometimes our sheep destroyed'. Another complained that he and his workers 'were kept for years in a perpetual state of alarm', and boasted of firing 60 rounds during a skirmish that gave his opponents 'a notion of what sort of stuff the white man was made'. Not all white men, though. 'They murdered one of my servants and burned my huts and stores, and all my wheat', one cried later. The struggle that ended in unchallenged white victory left him 'an invalid for life', he claimed, and 'comparatively a poor man'.[19] Similar cries were heard from veterans of later wars.

Frontier conflict wasn't war as those later veterans knew it, or even war as other colonists waged in the eighteenth and nineteenth centuries against the native populations of North America and southern Africa. No long columns of regulars ever wound through the Australian bush, no white men mustered as a militia, no great forts were built, and no treaties settled the squalid, confused conflict. A minor drag on colonisation, frontier fighting was too puny to encourage anything like a war industry beyond the importation and sale of more than the predictable number of shotguns and pistols. Victory brought no shouts of triumph. The dead earned few memorials beyond some stone plaques inside Sydney's St James's Church. Yet a final death toll proposed by historian Henry Reynolds – of 20 000 black Australians and more than 2000 white – is increasingly accepted.[20] That's about as many as were lost in 1917, Australia's worst year at war. It also represents an average of 200 dead every year from 1788 to 1901, and if that seems insignificant, it still exceeds Australian losses in any year in Vietnam. Puny and petty as it was, frontier fighting was much more a 'Battle for Australia' than the fighting in 1942 that lobbyists and politicians have recently elevated out of all proportion.[21]

The redcoats who occasionally arbitrated in frontier struggles were never mobilised for a serious campaign against the Aborigines, although Nathaniel Lowe of the 40th regiment had the dubious distinction of committing Australia's first war crime by having a black prisoner shot in 1826. British soldiers were never called upon to repel an attack by a rival empire on the Australian colonies, but they shot down rebel convicts outside Sydney in 1804 and miners at Eureka fifty years later. When the last British regiment left Australia in 1870, the civilian response was famously muted. But this brief catalogue of apparent irrelevance and alienation disguises the fact that the redcoats were not merely the first soldiers in Australia, but the first to belong to Australians.

In 1832 a Sydney newspaper pronounced the redcoats to be 'as much naturalized as the bulk of the community'.[22] It was an exaggeration, but not by much. British soldiers formed a significant proportion of early colonial enclaves, and as late as 1828 one in twenty white Australians was a redcoat, his wife, or his child. The border between soldier and civilian was even more porous than this reminder of the presence of military families suggests. Only a trickle of civilians enlisted in the garrison, but hundreds of

Australian military history doesn't begin on Gallipoli

thousands of civilians were former soldiers, some granted farms or town allotments in a strangely neglected first chapter in the history of soldier settlement in Australia. Relations between civil and military society were close, indeed intimate, at the time, with bonds of friendship and enmity, of love and sex. Sydney, Hobart and (although some residents snootily pretended otherwise) Melbourne were British army garrison towns in much the same manner as Colchester and York. Civilian residents lapped up the free spectacle of parades and salutes, flocked to military balls and concerts, played against the soldiers in football and cricket, consulted their engineers, surveyors and doctors, took on lucrative contracts to provide barracks with food and fodder, opened hotels to ply the rank and file with drink, and above all befriended soldiers and married them. The lack of fanfare accompanying the last regiment's departure reflected not so much public indifference as an uneasy acceptance of the inevitable. Previously, when British troops had sailed from Australian ports to war on some other frontier of the empire, they had been routinely hailed as 'our gallant soldiers'.[23] Most of the men, women and children cheering the redcoats would have dismissed out of hand any suggestion from us that they should have saved their martial loyalties for some home-grown army of the future.

These soldiers bequeathed as much tradition to the Australians of their day as any slouch-hatted troops would later do. They represented an army that had bled on a hundred famous battlefields. Its 'glorious and brilliant achievements', one South Australian said, were 'an heirloom to successive generations' and a challenge to them to emulate 'the noble deeds of their ancestors'.[24] Copies of famous battle paintings hung in middle-class parlours, preachers and governors lectured audiences on red-coated bravery. Towns and streets were named for hallowed battlegrounds on the other side of the globe, and for generals whose names were household words. 'A crowd of places in New South Wales bear the names "Waterloo" and "Wellington"', a French visitor observed in 1824,[25] and today there are twice as many Wellingtons as Jackas in a Melbourne street directory. The first Victoria Crosses worn in Australia graced the chests of redcoat veterans: three were presented to soldiers or former soldiers in Sydney and Melbourne. One of these men, Frederick Whirlpool, long preceded Neville Howse from the Boer War as Australia's first recipient of the medal.

Similar kinship and respect applied to the Royal Navy, ruler of the waves and with a base in Sydney until the eve of World War I. The first colonial governors were naval officers, the First Fleet was a naval expedition, and the first visit of a navy squadron (in 1824) was an occasion for wonder and verse. While military officers surveyed the land, naval officers surveyed the coast. Sydney became as much a naval town as visiting regiments made it a garrison town – to the annoyance of some politicians but the delight of many merchants, publicans and prostitutes. From 1891, Sydney hosted a so-called auxiliary squadron partly paid for by Australians. Its ships, bearing names like *Wallaroo* and *Boomerang*, blurred any distinction between imperial and local.

Not that everyone loved the British army and navy, or even gave a damn about them. But most of the predecessors of today's journalists, radio hosts, politicians and authors who shape our national military story were devoted to them and the wider imperial military story they embodied and inculcated. The centenary of the Battle of Trafalgar in 1905 was marked in Australian cities by victory arches, newspaper supplements and special sporting matches. Four years earlier the red coats of visiting British soldiers formed the centrepiece of the great Federation parade through Sydney. 'Australians were glad the imperial soldiers had come here', the nation's first prime minister said, 'for they were proud of them, and they hoped the imperial soldiers were proud of the Australians'. The city's mayor found it 'very difficult for any man to find words to sufficiently express the intense pleasure which the visit of the imperial troops had given the people of Sydney', especially because the 'glorious traditions of their regiments were well known to Australians'.[26] That's hardly true of the army that Australia has fielded since World War II, with its marginal presence in most capital cities. Few civilians habitually encounter soldiers and sailors today, let alone drink with them, marry them or brawl with them as their predecessors did with redcoats and bluejackets. The British army and Royal Navy were more truly at home in Australia, far more a part of everyday Australian life, than our servicemen and women today.

The real first world war for Australia was the long struggle against Revolutionary and Napoleonic France from the early 1790s to 1815. Few Antipodeans joined in the actual fighting – John Macarthur's eldest son and William Charles Wentworth's younger brother were the notable ones – but the result determined Australia's future nonetheless. In securing Britain's naval supremacy, Trafalgar promised the whole of Australia to British settlers. The red-coated contribution to the run of allied victories on land from 1812 ensured the promise was kept. The British empire would face no serious threat for another century, by which time its Australian territories had reproduced Britain's political and legal system and were permanently and prosperously integrated into the global economy. The 'battles that shaped Australia', to adopt the title of a 1990s celebration of later, better-remembered struggles, should include Trafalgar and Waterloo.[27]

Some colonial Australians barracked from the sidelines during the long war against France, and many more kept on barracking during Britain's wars throughout the nineteenth century. They marked victories with subscription dances and defeats with solemn church services. They established and donated to patriotic funds as early as 1816, if not before. Great battles like Balaclava, and boutique ones like Rorke's Drift, sent shudders of excitement or despair through Australia almost as deep as the fall of France and victory at El Alamein would do during World War II.

In the middle of the nineteenth century, fear of a new war between the British and French empires prompted English-speaking men around the globe to do more than simply barrack for their armies. When the wave of martial excitement rolled across Australian towns and suburbs in 1860, it prompted a rush to enlist that predated by half a century the more celebrated queues before Gallipoli. Within a year many localities had established a volunteer corps — a part-time military unit closer to a fire brigade than a unit of regulars — and a rifle club that trained for war as much as it shot for sport. These volunteers and riflemen were soon joined in the capital cities by tiny naval brigades that imitated Royal Navy landing parties. Hitherto serene mornings and evenings were disturbed by the sounds of military commands being shouted in parks and at racecourses. Strange new uniforms, not always well-tailored, enlivened parlours, ballrooms and church pews. New military ideas were borrowed from citizen soldiers in England and vigorously asserted. Discipline should not infringe a man's dignity; military punishment must not extend to flogging, let alone execution; the Crown could not force men to fight overseas. These ideas, not conceived to limit British control over Australian soldiers but inherited from England long before Australians ever went into battle, reflected the fact that communities, not colonial governments or the British army, had taken the initiative in forming and filling the volunteer corps.

The existence of a local volunteer corps instilled the same kind of communal pride as the creation of a local council and football team. Pride grew further after 1885, when some units began to ride horses – for mobility rather than the charge – and to replace colourful military clothing with khaki and slouch hats. Forgetting that the new tactics and uniforms were copied from other British imperial frontiers, some Australians hailed these 'buff-coloured boys' for introducing to war 'two of the natural habits of the Australians – riding and shooting'.[28] The search for the supposedly distinctive qualities in Australia's fighting men began a generation before Gallipoli.

Not that the search was widespread at the time. Indeed its preliminary results were challenged. In a way strangely unthinkable in our multicultural age, some volunteer units paraded defiantly ethnic identities. There were Irish and Scottish corps in the capital cities, a German one in Geelong, an exclusively English one in Sydney. (There would have been a Chinese corps had the idea not so spooked the New South Wales government.) Ethnic units wanted nothing to do with khaki, slouch hats and a common colonial identity. Nor were the new uniforms popular with mainstream urban volunteers, even after a visiting British general praised them for constituting a 'distinctive national dress'.[29] As one colonel explained, it was scarlet, not khaki, that symbolised 'actual soldiering'.[30]

The 700 New South Wales men who went to war with the British army in Sudan in 1885 were forced to give up their red coats – at the insistence of British generals. They served in the brief and, for them, bloodless campaign as dutiful apprentices to some of war's most highly skilled tradesmen. Such was the vision for the first Australian contingents to the Boer War fourteen years later. Few expected a handful of South African farmers to do more than delay a triumphal British march on their capital cities. This was one reason why most Australians seemed less than gripped by the outbreak of war in 1899. But historians in the 1970s who studied this languid reaction, and who concluded that imperial manipulation must have edged an essentially reluctant Australia into the war, were strangely blind to the subsequent mass public engagement with the conflict.[31] After the Boers fought back hard – in one 'Black Week' late in 1899 defeating three British columns – Australia plunged into its first active participation in an imperial war. New patriotic funds were established and public attention, as Tasmania's governor reported, 'centred practically on one subject, the war in South Africa'.[32] This was nothing new by nineteenth century standards. The novelty lay in the sudden enlistment of more than 30 000 men into new contingents, volunteer corps and rifle clubs.[33] Some said that number was far too small, thus prompting the first real arguments about raising a compulsory militia and anticipating the 1916 and 1917 conscription debates. The violent attacks on some German migrants that blighted Australia's record during World War I were likewise anticipated after Black Week, largely by hooligans angered by Berlin's sympathy for the Boers.

Many of the new contingents were sent at first to one of the Boer War's sideshows. Still, they made history there. Marched with deliberate slowness through Rhodesia, they helped deter both a Boer invasion of that new colony and an African revolt, fixing the country's future for seven decades as an apartheid state outside South Africa.[34] It was also in Rhodesia that another historical first occurred: the creation of the first Australian brigade in war, 1300 strong, under an obscure and overwhelmed English colonel who was anxious to lead his 'splendid Australians' at the enemy then let them 'go home happy'.[35]

The idea of dutiful apprentices patiently waiting while the regular army showed the way was one more casualty of early Boer successes. Replacing it was an expectation that, if Boer farmers riding nimble ponies could outwit or at least outrun professional soldiers, then amateurs from Australia, Canada, New Zealand

Australian military history doesn't begin on Gallipoli

and England itself should be able to do the same, and so tip the balance the empire's way. Thus Australians came to fight in South Africa as buff-coloured boys were supposed to do, riding out far from supply lines and dispersing small bands of Boers, although all too rarely crushing them. A year or two earlier, most of the Australians had been riding trams or bicycles to work, not horses. Still, they seemed handy enough on campaign, and some were truly at home in the outdoors. A few were wild, but their wildness was encouraged as, well, natural among frontiersmen. Years before official historian Charles Bean spied their descendants on Gallipoli, the poet Banjo Paterson rejoiced at seeing such 'long-legged fellows, brown and hard-faced' in a South African town, with 'the alert wide-awake look that distinguishes the Australian soldier from the more stolid English "Tommy"'.[36] Rudyard Kipling similarly summed them up as 'Dark, tall men, most excellent horsemen, hot and angry, waging war *as* war, and drinking tea as a sandhill drinks water'.[37] The Australian soldier entered the consciousness of the rest of the world as a bushman in khaki, and the slouch-hatted larrikin began to replace the dutiful, red-coated military apprentice as the stereotypical Australian in uniform.

The new image was a flash and flattering one, but the Boer War brought bad news as well. The squalid fighting on Australia's frontiers could be dismissed as nothing to do with real war; the squalid fighting in South Africa could not. Australians had to accept that war could be unrelieved by glory, that it could be simply brutal. This explains both the apologies given for 'Breaker' Morant, found guilty of murdering unarmed Boers, and also the wider acceptance that his execution was well deserved. Then there was the whiff of alienation, even antagonism between the British army and its wartime colonial recruits. For the first time, thousands of Australians were fighting beside the soldiers they had so long venerated, and found them to be ordinary men after all. British colonels and generals usually complied with the Australians' expectations that men who had come to help the army should be praised to the skies and, in all but a few cases, protected from military discipline and punishment – but there was friction when the brasshats acted like brasshats. A popular campaign effected the released from gaol of an accomplice of Morant who was popularly but mistakenly judged not to have been responsible for his part in the murders. A similar campaign and the same result, with greater justification, followed the incarceration of three Victorian soldiers who had challenged an overbearing general.

The Boer War also brought a heavy casualty list. The usual number given for Australia's dead, around 600, seems modest enough until supplemented by the likely toll among the thousands of men who fought in units raised in South Africa. If, as seems likely, a thousand Australians died in the Boer War, it was a noticeable loss in a male population only a third of the size of the Vietnam War generation. And like Vietnam, there was no great victory to point to, no moment when Australians seemed to have tipped the balance, no higher cause that seemed to make it all worthwhile. It became more satisfying to see the conflict not as a dull, disappointing drama in itself but as a forgivably patchy rehearsal for something greater to come. Australia had federated halfway during the war and could look forward, as nations and perhaps even proto-nations were supposed to do, to a bloody test of their worth. Australians were ready to embrace the next war as a new beginning.

Preparations for that war began soon after Federation, well before it was clear where the fighting would be and who the enemy was, and the result was a social and financial upheaval. Contrary to the folk tales of C.J. Dennis and Charles Bean,[38] the soldiers and sailors who came to fight in World War I were not so much products of rough city neighbourhoods and the self-reliance bred in the bush, but of much costly and uncomfortable military reform.

Talk of such reform began in 1905, but the hard and expensive work kicked off only in 1911, when teenage boys were forced into compulsory cadet drill. A year later the old force of volunteers, already reformed and partly transformed into a voluntary militia, gave way to a real, compulsory militia organised and funded by government, and trained and administered by professional soldiers. Half of all young men who turned eighteen in 1912 were obliged to serve. Slowly, year by year, a part-time army of seven infantry divisions and seven cavalry brigades emerged. One of its aims was to give Australia something like the military clout of Belgium or Romania – enough to warn off Japan, planning an empire in east Asia, and to prepare men to fight in a likely war in Europe against Imperial Germany, the British empire's most serious rival since Napoleonic France. There was also a domestic motive, particularly popular with some parents and clergymen, of inculcating toughness and patriotism among a new generation widely suspected of addiction to sport and cigarettes, to cinema and soft living. Perhaps best of all, the militia would be strictly territorial in its organisation, with just one unit for each town or suburb, leaving no room for the ethnic regiments that many Australians now feared as divisive. Whatever its motives, it all seemed a bold initiative – 'a proclamation of historic importance', as Boston's *Christian Science Monitor* put it[39] – and another example of how a newly federated Australia was becoming a laboratory of political and social reform.

But the experiment was nearly compromised. Historian John Barrett showed long ago that resistance to militia service was smaller than critics of the system claimed at the time;[40] the real problem was subtle but widespread resistance while in uniform. Many young men were reluctant to learn the unglamorous basics of soldiering or to obey unpopular superiors – or any superior. One officer described his cadet company as 'an involuntary association of stone-throwing criminals'.[41] What he would have thought of the whole battalion that broke out of its camp at Liverpool in 1913, and had to be returned at bayonet point, can only be imagined. Outside of the ranks, employers objected when workers were lost to militia duty, and parents protested when their sons were sent to camp, or made to drill on cold nights. Ian Hamilton, the British general who would later command the Australians on Gallipoli, inspected the new militia early in 1914 and guessed it was capable of resisting an enemy only half its size.[42] Still, by winter that year an army of 62 000 learners, loafers, leaders and larrikins was under some sort of training and discipline. Not until the 1950s would Australia have again a peacetime military force as large or as uncomplicatedly focussed on the basics of war.

By 1914 Australian also had a navy of sorts. Although the redcoats had left in 1870, the Royal Navy continued to crew an Australia Station. But the ships were small and few, sufficient for suppressing human trafficking in nearby Pacific Islands (their usual duty) but not much else. In any case, strategic orthodoxy was calling for concentration in European waters to face the growing German fleet. Some Australians saw the sense of this. During the so-called Dreadnought Crisis of 1909, as newspapers screamed that Berlin was outbuilding Britain in the construction of the latest capital ships, five rich men and countless poorer folk across New South Wales offered more than £90 000 – nearly the size of Queensland's entire defence budget a decade earlier – to reinforce the fleet in the North Sea. But more Australians feared Japan, or more precisely that the imperial government in London couldn't or even wouldn't help them fend off a Japanese attack. They wanted their own navy tied to local waters, and to hell with the cost. The final decision was a compromise – an affordable

Australian military history doesn't begin on Gallipoli

navy within a navy that would secure Australian shores in peace, and in war (provided Japan kept out of it) would reinforce the Royal Navy's main battle fleet. When the first Royal Australian Navy ships, built in England and partly crewed by British sailors, reached Sydney in 1913 they sparked the same proud comments as news of the Gallipoli landing would later. Australia, the Labor Party heavyweight William Morris Hughes pronounced, had 'assumed the toga of nationhood'.[43] With 16 ships, one of them a battle cruiser, our navy was a more formidable force in 1914 than it would be in 1939, and a relatively more powerful fleet than Australia has put to sea since the 1980s.

On the eve of World War I, then, Australia had the beginnings of a navy and a militia it was starting to think of as an army. When war came, the new ships and sailors proved themselves immediately, making possible the conquest of German New Guinea, running aground a German light cruiser, escorting the Australian Imperial Force (AIF) to war, and then reinforcing the Royal Navy's main battle fleet. The militia fell into neglect during the war, and wasted away as the tide of combat refused to break on Australian shores. But the vast effort of raising, organising and disciplining it, and the experience gained by its officers, administrators and suppliers, ensured that the AIF could be smoothly and quickly formed in 1914, and that more men than a few thousand Boer War veterans knew what to do once the shooting started.

If Australians were poised by 1914 to recast themselves as a distinct people by some act of military endurance, they continued to draw strength and to derive a sense of themselves from their long pre-Gallipoli military heritage. The best-selling book by an Australian at the time wasn't a volume by Banjo Paterson or Henry Lawson, but probably the Reverend W.H. Fitchett's *Deeds That Won the Empire*, a stirring account of heroism by Englishmen in red coats and blue jackets. The book, first published in Melbourne in 1896, was conceived for a purpose his successors like Peter FitzSimons share today – to bind Australian society with gripping popular stories of ancestral martial bravery.[44] A little more scholarly but no less purposeful was a 1908 lecture on the Royal Navy's contribution to Australian history by James Watson, a former volunteer captain and a leading light in the newly formed Royal Australian Historical Society.[45] Joseph Forde, another literary bowerbird plundering the past, narrated a lively history of British regiments in Sydney to amuse readers of the scandal-sheet *Truth* from the late summer to the late spring of 1909.[46] Not that Australia's military heritage was only clad in red and blue. Boer War memoirs and histories such as *Australians in War*, *Australians at the Front* and *Tommy Cornstalk* had sketched the achievements and attitudes of a new breed of British soldier from the fringes of empire, someone scarcely different from the one soon to be dubbed a 'digger'. Fitchett spied in a somewhat hapless defence of an obscure spot in the western Transvaal the same qualities about to revealed on Gallipoli,[47] with the result that the fighting at Elands River Post was already set to become a prequel to the national military story.

Still, in 1914 the old British army was still Australia's ancestral military force, its default image of the real soldier. Two months after the war began, the Sydney magazine *Lone Hand* covered its October issue with a picture of an Australian soldier striding off to war and saluting his predecessor – a soldier in the red coat worn at Waterloo. When news came of the Gallipoli landing, Fitchett pleased everyone by announcing that Australians were like Wellington's army almost exactly a hundred years before – young fresh-faced militiamen, ignorant of the sound of gunfire – except that 'Wellington's lads would not have had the initiative and daring to climb that cliff. That was the "Australian touch".'[48] The reverend's benediction helped Australians to shift

Australian military history doesn't begin on Gallipoli

their affections seamlessly from red coats to slouch hats, and from a military past to a military future that no longer needed a past before 25 April 1915.

But there *was* a past, more substantial than even our historians usually allow. Not as substantial as the Australian immersion in the two World Wars, of course, but more so than our military experiences since. It is customary, when calculating such experience, to tally up the number of people wearing uniform. But if we also count Aborigines likely to have engaged in *ganygarr*, and also the members of rifle clubs, then martially active men in Australia might have numbered more than 50 000 early in the nineteenth century,[49] perhaps 70 000 at the height of the Boer War,[50] and certainly more than 90 000 in mid-1914.[51] Such numbers were exceeded only during the World Wars and from the 1950s to the 1970s, but really only in the 1940s if we adjust for an increasing population. Deaths in combat were notoriously heavy during the World Wars, but more than 20 000 dead from frontier fighting and Boer War service is not to be sneezed at – and far exceeds all our battle deaths since 1945. On the grounds of human cost alone, the Australian War Memorial's colonial and Boer War rooms ought to be larger and more prominently placed than its Korea and Vietnam galleries.

While cost is one reason for pondering Australia's military history before Gallipoli, an equally good one is the alternative and perhaps unsettling vision opened up by looking at our military experience from a different vantage point from that of Anzac Cove. Looking from Gallipoli, we see Australians dying beside their New Zealand cousins. We hail them all as Anzacs and leave the connection at that. But as Grace Hendy Pooley understood – and as later historians like me, even in this chapter, have pretended not to notice – our national military story from the First Fleet to the First World War and probably beyond, has artificial if not ahistorical boundaries unless it spans both sides of the Tasman to take in New Zealand, that seventh former British colony at the Antipodes.

Looking from Gallipoli, we also see Australians fighting and dying against the odds and always in a good cause. That's fair enough when considering the two World Wars. But looking again at the squalid frontier, and past the blunders of the Boer War, opens our minds to the thought that our soldiers often fight safely on the side of the big battalions against puny enemies for causes which, however politically pragmatic and even necessary, are not entirely virtuous.

Looking from Gallipoli also places us within a national love affair between citizens and slouch-hatted soldiers. But looking from, say, the celebrations that marked the arrival of news of Waterloo, we know the love affair predated Federation and that the earliest object of civilian affection was an army in red coats recruited outside Australia. The tradition that slouch hats gave us had to be chalked in big letters over an old and well-used slate, not a blank one, and there was still room for other scribbles. A romance with the troops of great allies and old homelands has endured at the margins of Australian military engagement. It encompasses respect and affection for, say, British fighter pilots during World War II, and the secret admiration among some migrant communities for national enemies from the Kaiser to the Taliban.

Within some marginalised sections of Australian society the understanding and experience of war largely remains a privately inherited one, sometimes indifferent to the public story, or even at odds with it. Just as redcoat settlers passed their stories of Waterloo and the Charge of the Light Brigade into their community's consciousness, migrants from Vietnam, Somalia and Afghanistan transplant their own memories of recent wars that have little to do with the bravery of men and women in bush hats or Kevlar vests. But these alternative understandings also hold out hope for strengthening Australia's military forces – if the enormous popularity of the old ethnic volunteer units is any guide. Colonial military forces were attractive to civilians and healthily bustling in themselves partly because of their acceptance of Irish, Scottish and similar units. Perhaps today's socially isolated and chronically under-strength Australian Defence Force should consider raising Lebanese and Vietnamese regiments?

No one thinks our military experience really began in 1915. But we ought to acknowledge the earlier and sometimes contrary military strands to that experience. Even on Anzac Day we should admit that our martial story doesn't begin on Gallipoli.

Further reading

J. Bach, *The Australia Station*, UNSW Press, Sydney, 1986.
J. Barrett, *Falling In: Australians and Boy Conscription 1911–1915*, Hale & Iremonger, Sydney, 1979.
J. Connor, *The Australian Frontier Wars 1788–1838*, UNSW Press, Sydney, 2002.
J. Grey, *A Military History of Australia*, 3rd edn, Oxford University Press, Melbourne, 2008.
K.S. Inglis, *The Australian Colonists*, Melbourne University Press, Melbourne, 1974.
M. McKernan & M. Browne (eds), *Australia: Two Centuries of War and Peace*, Australian War Memorial, Canberra, 1988.
H. Reynolds, *The Other Side of the Frontier: Aboriginal Resistance to the European Invasion of Australia*, UNSW Press, Sydney, 2006 (first published 1981).
G. Souter, *Lion and Kangaroo*, Text, Melbourne, 2001.
P. Stanley, *The Remote Garrison: The British Army in Australia 1788–1870*, Kangaroo, Sydney, 1986.
C. Stockings, *The Torch and the Sword: A History of the Army Cadet Movement in Australia*, UNSW Press, Sydney, 2007.
C. Wilcox, *Australia's Boer War*, Oxford University Press, Melbourne, 2002.

C. Wilcox, *For Hearths and Homes: Citizen Soldiering in Australia 1854–1945*, Allen & Unwin, Sydney, 1998.
——, *Red Coat Dreaming: How Colonial Australia Embraced the British Army*, Cambridge University Press, Melbourne, 2009.

[2]

THE 'SUPERIOR', ALL-VOLUNTEER AIF

John Connor

Every Sunday night in homes across the country, procrastinating students – and harassed parents – hunch over computers frantically Googling to finish school assignments due the next day. For students studying World War I, such internet searches invariably produce this statement: the Australian Imperial Force (AIF) was the only all-volunteer army in the war of 1914–1918. This fact sounds significant. It proves the uniqueness of the Australian soldier, and can be guaranteed to appear in most students' assignments. The only problem with this important and well-known fact is that it is totally false. The AIF was not the only all-volunteer army in World War I. Every Irish member of the British Army was a volunteer. No conscripts served in either the South African or Indian armies, or in British colonial forces such as the King's African Rifles and the British West Indies Regiment. Another, perhaps even more insidious myth has developed out of this basic factual error: that the volunteer status of Australian troops in World War I made them inherently superior to their conscript counterparts.

Both mistaken notions may be attacked on two fronts. Leaving aside the erroneous idea that Australian soldiers were the only true volunteers during the war, the first is that many men who joined the AIF were not volunteers as the term would be understood in twenty-first century Australia. Unlike today, when individuals generally make their choices according to self-interest, free from external pressure, the Australians of a century ago were less individualistic. The decision whether a man did or did not join the AIF was often made not by him, but for him by parents who selected which sons would go to war and which would stay at home. Employers, workmates, fellow church-members and friends also helped determine enlistment. At a time when the unemployed received little financial assistance, and the Australian economy was faltering due to drought and the wartime disruption of trade, many men joined up simply because they needed a job.

The second argument against the myth of Australian uniqueness in this regard is that wars throughout history have shown that volunteers are not necessarily superior soldiers to conscripts. For example, the British volunteer professional soldiers led by the Duke of York to northern France in 1793 were defeated by the mass conscript army of the French Republic. The myth of the superior AIF volunteers appears to have originated in the latter part of World War I as a consequence of the conscription debate. The failure to introduce conscription in Australia in the referenda of 1916 and 1917 led some to claim that the 'No' vote meant most Australians were opposed to war and disloyal to the British Empire. In response, other commentators turned the all-volunteer nature of the AIF into a virtue, and created this special – although mythical – status for the force.

It was General Sir John Monash, commander of the Australian Corps on the Western Front, in his 1920 book *The Australian Victories in France* who first made the claim that the AIF was 'the only purely volunteer army that fought in the Great War'. Monash went on to assert that the Australians in the offensives in 1918 were, at least partially as a consequence, a superior type of force in that they 'contributed ... in the most direct and decisive manner, to the final collapse and surrender of the enemy', playing 'an important' and sometimes 'predominating part' in the Allied victory.[1] Monash's claim has been repeated as fact by subsequent authors. Patsy Adam-Smith, in *The Anzacs* in 1978, compared the all-volunteer Australian army to those of 'other Commonwealth countries, all of whom were conscripted'. Ken Inglis, in a 1988 article, stated: 'In 1915 an army composed entirely of volunteers was not unusual. By 1918 the Australian force was alone among armies on either side in remaining so.' Jonathan King, in *The Western Front Diaries* in 2008, describes the AIF as 'the only all-volunteer army in World War I'. The mistaken claim can also be found on the internet on websites ranging from 'Sands of Gallipoli' (which sells medallions and other items featuring vials of Gallipoli beach sand) to the Dynamic Learning Online site (that offers an 'inexpensive online library ... designed for use by schools, parents, seniors').[2]

It is true the AIF was made up entirely of volunteers, but it is not true that the Australians were the only such force in World War I. Charles Bean, Australia's official historian of this conflict, certainly described Australian soldiers as volunteers, but he was careful not to say they were the only ones. Bean does not explicitly state why, but it would have been because he knew that the 1st South African Infantry Brigade serving on the Western Front was also an all-volunteer force. Both Australian and South African units faced the difficulties of declining recruitment as the war went on. In the final volume of the official history, Bean commented on the under-strength nature of Australian infantry battalions in 1918. He made the same point about the South Africans, where the brigade (consisting of four battalions) ended the war with its formation strength equivalent to just one battalion.

Jeffrey Grey, in his *A Military History of Australia*, first published in 1990, and in his 2001 history of the Australian Army, explicitly described the South African Brigade as an all-volunteer force and pointed out that the 'popular perception' of the AIF as being the only all-volunteer army in World War I 'needs to be modified'. *The Oxford Companion to Australian Military History*, and the Australian War Memorial's website make similar clarifying statements.[3]

Other British Empire forces consisting of volunteer soldiers and auxiliary troops need to be assigned their places alongside the Australians and South African Brigades on the list of all-volunteer forces of World War I. But first, the extent of conscription within this conflict needs to be briefly outlined. With the exception of the United Kingdom, all the major combatant nations fought the war with conscript soldiers. The 'Great 'Powers' of France, Russia, Italy, Austria-Hungary, Germany and the Ottoman Empire had long traditions of compulsory military service, as did smaller European nations such as Serbia, Belgium, Bulgaria and Romania. When the United States entered the war in 1917, it too created a conscript army under the *Selective Service Act*.

For its part, the United Kingdom entered the war with a small volunteer professional army of about 250 000 men that was largely destroyed in the initial battles of 1914. In its place, the 'Kitchener army' of 2.4 million volunteers was raised, trained and suffered heavy losses in the battles on the Somme from July to November 1916.[4] With the decline in voluntary enlistment, conscription was introduced in Britain – but not in Ireland – in January 1916. Initially limited to single men and childless widowers between the ages of 18 and 41, within six months all men in this age range became liable for military service, and the upper age limit was extended to 50 in April 1918.[5] Two and a half million men were thus called up in Britain, joined the remaining veterans of the

The 'superior', all-volunteer AIF

pre-war regular army and the surviving wartime volunteers to fight the indecisive battles of 1917; to face and stop the German offensive of March 1918; and to take part in the Allied 'Hundred Days' offensive that brought final victory in November 1918.[6]

Of the five self-governing Dominions in the British Empire during World War I – Australia, Canada, Newfoundland (now a part of Canada), New Zealand and South Africa – three followed Britain's lead in introducing conscription: New Zealand in June 1916, Canada in January 1918 and Newfoundland in May 1918.[7] These Dominions conscripted far fewer men than did Britain, even when the differences in population are taken into account. The New Zealand government decided to limit its Western Front commitment to one infantry division of three brigades (temporarily supplemented by a fourth infantry brigade created in March 1917 and disbanded February 1918). For this reason New Zealand conscripted only 32 270 men – less than half the number who voluntarily served in the New Zealand Expeditionary Force.[8] In Canada, 124 588 men were called up into the Canadian Expeditionary Force (in comparison to about 600 000 volunteers), but only 24 132 conscripts had gone overseas before the end of the war, and of these only a few thousand actually reached the front line. Although the Newfoundland government did introduce conscription, none of the conscripts left home before the Armistice, and the Royal Newfoundland Regiment serving on the Western Front retained its all-volunteer identity to the end of the war.[9]

With the Australians having being joined on the list of all-volunteer forces by the South African Brigade and the Royal Newfoundland Regiment, it is now time to add another group. As mentioned above, conscription was never instituted in Ireland, so all 210 000 Irishmen who served in the British Army in World War I were volunteers.[10] The 10th (Irish) Division served alongside the Anzacs at Gallipoli. The 36th (Ulster) Division, formed out of the Unionist (wanting Ireland to remain united with Britain) paramilitary Ulster Volunteer Force, lost about 5000 men on the first day of the Battle of the Somme. The 16th (Irish) Division, which included many prominent Nationalists (who wanted Ireland to have its own government, separate from Britain), also served on the Somme. On 7 June 1917, the 16th (Irish) and the 36th (Ulster) Divisions put aside their political differences and fought alongside each other in the successful attack on Messines. As voluntary enlistment in Ireland declined, Irish battalions were bolstered with British conscripts.[11] An attempt to introduce conscription in Ireland in 1918 failed when it met with strong public opposition that can be compared in many ways to the opposition to conscription in Australia.[12]

The remaining all-volunteer forces to be considered came from South Africa, India and several British colonies. These soldiers were mostly non-White, and Australian World War I-era racial attitudes probably explain why these men, even when they fought alongside the AIF at Gallipoli and in the Palestine campaign, were ignored when making claims about all-volunteer forces.[13]

That the 1st South African Brigade that fought on the Western Front was composed entirely of volunteers has already been noted. This brigade was composed almost entirely of English-speaking whites, but all South African units – whether recruited from English- or Afrikaans-speaking whites, mixed-race 'Coloureds' from Cape Province, ethnic Indians from Natal, or the African majority – were volunteers. A force of 45 000 white volunteer combatants and 33 000 African, 'Coloured' and Indian volunteer auxiliaries took part in the South African invasion of the neighbouring German colony of South-West Africa in 1914. Twenty-one thousand African volunteers served with the South African Labour Contingent in France and carried out vital mili-

The 'superior', all-volunteer AIF

tary tasks such as building roads and unloading supplies at the Channel ports. A further 18 000 Africans served in East Africa. About 7000 'Coloureds' enlisted in the Cape Corps and members of this formation's 1st Battalion fought as infantry alongside Australians in the Palestine campaign.[14]

The largest all-volunteer army in World War I was, in fact, the Indian Army. In 1914, this force, in which almost all officers were British, consisted of 155 423 soldiers and 45 660 non-combatant troops who carried out logistics, transport, medical, veterinary and remount tasks. In 1914 and 1915, Indian volunteers served on the Western Front and alongside Australians at Gallipoli. From 1915, the Indian Army provided the bulk of the British Empire force fighting the Ottoman Empire in Mesopotamia (now Iraq) and alongside Australians in Palestine. By the end of the war, the Indian Army had expanded to over 1.4 million volunteer troops – one million more than the entire number who enlisted in the AIF in the whole of the war – composed of 877 068 combatant and 563 369 non-combatant soldiers.[15]

Military units raised in other British colonies were also all volunteers. In the Caribbean, 15 601 men enlisted in the twelve battalions of the British West Indies Regiment. The battalions of the regiment sent to Europe were deployed as labouring troops, but those sent to Palestine fought as infantry alongside Australians.[16] The Nigeria Regiment raised about 17 000 volunteers who served in the campaigns in German Cameroons and German East Africa. A further 38 500 Nigerian volunteers served as auxiliaries.[17] The King's African Rifles, recruited from Britain's various east African colonies, expanded from three battalions in 1914 to twenty-two battalions in 1918, with 31 000 volunteer infantrymen.[18] These soldiers fought German forces in the East African campaign that began in 1914 and did not conclude until the German commander, General Paul von Lettow-Vorbeck, was told that the war in Europe had ended and he subsequently surrendered on 23 November 1918.

The gross misconception that arises out of the erroneous belief that the AIF was the only all-volunteer force in World War I is that Australian volunteers, because they chose to enlist, inevitably made better soldiers than those who were compelled to join up. This idea is a myth for two reasons. Firstly, it projects current ideas of individualism and autonomy back almost one hundred years onto young men living in a more hierarchical and deferential society. In this time, the choice of whether or not to enlist was not necessarily an act of self-determination, but was often a decision made for the individual within a family or wider community. As one AIF veteran wrote in 1965, Australia in the period of World War I 'was an old man's world – a chap of twenty-one was considered a boy and not given responsibility, nor much notice'. Young people were used to decisions being made for them and following the directions of others. A clerk in a Ballarat solicitor's office recalled of his decision to join up: 'I hardly thought about it. The adults around me all seemed to be of the opinion that enlistment was the right thing for an eligible male to do and I just seemed to conform to that idea without attempting to weigh the pros and cons of the matter.'[19]

Australian males in this period did not act individualistically without reference to others to the extent that their contemporary equivalents do. Instead, the Australians of 1914–1918 were more likely to view themselves as members of wider groups such as a church congregation, trade union or professional organisation, political party or sporting club. One under-aged Balmain apprentice printer enlisted in November 1915 because he had heard the news that several men from his church had been killed at Gallipoli. Employers played a major role in deciding which of their employees went to war and which stayed at home. One man working for the Melbourne city branch of the Bank of New South Wales was prevented from enlisting in 1914 because he was not one of the five employees the bank manager was willing to release from the branch's staff. In the same way, at the beginning of the war a station manager on a property in the north-east of South Australia allowed several stockmen to go to Adelaide to join the Light Horse because drought had reduced stock numbers and their services were not needed. The man in charge of maintaining the dams, however, was vital to ensuring the survival of the remaining sheep and cattle, and he had to stay until heavy rains in 1915.[20]

Family responsibilities generally loomed much larger in a young man's life in Australia in 1914 than it does today. In a time before pensions, superannuation, retirement villages and nursing homes, parents required their children to keep and care for them in old age. Most boys and girls generally finished school around the age of 12 and started working either in paid jobs or in doing all the unpaid work that needed to be done around homes, family businesses or farms. Parents therefore often saw children less as individuals, with their own rights and ambitions, and more as economic units to be deployed for what they saw as the greater interest of the family unit.

Some parents directed their sons to enlist. One mother, an English migrant living in Ballarat, told her children: 'Well boys, MY COUNTRY is at War and you know what is expected of you'. The father of Robert Menzies (who would become Australia's longest-serving prime minister) held a 'a family conference' at which he decided that his two eldest sons should join the AIF and that Robert, who was studying law at Melbourne University and therefore had better financial prospects, should remain at home to provide for his aging parents.[21]

Other parents refused to allow their sons to go to war. In

1915 the Federal Government issued war census cards to all adult males and asked those aged between 18 and 44 whether they were willing to enlist and: 'If you are not willing to enlist, state the reasons why'.[22] One dairy farmer — the most labour-intensive form of farming in this period, since the twice-daily milking had to be done by hand — was so determined to keep his adult son on the farm that he filled out the his card for him, stating that he could not enlist, and demanded his son sign it. As the son later wrote: 'I signed as he directed but made a private vow to leave home and join up under another name. I felt that only by doing so could I regain the loss of dignity and pride that I had suffered by submitting to such treatment. I felt most dreadfully shamed and humiliated.'[23]

In some rural areas the older men of the district decided how many men needed to stay to provide sufficient labour to work the farms and how many could join the AIF. As John McQuilton found in his study of north-east Victoria in World War I: 'Once local communities were satisfied that their "eligibles" had gone, they resisted any further attempts to force the men remaining to enlist'. McQuilton provides the example of the rural district of Wooragee, just north of Beechworth: 14 men had enlisted from Wooragee by the time the first conscription referendum has held in October 1916, and the local community had decided that this was enough. When members of the Beechworth branch of the pro-conscription National Referendum Council visited Wooragee in the lead-up to the referendum, they received a hostile reception. Only four men enlisted from this district in the remaining two years of the war.[24]

Strongly-held societal values also influenced the decision to enlist. The idea of 'duty' was dominant in Australia in this period. As an engine cleaner in the New South Wales Government Railways later wrote: 'My motive for enlisting was, as Australia was at war, it was my duty as a Free young able Man to enlist'. When men considered 'eligible' to enlist by the rest of the community did not do so, they were sometimes sent white feathers – a symbol of cowardice – to pressure them to 'do their duty' and join up.[25]

The second reason why enlistment in the AIF in World War I was not necessarily a free choice was the poor state of the Australian economy in this period. Between 1911 and 1916 much of the country was devastated by drought. An editorial in the *West Australian* in 1915 rightly described drought as 'the formidable enemy within our gates'. The outbreak of war exacerbated these economic problems, especially after the amount of shipping sailing to Australia fell to half. As economic historian Marnie Haig-Muir puts it, for an economy so reliant on exporting commodities and importing manufactured goods, this was 'little short of disastrous'. The war also led to high inflation. In Melbourne, from mid-1914 to mid-1915, the price of meat increased 200 per cent, flour 87 per cent, butter 63 per cent and bread 50 per cent.[26]

With this weak Australian economy, many men worked irregularly or not at all, and there were no government payments to the unemployed. For many, the decision to enlist was thus determined by economic circumstances. One 16-year-old in Melbourne, who had been working to help support his mother since the age of ten, enlisted in June 1915 to improve on the 30 shillings a week he brought into the household by delivering newspapers and milking cows. He calculated that if he joined the AIF he would be able to give his mother the bulk of his private's pay of 42 shillings a week 'and mum didn't have to feed and clothe me'. In another example, an English coalminer who had migrated to Australia with his wife in 1913 was unable to secure regular work due to constant union strikes and company lockouts in the New South Wales coalfields of the Hunter Valley, Illawarra and Lithgow. His middle-class wife had brought 'a considerable amount of money' with her to start their new life in Australia, but when this had been spent on living expenses they faced 'poverty caused by constant unemployment'. This man, a stalwart unionist and a staunch member of the Methodist Church, decided to enlist for three reasons. First, he doubted he would be able to work again at his Lithgow colliery which had re-opened with non-union labour. Second, he 'salved his conscience' over the morality of war with the belief that Britain had a just cause in mobilising to protect Belgium against German aggression. Third was what he described as the 'financial issue': 'In the army, at least, I would be fed, and my wife with a 3 [shilling] a day allotment would be able to live without getting into further debt'.[27]

The last problem with the mythology surrounding the voluntary status of the AIF is the spurious notion that a volunteer will always be a better soldier than a conscript. As Elizabeth Greenhalgh wrote in her chapter on the myth that the AIF broke the Hindenburg Line in 1918 in the original *Zombie Myths of Australian Military History*: 'The idea that Australian volunteers had developed specifically Australian racial characteristics well suited to modern industrial war, in contrast to the class-ridden, stunted, conscripted infantry of the "Mother Country", is quite ridiculous'.[28] The AIF was successful on the Western Front in 1918 not because they were all volunteers, but because they were a component of a British Empire army and wider Allied force that was by that stage in the war well trained and well supported, particularly with artillery – and especially in contrast to its enemy.

Rob Stephenson, in his study of the 1st Australian Division in 1917, argues that the ability to successfully attack on the Western Front relied '[n]ot so much on the individual courage of the front line digger, although this was of course still vital, but rather the intellectual and moral power' of the Division's commander, Harold Walker, a British Regular officer who had served with the

Indian Army, and his chief of staff, Thomas Blamey, an Australian Permanent officer. Just as significantly, according to Stephenson, Walker's and Blamey's improvements in the 1st Australian Division were replicated 'in dozens of divisions' through the British Empire's army as 'like-minded professionals grappled with the implications of new technology, experimented with new tactics to exploit it and adapted the way they organised and trained their troops'.[29]

This development of technology and tactics to successfully attack the German army on the Western Front has been described by British historian Gary Sheffield as a 'learning curve' or 'learning process'.[30] Central to this notion were improvements in the use of artillery so that the British (and their allies) were able to suppress the German infantry and its artillery, and enable their own soldiers to advance with hitherto unknown 'protection'. Allied artillery fire was made much more accurate by a number of measures. These included: compiling mathematical tables that took account of the effect of barrel wear of a gun so it could be gradually re-aimed in order to continue hitting the same target; compiling similar tables that took account of the effect of shell weight variation, weighing a sample of each batch of shells and accordingly adjusting the aim of guns using these shells; meteorologists making weather reports on wind, temperature and atmosphere that were sent to all artillery batteries six times a day; using flash-spotting and sound-ranging to identify the location of German artillery batteries; and developing counter-battery tactics to prevent these guns from firing when Allied troops attacked.[31]

The importance of artillery on the Western Front in 1918 can be illustrated by one minor operation: the 7th Australian Brigade's capture of a small area of high ground at Morlancourt on the evening of 10 June 1918. In this attack, the advance of 2000 Australian infantrymen was made possible by the artillery fire provided by 7000 mostly British gunners.³² By the time of the Allied 'Hundred Days' offensive in 1918, the British Empire infantry on the Western Front had all received the same type and level of training whether they were British, Canadian, or Australian – and whether they were volunteers or conscripts. As Sheffield has pointed out, the British 46th (North Midland) Division did not have the reputation of elite troops accorded to the Australian, Canadian or New Zealand divisions, yet with the guns of the British Army behind them, the mostly conscript soldiers of the 46th became the first troops to break through the Hindenburg Line on 29 September 1918 with an audacious crossing of the St Quentin Canal by men wearing floatation vests and carrying scaling ladders to ascend the steep far bank.³³ The Allied victory on the Western Front in World War I was a team effort. National governments and private industries, civilians and soldiers – both volunteers and conscripts – combined to defeat Germany. As Elizabeth Greenhalgh wrote:

> Breaking the Hindenburg Line … required a co-ordinated weapons system. It did not matter which part of the world, which part of the British Empire, or which part of England the infantry came from; these infantry troops formed one element of a weapons system that included tanks, aircraft and, above all, artillery. The guns were made in Britain or Canada, with steel imported from the USA, and they fired shells packed by women munitions workers.³⁴

As the centenary of World War I approaches, it is important that the commemoration of this conflict is based on the real Australian war experience, and not the perpetuation of myths such as that of the AIF being the only all-volunteer allied army that took part. True, this war was a defining national experience for

Australia; but, as we remember the men of the AIF, we need also to remember how their world differs from our own. With Anzac Day becoming the *de facto* national day, and the increasing interest by Australians in their military past, the best form of commemoration will be based on a solid base of fact and not the shaky foundations of myth.

Further reading

E.M. Andrews, *The Anzac Illusion*, Cambridge University Press, Melbourne, 1993.

J. Beaumont (ed.), *Australia's War 1914–1918*, Allen & Unwin, Sydney, 1995.

C. Bridge, *William Hughes, Australia: The Paris Peace Conferences of 1919– 1923 and their Aftermath*, Haus Publishing, London, 2011.

J. Connor, 'Some examples of Irish enlistment in the Australian Imperial Force, 1914', *The Irish Sword*, 83, 1998, pp. 85–89.

——, 'The Empire's war recalled: Recent writing on the Western Front experience of Britain, Ireland, Australia, Canada, India, New Zealand, South Africa and the West Indies', *History Compass*, 7(4), May 2009, pp. 1123–45.

——, *Anzac and Empire: George Foster Pearce and the Foundations of Australian Defence*, Cambridge University Press, Melbourne, 2011.

J.N.I. Dawes & L.L. Robson, *Citizen to Soldier: Australia before the Great War ~ Recollections of Members of the First AIF*, Melbourne University Press, Melbourne, 1977.

J. Grey, 'Cuckoo in the nest? Australian military historiography: The state of the field', *History Compass*, 6(2), March 2008, pp. 455–68.

K.S. Inglis, (ed J. Lack), *Anzac Remembered: Selected Writings of KS Inglis*, Melbourne University History Department, Melbourne, 1998.

M. McKernan, *The Australian People and the Great War*, Thomas Nelson, Melbourne, 1980.

J. McQuilton, *Rural Australia and the Great War: From Tarrawingee to Tangambalanga*, Melbourne University Press, Melbourne, 2001.

A. Thomson, *Anzac Memories: Living with the Legend*, Oxford University Press, Melbourne, 1994.

R. White, 'Motives for joining up: Self-sacrifice, self-interest and social class 1914–1918', *Journal of the Australian War Memorial*, 9, October 1986, pp. 3–16.

—— , 'The soldier as tourist: The Australian experience of the Great War', *War & Society*, 15(1), May 1987, pp. 63–77.

[3]

WHAT ABOUT NEW ZEALAND? THE PROBLEMATIC HISTORY OF THE ANZAC CONNECTION

Chris Clark

Of the many myths surrounding Gallipoli and the enduring historical tradition spawned by the Anzac landing of 25 April 1915, none is more puzzling than the treatment of the Australia–New Zealand connection. On the one hand there is the mistaken notion that, as a result of that terrible eight-month campaign, a unique affinity amounting to an unbreakable social and military bond was forged between the two nations which has seen them operate as virtual brothers-in-arms ever since. On the other is the actual situation that has developed over recent times, where Australians have taken almost complete possession of the Anzac tradition as though the events at Gallipoli related solely to their country alone. Bad enough that Australians have arrogated to themselves the term 'digger', which was supposedly first applied by New Zealanders about themselves in France in 1917, but to speak of 'Anzac' – the name given first to parts of the Turkish landscape, and ultimately to the men of the Australian & New Zealand Army Corps – as though the New Zealanders were not even part of it, is galling in the extreme.[1]

Such feelings have been around for a good many years. These

days, most New Zealanders are not particularly fussed by the way Australians have taken over the term 'digger', since it is now seldom used as a military term on their side of the Tasman. Instead, as Frank Glen observes, 'New Zealanders use the more ethnic term "Kiwi" to describe members of our armed forces'.[2] Appropriation of the term 'Anzac' is, however, a different matter. As long ago as 1921, one New Zealand writer was moved to issue a reminder of an obvious fact about the word, that 'if the initial "A" stands for Australia, New Zealand furnished the very necessary pivotal consonants'.[3] The point is that the New Zealanders were part of the Gallipoli story from the very first day until the bitter end, and any omission of them by Australians will rankle for as long as the two sides continue to engage in joint military endeavour – as they frequently have since World War I.

So how has such a situation come about? Is it simply another example of big inevitably subsuming small, or could it be that there have been other unrecognised historical forces at play? Could it be that there are elements of the Gallipoli story that do not naturally add up to the tradition as it has evolved? Certainly, when what each side has said about the other on various occasions is considered, it is easy to form an impression of two separate nationalities that have viewed each other as rivals as much as 'cousins' – let alone brothers-in-arms. So is the widely accepted fraternal interpretation valid at all, and if so how and why did it arise? Conversely, if it was an invention and remains a lingering misconception, what has been the long-term impact of what might be a very wrong-headed or misinformed view of each other? Have military connections across the Tasman been of popular imagining only? Could it be that this aspect of the Anzac tradition has grown out of proportion to the facts, as much myth as legend?

A look at events during the lead-up to the operation against the Dardanelles in 1915 reveals little sign of the fraternal regard enshrined in the dominant contemporary Anzac tradition. Indeed, the pattern of the era suggests there was little reason to imagine that a unified response from 'Australasia' ought to have been expected at all. World War I was not the first occasion that Britain's Dominions had rallied on the battlefield in the cause of Empire, but during and after the earlier conflict in South Africa (1899–1902) each of the Australasian nations had been keen to emphasise the separateness (and uniqueness) of their contributions and achievements. New Zealand's attempts to claim the credit for having made the most fulsome colonial response, in proportion to its size, to that war effort won it few friends elsewhere.[4] Nor did New Zealand's willingness to break ranks with Canada and Australia and embrace British efforts to lock in Dominion support for future imperial military enterprises.[5] Even while the two countries managed to co-operate over some practical matters (such as sharing the military college at Duntroon in Canberra to train officers for their respective armies), in the ten years following the Boer War there was a serious divergence between Australia and New Zealand over issues of strategic and imperial defence policy.[6]

It was certainly true that, during military talks in Melbourne in November 1912, Australia and New Zealand consulted about making a co-operative response in the event of a European war, and agreed to raise a joint expeditionary force of divisional size drawn two-thirds from Australia and the rest from New Zealand.[7] On the outbreak of World War I in August 1914, however, these arrangements were promptly and unilaterally disregarded by Australia. The Commonwealth Government, not wanting to be overshadowed by the reported generosity of a Canadian offer to send forces, opted to raise a much larger and all-Australian contingent.[8] Australia gave little thought, it seems, as to where this left the New Zealanders, who planned to stick to the original scheme. Despite British Admiralty plans to escort both contingents overseas in a single convoy, the Australian approach ensured that both countries sought to make their names on the battlefield as separate national forces rather than a single antipodean entity.

There is further evidence of the less-than-close military relations between Australia and New Zealand at the onset of World War I. Before the separate national contingents sailed from their assembly point at Albany, Western Australia, a Boer revolt in South Africa raised the prospect of the convoy being diverted to the Cape. The commander of the Australian Imperial Force (AIF), Major General William Bridges, quickly proposed a solution to putting down the rebellion: he was quite ready to 'sacrifice' the New Zealanders, as well as the Australian Light Horse Brigade, if only this would enable the complete Australian division under his command to proceed intact to Europe as planned.[9] And when the Australian High Commissioner in London, alarmed at the adequacy of facilities in England to accommodate his country's troops, succeeded in having the AIF disembarked in Egypt, the New Zealand Expeditionary Force (NZEF) found itself lumped in under these arrangements as well. The NZEF commander, Major General Sir Alexander Godley, was greatly annoyed to learn of the change at second-hand, from Bridges.[10] To Godley, nothing could have highlighted so clearly the irritating fact that the New Zealanders were generally regarded as affiliates of, or mere adjuncts to, the Australians.

The period during which the two contingents trained in Egypt prior to the Gallipoli landings brought a new edge to their developing mutual antagonism. The loutish behaviour of many Australian troops while enjoying leave in Cairo brought relations to a new low. The diaries of New Zealand soldiers often contain a range of descriptively disparaging observations about their trans-Tasman neighbours. One wrote that whenever Australians were encountered in restaurants or similar places about town 'there is generally a row of some kind', while another commented of the Australians he met that 'the town bred man is a skiting bumptious fool'.[11] Small wonder that some New Zealand officers began encouraging their men to have nothing to do with the Australians, but instead to demonstrate the difference between the two contingents by their own exemplary example. As Charles Bean, then Australia's official press correspondent, later recorded in the official war history: 'This attitude, which was to some extent supported by the New Zealand commanders, led to a certain coolness between Australian and New Zealand troops in Cairo'.[12] For his part, Bean regarded the New Zealanders as colourless and lacking the 'extraordinarily good points' which he felt made up for the Australians' more visible behavioural defects.[13]

In truth, much as New Zealanders might have liked to imagine themselves superior in their conduct to the Australian, misbehaviour also came from their ranks. The notorious 'Battle of the Wasser', so-called after a riot in Cairo's Haret el Wassir district on Good Friday 1915, was (and is still) frequently held to have been attributable solely to Australian troops. New Zealanders, however, were no less involved.[14] While each contingent blamed the other for the episode, the last word on the subject might be gauged from the fact that, of the four soldiers injured in the affray, three were Australians and one New Zealander. Since these numbers matched the proportion of the respective contingents, it can be said – as indeed one New Zealand historian has noted – that 'honours' were equally shared.[15] So too was the damages bill of £1700.[16]

Not only were relations between the AIF and NZEF brittle at this time, other factors pushed them into a relationship which neither side particularly sought. The British high command, acting on the fact that both contingents were conveniently available in

Egypt, and from an assumption that because they came from the same part of the world they were essentially all the same anyway, took the decision to link them in a single formation – the now famous Australian and New Zealand Army Corps (ANZAC).[17] To be fair, there was some justification for the British attitude, since each contingent contained a large number of each other's nationals.[18] To an extent, this merely reflected the make-up of the populations of the two countries: for instance, figures show that 5 per cent of New Zealand's total population in 1911 was Australian-born.[19] But the formation of the original ANZAC did not make instantly for a close and indistinguishable union of forces. The AIF and NZEF continued to be acutely conscious of their separateness and their individual characters.

Regardless of this continuing friction, with the inauguration of ANZAC an important step had been taken in the creation of a popular myth. The same British guiding hand was to give the Anzac legend a helpful push during the landing at Gallipoli. The troops which assaulted the beach north of Gaba Tepe before dawn on 25 April came from the 1st Australian Division alone. The mixed NZ & A (New Zealand and Australian) Division, which Godley commanded, formed the reserve force for the landing, and it was not until nearly five hours later, after 9.00 am, that the first companies of New Zealanders from this formation were put ashore.[20] Although they saw some heavy combat off the beach, to virtually everyone present the day was regarded as Australia's. Even the New Zealanders acknowledged that it was the Australian achievement which deserved the praise.[21]

This view was reflected, too, in the dispatch drafted by the British official correspondent, Ellis Ashmead-Bartlett, in which he described the exploits of the landing. As luck would have it, the British naval staff officer to whom he submitted his copy for censorship was a friend of Godley's, and he performed an entirely different role than that officially required of him. Noticing the omission of any mention of the New Zealanders' presence, he assiduously added references to them wherever he thought appropriate. As one New Zealand historian has remarked: 'It is by such actions that legends are born'.[22] While initial press reports of the Gallipoli landing arguably provided the origins of the Anzac tradition, others soon joined the process of myth-making. In the Australian official history of the war, Bean maintained that co-operation between the men of the two forces over the next few days effectively wiped away all the petty jealousy and antagonisms remaining from their period in Egypt. From this point on, he believed, Australians and New Zealanders were bound together in a close brotherhood-of-arms.[23]

Bean's perception was based on what he believed he knew of bitter fighting which occurred on the left of the shallow beachhead established by the ANZAC landing forces, on a feature called Russell's Top. Here, the Australian 2nd Battalion, commanded by Lieutenant Colonel G.F. Braund, was intermixed with the Wellington Battalion under Lieutenant Colonel W.G. Malone. By the time the Australians were withdrawn on 28 April, a solid bond of mutual respect – according to Bean – had been forged. In his first volume of the official war series, Bean declared that:

> The feeling of the New Zealand infantry, as Braund and his battalion left them, was one of warm and affectionate admiration. Day and night Australians and New Zealanders had fought together on that hilltop. In this fierce test each saw in the other a brother's qualities. As brothers they had died; their bodies lay mingled in the same narrow trenches; as brothers they were buried ... Three days of genuine trial had established a friendship which centuries will not destroy.

Visiting the New Zealand trenches a few hours later, Bean claimed that he had found the men 'overflowing with warm references to the 2nd Australian Battalion'.[24]

But there is evidence that Bean may have got things seriously wrong in his description of the defence of Russell's Top. Colonel Malone's diary presents a different view of the qualities of the Australian troops that he encountered here. In one case he recounted that, to move some that he came across, he 'ordered them up and drove them ahead pelting the leading ones on the track where they stopped with stones and putting my toe into the rear ones'.[25] More seriously, Malone was so incensed at Braund's combat tactics that he complained to Braund's brigadier, insisting that all the Australians should be withdrawn – which they subsequently were – declaring them to be 'a source of weakness'. Bean is also simply wrong in claiming that the shared experience of defending the Anzac beach-head ended all criticism of each other. Malone, in particular, continued to nurse an anti-Australian bias which he frankly confessed in his diary. Welcoming the transfer of his battalion south to the site of the British and French landing at Cape Helles in early May, he wrote that it was a 'relief to get in where war is being waged scientifically and where we are clear of the Australians. They seem to swarm about our line like flies. I keep getting them sent out. They are like masterless men, going their own ways.'[26] Malone, it must be admitted, was an unusual officer even within the NZEF. An Englishman by birth, his approach to soldiering was probably more typical of a British regular, and he was recognised for being difficult, a perfectionist and a martinet. Nonetheless, it is unlikely that he was alone in his views about the Australians.

Although NZEF members like Malone decried the fact that their contingent was 'being absorbed in the word Australasian ... if not Australian', after several months on Gallipoli a special form of acceptance had undoubtedly evolved between the New Zealanders and Australians.[27] It may have been simply the fight for the Anzac beachhead had engendered 'the mutual confidence and esteem' – in the opinion later expressed by the ANZAC's British commander, Sir William Birdwood: 'Going round, as I did, the trenches ... it was to me a constant source of satisfaction and delight to find New Zealanders and Australians confiding in me the highly favourable opinion which, apparently to their surprise, they had formed of each other!'[28]

Plainly Australians and (perhaps more particularly) New Zealanders did not cease finding fault with each other, while both at the same time considered themselves to be the elite among the Dominion troops engaged. But like it or not, the identities of the two contingents had to some extent become merged. Perhaps nothing typified and highlighted this fact more than the later episode when a watercolour image of AIF Private John Simpson Kirkpatrick – more famously known as 'Simpson' or 'the man with the donkey' – was painted by NZEF artist Horace Moore-Jones, using a photograph which he believed showed this 'hero of Anzac' engaged in his mercy role. Unfortunately, the photo was not of Simpson but a New Zealand stretcher-bearer, Private Richard ('Dick') Henderson, even though Moore-Jones' rendition was later hailed as an excellent likeness of the Australian.[29]

After Gallipoli, the subsuming of 'Anzac' by Australia began, while at the same time evidence of friction and/or separateness between the two nations was ignored. Following the allied abandonment of the Gallipoli peninsula in December 1915, both the AIF and NZEF underwent radical restructuring before moving to France. This changed, for all time, the nature of the relationship which was possible between the two forces. The AIF was expanded to a force of five infantry divisions, the NZEF to a complete division. These now were formed into two corps –

I Anzac and II Anzac. Since the one New Zealand Division was obviously in the minority even within its corps, the Anzac tradition was from this point well on its way to being appropriated by the Australians. In November 1917, the New Zealand Division was transferred to the British XXII Corps and the Australian divisions reformed into their own corps. From this point, the Anzac connection on the Western Front effectively disappeared entirely.

Only in the secondary Middle East theatre could it be said that the Anzac bond retained any meaningful form, through the mixing of Australian and New Zealand mounted troops. In March 1916 brigades from the two Dominions were brought together into an Australian and New Zealand Mounted Division, commanded by Australian Major General Harry Chauvel until he was promoted to command the Desert Mounted Corps a year later, whereupon command of the division passed to a New Zealander, Major General Edward Chaytor. The division was known from the start as the 'Anzac Mounted', and the formal linking of Australian and New Zealand horsemen in this formation was continued throughout the campaign in Sinai and Palestine.[30] At the end of 1916, Australians and New Zealanders were also brought together, along with British troops, within a Camel Corps. This force was called 'Imperial', but the three of its four battalions recruited from the colonies were dubbed Anzac units: for instance the 4th (Anzac) Battalion contained a mixture of Australian and New Zealand troopers.[31] The 'Camels' stayed in existence until mid-1918, when it disbanded and its Australians and New Zealanders transferred to form a new 5th Light Horse Brigade.

In Mesopotamia (modern-day Iraq) there was another minor but quite symbolic association between Australian and New Zealand aviators which curiously overlapped with the events taking place on Gallipoli. Lieutenant George Merz, the

What about New Zealand?

first Australian Flying Corps pilot to be killed, perished in July 1915 alongside Lieutenant William Burn, a pilot attached from the New Zealand Staff Corps (although by coincidence Burn happened to be Australian-born).[32] Also in Mesopotamia, the 1st (Anzac) Wireless Signal Squadron was formed during 1916 by combining Australian and New Zealand signals troops to support British operations against the Turks in that country. This unit remained in existence until late 1917, when the New Zealanders were withdrawn to go to France.[33]

Although the Anzac tradition had its most real (but nonetheless questionable) basis for no more than an eight-month period in 1915, the legend created at this time retained a potency which – perhaps surprisingly – has endured ever since. Why this should be so might be argued endlessly, but what may be noted here is the tenuous factual nature of the legend in subsequent years. The reality was that Australians and New Zealanders continued to be at least as much rivals as they were comrades. Despite the invocation of the Anzac name at various points during World War II, for example, the fact remained that Australian and New Zealand forces operated for the most part as entirely separate national forces, and later in separate theatres of operations.

During the short Greek campaign of April 1941, an Anzac Corps existed for less than a fortnight, essentially by renaming Lieutenant-General Sir Thomas Blamey's 1st Australian Corps headquarters to acknowledge that it had the 2nd New Zealand Division under its command.[34] Even this briefest of associations was not trouble-free: in the confused withdrawal following a German breakthrough at Pinios Gorge, for example, Australian and New Zealand soldiers traded accusations against the other of having deserted their posts and abandoning vital gun positions.[35] A month later, plans were being debated for a new Anzac Corps to be formed in the Middle East under the NZEF commander,

Major General Bernard Freyberg. Blamey's idea on this occasion was to form the Australian 7th and 9th Divisions into an additional Australian Corps, with himself in command of both corps as an army commander.[36] This scheme found little favour with the Australian government, however, which feared that it could actually 'result in a splitting of the Australian Force', and consequently nothing came of it before Japan entered the war and overturned the basis of Australia's military effort in the Middle East to focus on the Pacific theatre. Despite the fact that New Zealand was no less under threat from the Japanese, the major part of the NZEF stayed in Europe.

For quite understandable reasons, the Anzac mantle has rarely assumed a naval dimension in either Australia or New Zealand (see Chapter 8). During World War II, however, one such occasion arose late in January 1942, when the Allies established ABDA (American, British, Dutch, Australian) Command covering most of South-East Asia, the Netherlands East Indies (later Indonesia), and even a slice of northern Australia. East of this zone was another called 'ANZAC Area', taking in the east coast of Australia and the whole of New Zealand, patrolled by a seagoing squadron known as Anzac Force. Although half the ships of this squadron were American, the flagship was Australian and two light cruisers were from New Zealand.[37] The existence of Anzac Area lasted barely three months before it was submerged within new allied arrangements which saw New Zealand – despite objections from Wellington – placed in a naval command area that was quite separate to that containing Australia.

The difference in outlook which had emerged in Australia and New Zealand during World War II, at least at the level of high command if not on the part of the ordinary soldier or the man-in-the-street, was expressed most forcefully and starkly by General Blamey. As Australian commander-in-chief, Blamey was concerned to ensure that post-war policy in the Pacific was firmly based on realities and not sentiment. On these grounds, he was worried about the Curtin Labor government's negotiation of the 1944 Anzac Pact with New Zealand, under which the two countries proposed to establish a regional organisation called the South Seas Regional Commission. While part of his opposition to such schemes stemmed from his reservations about associated ideas for establishing 'well-defended forward bases' (which he thought could be bypassed and would be difficult to maintain), his more fundamental objection concerned the wisdom of Australia making far-reaching and irrevocable defence commitments.[38] Blamey put his views in forthright terms when he told the Minister for the Army, Frank Forde, that:

> Militarily, of course, New Zealand is of very little real interest to Australia. On the other hand, Australia is of the very greatest interest to New Zealand from the military point of view. As long as Australia is safe, New Zealand is completely safe in the present world set-up, so that any Australian military commitments should be solely designed to Australian requirements, without any consideration to New Zealand's position at all.[39]

Blamey, at least, recognised that invoking the emotional pull of the Anzac name was a tactic which suited New Zealand interests, but which offered nothing to Australia as the bigger partner. Had he lived beyond 1951 – when Australia, New Zealand and the United States signed the ANZUS Treaty – it would have been interesting to know what Blamey thought about the similar attempts by later Australian governments to claim the attention and support of Australia's bigger ally, the United States, by invoking the ANZUS rather than Anzac catchcry.

Blamey's perspective on the Australia–New Zealand connection was, however, neither widely understood nor shared: to generations of ordinary Australians it has seemed that co-operation with New Zealand in conflicts after World War I simply represented further glorious chapters in an ongoing Anzac tradition. Most Australians, for instance, appear unaware of many of the attempts, mainly at the instigation of third parties, that were made to manufacture an Anzac connection after 1945 even where none naturally or necessarily existed. A number of these minor episodes involved units of the two countries' air forces. During the Berlin Airlift of 1948–1949, for example, an apparently British initiative grouped the ten transport aircrews sent from Australia and the three New Zealand ones into a single entity referred to as No. 1 Dominion Squadron, to distinguish them from South African Air Force crews who were put into No. 2 Dominion Squadron.[40] This mixed 'Anzac' unit (although that specific term was never used) was placed under command of the senior officer of the Royal Australian Air Force (RAAF) contingent, although he had no idea why.[41] Apparently the arrangement was no more than an administrative convenience, taken without knowledge or consent of the countries which had sent the personnel in the first place.

A similar situation arose again when both Australia and New Zealand acceded to British requests in 1952 that they contribute forces to assist the Royal Air Force in garrisoning the Mediterranean region. Australia responded by dispatching its No. 78 (Fighter) Wing, comprising two half-strength squadrons to operate Vampire jets – leased from Britain – from bases on Malta. New Zealand sent its No. 14 Squadron, also operating Vampires but from the island of Cyprus, under the same terms as the RAAF. It came as no surprise that for major air exercises in which the two contingents were involved, the New Zealand unit flew as the third squadron of the Australian Wing.[42] This arrangement lasted until 1955, when No. 78 Wing returned to Australia and No. 14 Squadron moved to Singapore. Both the Berlin and the Mediterranean cases reflect a British desire and tendency to create an artificial linkage, regardless of the wishes or inclinations of the two nationalities involved.

In between these two examples came the Korean War, perhaps the one post-World War I opportunity to recreate the Anzac connexion in more substantial form. Immediately after conflict began on the Korean peninsula in June 1950, there was discussion and deliberation in Canberra about the size and form of Australia's involvement. The Americans told Australian political leaders that they would be 'delighted if Australia and New Zealand together could send three battalions in the following three to four months' to help to form a British Commonwealth Light Division. Following this clear statement of preference for an 'Anzac' force, the focus of planning naturally went in this direction – until the New Zealanders made it known that their army was better placed to provide fire support rather than combat troops, and that they were more likely to offer a regiment of field artillery instead of an infantry battalion.[43] The promised unit, the 16th New Zealand Field Artillery Regiment, duly reached Korea late in January 1951 and joined the 27th British Commonwealth Infantry Brigade, where its 163rd Battery was allocated to support the 3rd Battalion, Royal Australian Regiment (3RAR). According to one Australian account, 'The spirit of Anzac was never stronger than the good feeling which existed ... between the New Zealand artillerymen and the men of the 3rd Battalion'.[44]

Such excellent relations, deriving from 'the old ANZAC affiliation' (in the words of the Australian official history), were never more important than during the famous battle of Kapyong, which took place, coincidentally, on the eve of Anzac Day 1951. The success of the gallant delaying action which 3RAR and a Canadian battalion mounted against a 10 000-strong Chinese division on 23–24 April was in no small part due to the fire support received throughout the battle from the New Zealand 25-pounder guns, which frequently helped break up enemy assaults as they were forming up. The Kiwi contribution was all the more remarkable for having been maintained in the face of a severe shortage of ammunition, and even after Chinese infiltrators had reached the defenders' rear positions and had begun probing the gun area itself, forcing the New Zealanders to move their batteries to a safer location further back.[45]

Having helped 3RAR to hold its ground, the New Zealand gunners were also instrumental in enabling the Australians to withdraw during the early hours of darkness on the night of 24 April. By then the Chinese had penetrated down the Kapyong Valley, more than four kilometres past the Australian battalion's position, and the unit was in peril of being completely cut off. The New Zealanders played a pivotal role in keeping the Chinese at bay as the Australian companies thinned out their positions and then allowed rearguards to break contact and get away. In the words of one Australian officer:

> Towards evening orders came to withdraw. We did so, ably supported by our Anzac friends of the New Zealand 16th Field Artillery. As D Company evacuated their positions Chinese troops were right behind them and many a Chinaman had a dead heat or a photo finish with a 25-pounder Kiwi shell. Sometimes the Chinaman won and sometimes only came second ... on Anzac Eve we dug in among friends. At last I felt like an Anzac and I imagine there were 600 others like me.[46]

What about New Zealand?

Invoking the Anzac tradition at this point also seemed appropriate to the Australian official historian of the Korean War: 'The combined Australian–New Zealand action [at Kapyong] was singularly appropriate on the eve of their first spectacular partnership in combat on Gallipoli Peninsula thirty-six years previously'.[47]

Later still, a new conflict in Vietnam provided yet another setting to revive the Anzac connection. Again, the push that developed for an Anzac Force to be established came chiefly from the United States, which desperately wanted a physical presence of supportive allies.[48] Initially, New Zealand was unable to commit infantrymen to the conflict, but agreed to send its 161st Field Battery to provide artillery support to the battalion group that Australia sent in June 1965, and the task force that followed a year later. This ensured a New Zealand connection with the action which has come to define Australia's combat experience in Vietnam: the battle of Long Tan on 18 August 1966. When a company of 6th Battalion, Royal Australian Regiment, found itself facing annihilation by a vastly superior enemy force, it was the supporting fire of the 1st Australian Field Regiment (which included the New Zealand 161st Battery) – directed, as it happened, by an attached New Zealand Army forward observer – which largely prevented such a dire outcome.[49] It was this circumstance, presumably, which prompted one Australian army historian to subtitle his account of the battle as 'The Legend of Anzac Upheld'.[50]

If lauding the Anzac connection at Long Tan in this way seemed a little extravagant, there was more justification for such portrayal from 1967 when New Zealand infantry companies – first one, and then a second – were incorporated into Australian battalions in Vietnam. The situation was formalised in March 1968 when the 2nd Battalion, Royal Australian Regiment was retitled 2RAR/NZ (ANZAC), and this naming practice continued with later battalions until the withdrawal in 1971.[51] The significance of this arrangement was not lost on the Australian official history:

> For the first time in the history of Australian–New Zealand joint military co-operation, dating back over 50 years to the Gallipoli campaign of 1915, infantry soldiers of the two nations were officially combined into a single battalion to fight side-by-side under a common name and in a common cause.[52]

'Bonds of comradeship' and 'a shared military tradition' may have counted for something in this case, but it could not prevent an 'amicable rivalry' from developing even here, with both sides considering themselves superior in their operating methods in the field. The New Zealanders found cause for complaint (once again) in the 'brash behaviour' of the Australians, and whenever they felt that their identity was being submerged or they were treated like 'poor relations'. For their part, the Australians based their attitude to their trans-Tasman colleagues on the reputation that Maori soldiers had acquired for serious indiscipline whenever they were within the task force base camp, which led to the Kiwis being assigned extra time in the bush on patrol.[53]

A decade after the Vietnam experience, Australian and New Zealand military elements were again brought together in a joint enterprise which bore, in a fashion, the Anzac mantle. On this occasion, however, the role was peacekeeping rather than war, and the forces involved were not mainly army. In 1981 the two countries agreed to provide a combined helicopter unit to support the US-led Multinational Force and Observers to monitor the provisions of the 1978 Camp David accord, and the peace treaty signed the next year, which returned the Israeli-occupied Sinai Peninsula to Egypt. When deployed in March 1982, the Rotary Wing

Aviation Unit consisted of eight Iroquois and 99 personnel from the RAAF, and a New Zealand contingent of two more Iroquois (leased from the US Army) and 36 personnel. Operating from El Gorah in the north-eastern Sinai, about 20 kilometres south of the Mediterranean coast, the unit – informally known as 'Anzac Airlines' – first took to the air on Anzac Day 1982. Within weeks of arriving, the two contingents had also set up an all-ranks bar known as the 'Anzac Surf Club (Sinai)', which came complete with surf boards.[54] For the next three years this composite unit of Australians and New Zealanders clearly saw themselves as continuing a hallowed tradition: they even took the 'ANZAC' name for themselves – although in this instance the acronym was held to stand for 'Australia and New Zealand Air Contingent'.[55]

Co-operation between Australian and New Zealand military forces continued despite the upset caused in the mid-1980s by New Zealand's abrogation of the ANZUS Treaty over the issue of visiting nuclear ships. In March 1987, after the navies of Australia and New Zealand identified a requirement for a new general-purpose frigate, both countries signed a Memorandum of Understanding for what became known as Anzac frigate project. As was often the case with the Anzac connection, this joint agreement did not meet universal acclaim, despite the fact that arrangements for sharing the modular construction of the new vessels meant work for shipyards on both sides of the Tasman.[56] By the mid-1990s there was considerable controversy in New Zealand due to perceptions in sections of the community and body politic that 'Australia was forcing New Zealand into buying more expensive ships than the country needed'.[57]

While such ructions caused problems from time to time within the Anzac partners' armed forces, they were still capable of working together at an operational level. New Zealand contributed a battalion group to the Australian-led intervention in East Timor from 1999 to 2002, and the two countries have also been joined together in the International Stabilisation Force which returned to East Timor in 2006 under arrangements which have seen command vested in an Australian Army officer, deputy command with a New Zealander. During the changeover of command in Dili in July 2011, the outgoing Australian officer was quoted as saying, 'It is a privilege to have led the combined Australian and New Zealand Force that performed in the true spirit of the ANZAC legend forged so many years ago'.[58] This was a fine and noble sentiment, but one is left to wonder whether those uttering such words understood the full background to the tradition they were embracing.

And if the top brass seem to have an overly rosy impression, several recent efforts to memorialise the Australian–New Zealand connection on Australian soil also appear misinformed. One such commemoration, apparently the result of a local initiative, saw Sydney's recently constructed Glebe Island Bridge renamed the 'Anzac Bridge' in 1998. An Australian flag flies atop its eastern pylon with a New Zealand flag from the western pylon, and a bronze memorial statue of an Australian soldier placed at the western end of the bridge was followed in 2008 by a similar statue of a New Zealand counterpart directly across the road – both statues by the same New Zealand sculptor. At the dedication of the second statue, New Zealand Prime Minister Helen Clark announced that the original bronze Australian was now 'joined by his mate, symbolising the extraordinary and close friendship between New Zealand and Australia in times of war and peace'.[59]

In the meantime, the New Zealand Memorial was also dedicated on Anzac Parade in Canberra – on 24 April 2001. One commentator more cautiously observed that 'The memorial gives rise to a range of possible meanings' and suggested 'it is the clean, consensual collective memory that is being assisted by this memorial, the seemingly unproblematic ANZAC relationship'. An interpretive plaque nearby states that its purpose is to commemorate 'the unique friendship between New Zealand and Australian people', yet everything about the memorial – from its position in the heart of Australia's national capital, to the inclusion of inscriptions of battlegrounds where the men and women of both countries have fought together on foreign soil, along with buried boxes of earth from two of those contested fields at Gallipoli (Chunuk Bair and Lone Pine) – serves to proclaim that this is specifically a war memorial.[60] If nothing else, the memorial stands as a visible and irrefutable reminder, to any Australian who may be inclined to forget, that New Zealanders were also Anzacs – not just Australians – and the Anzac tradition is not the national possession of Australia alone.

Further reading

C.E.W. Bean, *The Story of Anzac*, The Official History of Australia in the War of 1914–1918, 2 vols, Angus & Robertson, Sydney, 1921 & 1924.

A.G. Butler, *The Digger: A Study in Democracy*, Angus & Robertson, Sydney, 1945.

J. Crawford (ed.), *No Better Death: The Great War Diaries and Letters of William G. Malone*, Reed Books, Auckland, 2005.

F. Glen, 'ANZAC today: What does ANZAC mean to contemporary New Zealanders?', *Wartime*, Official Magazine of the Australian War Memorial, 14, Winter 2001.

H.S. Gullett, *The Australian Imperial Force in Sinai and Palestine*, The Official History of Australia in the War of 1914–1918, vol. 7, Angus & Robertson, Sydney, 1923.

K. Hunter, 'States of mind: Remembering the Australian–New Zealand relationship', *Journal of the Australian War Memorial*, 36, May 2002, < www.awm.gov.au/journal/j36/nzmemorial.asp>.

P. Londey, *Other People's Wars: A History of Australian Peacekeeping*, Allen & Unwin, Sydney, 2004.

L. McAulay, *The Battle of Long Tan: The Legend of Anzac Upheld*, Arrow Books, Sydney, 1987.

J. McLeod, *Myth & Reality: The New Zealand Soldier in World War II*, Heinmann Reed, Auckland, 1986.

I. McNeill & A. Ekins, *On the Offensive: The Australian Army in the Vietnam War 1967–1968*, The Official History of Australia's Involvement in Southeast Asian Conflicts 1948–1975, Allen & Unwin, Sydney, 2003.

R. O'Neill, *Australia in the Korean War 1950–1953*, 2 vols, Australian War Memorial, Canberra, 1981 & 1985.

C. Pugsley, C *Gallipoli: The New Zealand Story*, Hodder & Stoughton, Auckland, 1984.

[4]

OTHER PEOPLE'S WARS

Craig Stockings

In his recent documentary entitled *Other People's Wars*, filmmaker John Pilger described how Australians have 'a special relationship with war'. 'We fight', he contends, 'mostly against people with whom we have no quarrel and who offer us no threat of invasion', and Australians have thus 'paid a unique blood sacrifice in order to appease a great protector'.[1] In other words, Australia has largely fought other people's wars that have been as unnecessary as they have been costly. It has done so either out of unthinking fidelity to great power protectors (either Britain or more recently the United States) or as a consequence of being duped or otherwise manipulated by these 'big brother' allies. Pilger is certainly not alone in this view. Rather, he represents a continuing and pervasive perception of Australia's military past that runs through not only the popular media, but in wider social and scholarly circles as well.[2] On 26 April 1992, for example, Australian Prime Minister Paul Keating made a speech about the Kokoda Trail in which he claimed:

> Even though we fought in many conflicts where we felt pangs of loyalty to what was then known as the 'Mother Country', to Britain and to the Empire, and we fought at Gallipoli with

heroism and in Belgium, in Flanders, in France and in other places, this was the first and only time we've fought against an enemy to prevent the invasion of Australia, to secure the way of life we had built for ourselves.[3]

The inference is clear. According to Keating, all other wars before 1942 and after 1945 were consequences of misplaced loyalty and sentiment. Similarly, in an academic anthology published only last year entitled *What's Wrong with Anzac?: The Militarisation of Australian History*, Professors Henry Reynolds and Marilyn Lake make similar arguments: 'Engagement in foreign wars has been one of the most distinctive features of Australia's twentieth century history. Many of them have been what are now commonly called wars of choice rather than wars of necessity.'[4] Again the implication is that Australia ought to have kept its nose well out of conflicts that did not concern it. Many other authors and commentators over time have chosen specific wars and sought to demonstrate Australia's mistaken choice to become involved, decisions they see as often having been made for the wrong reasons, with an incomplete knowledge of circumstances, or even under external coercion. Collectively such sentiments capture one of the most powerful and widespread misconceptions of Australian military history.

It is not the purpose of this chapter to make moral judgment on the wars Australians have fought from the colonial era to the present. Nor is it concerned with the outcomes of those wars, and questions of whether or not the manifold 'aims' of various Australian military expeditions were met. Nor is there space to investigate what a concept like the 'national interest' might mean exactly – are these the interests of everyday Australians, for example, or else the interests of those in positions of power and influence with potentially quite divergent priorities? Rather, this chapter seeks specifically and singly to address the idea that these wars have belonged to 'other people'; that Australian policy-makers have consistently been victims of their own sentimentality toward 'great and powerful friends', or else been bullied or duped into appeasing these allies through military commitments better avoided and with little or no intrinsic consequence to Australia. This idea, while it may well have had (and no doubt still has) significant appeal to various political and intellectual agendas, simply fails to stack up to historical scrutiny or evidenced argument. Australia's wars have been her own. For better or worse, successive Australian governments have chosen to fight. They have done so in the main for cold, calculating, *realpolitik* reasons. This is not to suggest that powerful cultural and emotional connections, or appeals to the patriotism of Empire, or more recently to apparent need to impose 'freedom' or 'democracy', have not existed, nor played their part – especially as recruiting tools. Nor does it suggest that soldiers past and present have not ardently believed in the righteousness of their cause, or that these allies have not sought to shape Australian decision-making to serve their own ends. In all cases, however, there is need to pierce the shroud of propaganda and popular sentiment that inevitably surrounds decisions to participate in war. Private soldiers and private citizens do not choose when and where to commit themselves to armed conflict. They deploy, and die, on the orders of their government. Australian politicians have made such choices according to rational and realist principles – not sentiment.

In order to focus its argument, this chapter will first examine the decision to deploy the 2nd Australian Imperial Force (2nd AIF) to the Middle East in 1939. This is not at all a random choice. If ever there were a military expedition that should support the 'case for the prosecution', it is this decision. This was a choice to commit the nation's only fully armed and equipped regular (full-time) formation half-way around the world, at Britain's call, to protect British interests in North Africa from potential Italian aggression. Of what import was the fate of Egypt to Australia? Why should Australians be put in a situation where they might be forced to fight and die against an Italian enemy? The Germans were nowhere near Africa at this stage in the war. Even the Suez Canal was not of any real economic consequence to Australia.[5] Mussolini's reach could never seriously threaten the Pacific. Moreover, this decision was made in the context of an emerging and acknowledged threat to Australia from Imperial Japan. Why did arguments for keeping Australian soldiers at home to help balance this menace fail? To top it all off, of all the self-governing Dominions only Australia had taken the plunge of declaring war in the first place, immediately after Britain's decision to do so, without parliamentary approval. An unrepentant Prime Minister Robert Menzies justified his decision by pointing to public sentiment and the 'impossibility' of the King being at war and Australia being at peace – an 'impossibility' overcome in Eire (which stayed neutral) and one which did not stop parliamentary debate in the other Dominions.[6] Surely this was a case of committing to one of Pilger's 'other people's wars'?

Despite claims over time by prominent authors such as David Day, Australia did not move to war in 1939, nor decide upon the deployment of its troops to far-flung battlefields, as an automatic consequence of British decision-making, duplicity or pressure.[7] The choice was quite deliberate and had been forming for a number of weeks as the inevitability of hostilities in Europe grew. Neither naivety nor blind imperial loyalty tipped the government's hand. The decision was, in fact, congruent with what appeared to be the national interest, particularly the value placed on the idea of resistance to international aggression and the concept of 'imperial defence'. The traditional idea that British strength was the best guarantor of Australian security was a keystone principle: for the Empire to be strong anywhere, it needed to be strong everywhere. Australia, therefore, ought to fight any and all of the Empire's wars so that if the day of crisis ever came for Australia itself then Britain, and in particular the Royal Navy, would be there in the nation's hour of need. In the 1920s and 1930s this policy was encapsulated in the 'Singapore Strategy', whereby in a time of Australian peril British ships would sally forth from their base at Singapore and save the day.

The key problem for Australian political and civil figures, most of whom accepted the concept of imperial defence as an article of faith, was that by September 1939 – whether they chose to acknowledge it or not – Britain's power could no longer underwrite its promises.[8] Despite this, apart from a number of outspoken middle-ranking army officers, there had been little open dissent against the clear weakness of the Singapore Strategy throughout the 1930s. As the European crisis intensified, however, the possibility that British pre-occupation on that continent might leave Australia exposed to potential Japanese territorial ambition was a growing cause of concern, especially following Japanese advances against China from 1937. Very little stood in the way should Japan decide to exploit weakened European imperial positions in the Far East, and the open belligerence displayed by the Japanese during the Tientsin Crisis of mid-1939 was read by many as a statement of future intent. As a consequence, despite an early and outward appearance of solidarity, there were significant strategic divergences between Britain and Australia that would, given time and circumstance, drive the two nations apart. In 1939, however, the only real question was how far should Australia, with this potential local threat in mind, rally to the cause of imperial defence? The answer to this question sent Australian soldiers to the Middle East.[9]

With the declaration of war, the question of what action Australia ought to take beyond passive measures at home became a topic of heated parliamentary and public debate. There was no regular army in 1939 to despatch to a European battlefield. Nor was there legal provision, as there was for naval and air forces, to send part-time militiamen to fight beyond Australian shores. On top of all this, given continuing uncertainty over Japanese intentions, the physical defence of Australia could not be neglected. As had been the case in 1914, if the government decided to send troops overseas in the cause of imperial defence, but without amending legislation its only choice was to raise a 'special force' for that purpose.[10]

The first obstacle to the idea of such an expeditionary force was political. While ready to support Menzies' decision for war, the Australian Labor Party was initially less enthusiastic about the idea of forming a full-time force for potential overseas service, even though there were standing military plans for such a contingency. While outwardly maintaining the line that he would wait and see what Britain requested before making a decision, Menzies too was hesitant for strategic reasons, and what he perceived as public opposition to the idea. On 5 September he cabled Stanley Bruce, the Australian High Commissioner in London, to inform him that until Japanese intentions were clear it was pointless even to discuss the idea.[11] Menzies was, from the earliest stages, neither a British stooge nor inspired to make a decision by emotional imperial sentiment. There was, however, a long-term British expectation that Australia would send an expeditionary force should it be required.[12] Pressure from Whitehall began to mount – but with remarkably little impact in Canberra. Despite British assurances to the contrary, and on the advice of the Australian Military Board, a calculating Menzies remained more concerned about Japan and the potential for strategic disaster in the Far East.

The political pressure on Menzies ratcheted up another notch, however, when on 9 September the New Zealand government announced its intention to raise its own 'special force' in support of Britain. This was invaluable ammunition for the press, almost uniformly in support of an increased Australian commitment to the war. Eventually, under siege from all sides, an unsettled and reluctant prime minister made his choice. Again using radio rather than parliamentary procedure, Menzies announced during his regular Friday broadcast on 15 September the raising of the full-time force. He spoke of one division of 20 000 men to be used in Australia or overseas 'as circumstances permit'.[13] Although widely approved by the public, the announcement caught the army completely by surprise. It was left to the Minister for Defence, Geoffrey Street, to spell out the details in parliament. Executive direction to raise the force, to be known as the 6th Division, 2nd AIF (as there were already four infantry divisions and part of a fifth in the militia), was given in mid-October 1939.[14]

Steps to find the soldiers for the 6th Division began in the first week of October 1939. The initial intention was to recruit half the force from the militia, a quarter from ex-militiamen or those with other forms of military experience, and the final quarter from men with no previous military training. From the outset, however, such plans were derailed. For a range of reasons – including such issues as memories of the last war; the 'Phoney War' in Europe from September 1939 until May the next year, which was marked by a lack of major military operations; alternate avenues of service such as the Empire Air Training Scheme; and Menzies' call for 'business as usual' – there was no 1914-style rush to enlist in the 2nd AIF. By mid-October, only 1200 of 25 000 militiamen in New South Wales had volunteered. Of the 20 000-man target, around 7800 recruits were at hand by the end of the month. By November, only Queensland had met its state enlistment quota,[15] and although most other states had caught up a month later, the pace of recruitment had been much slower than had been anticipated. So much for the idea of blind sentimentality and an inescapable connection to Britain, even from the public. In fact in public and in parliament some opponents of the war began using derogatory labels for these volunteers, calling them 'Menzies' tourists', 'economic conscripts' or even 'five-bob-a-day murderers'.[16]

Meanwhile, the issue of whether the 6th Division should eventually be sent overseas, and if so where, remained a serious conundrum for the government. In military terms, any such undertaking represented a serious strategic risk. Unlike any air or naval expeditionary forces, the numbers involved would be high and, depending on where they were sent, the difficulty in getting them home if the British position collapsed or the Japanese threat materialised might be much greater. Potentially, Australia faced the unenviable but real prospect of losing a large proportion of its trained and equipped ground force just when it might be needed most. It was no surprise that September and November 1939 saw considerable political and military debate as to whether the 6th Division ought to be sent anywhere.[17] The choice was far from automatic.

The issue of despatching an Australian expeditionary force overseas if requested by Britain actually pre-dated Menzies' announcement to raise the 6th Division. As early as 8 September, Anthony Eden, British Secretary of State for Dominion Affairs, noted to the British High Commissioner in Australia, Sir Geoffrey Whiskard, that the British government hoped that Australia, in exerting its full national effort, would prepare and despatch an expeditionary force.[18] While it was unclear at this stage what form this force might take or where it might be employed, the intent and assumption was clear: from the outset Britain expected Australia to send troops. Equally, from the very beginning, early Australian military and political opinion was guarded. Lieutenant General E.K. Squires, a British officer acting as Chief of the Australian General Staff, believed that the possibility for despatching the 2nd AIF existed, but only when danger of attack on Australia was removed. Squires was supported in this by Menzies, who was similarly cautious about committing Australian soldiers to a faraway theatre of war.[19]

The slow transition from an attitude of careful regard for Australian security to one that placed the 6th Division on ships bound for foreign soil began to gather speed towards the end of October 1939, after the fall of Poland earlier that month. Increasing public pressure to despatch ground forces in support of Britain was mirrored by some prominent personalities in London, including Winston Churchill, who (although not yet representative of the official British War Cabinet position) made clear their desire to see Australians 'in France by spring'.[20] At this point R.G. Casey, Australian Minister for Supply and Development, went to London to meet with other Dominion and British officials to clarify Britain's wishes with regard to the Australian war effort, and to discuss concerns about Japan. Casey's visit initiated a string of nebulous and unspecific British pledges to underwrite Australian security in exchange for the despatch of troops. The iron-clad guarantee that Casey and Menzies sought, however, could not be given. The truth was that, depending on the fortunes of war, Australia could be sure of neither Britain's ability nor intention to fulfil any implied promises. The Australian government knew this. If the British were trying to dupe Menzies, they had failed.

Despite this, so deep-rooted was the idea of imperial defence, and so reliant was Australia on British intelligence estimates of Japanese intentions, that throughout November authorities in

Canberra began considering using the 6th Division to relieve British regular troops in Burma, Singapore or India. This would be training before the 2nd AIF entered the European theatre to stand alongside British troops against Germany. At the same time, London applied pressure for the force to go to instead to Palestine to finish its training, and swell British troop numbers there in the hope of deterring Italian aggression, before moving to France.[21] Menzies, however, remained hesitant to despatch ground forces anywhere while Japanese intentions remained unknown. The British response to this position grew gradually more pointed, stressing the need for more troops in France and the remoteness of the Japanese threat. Throughout this period the British message was consistently buttressed by advice from Stanley Bruce, the Australian High Commissioner in London. In spite of certain personal misgivings about the overly optimistic British picture of the strategic situation in the Pacific (which he saw at least partly coloured by Britain's desire to get the 6th Division despatched as soon as possible), Bruce was committed to making imperial defence work, and his advice reflected this position.[22]

At this point, although the 6th Division was still short of its enlistment target, British lobbying finally bore fruit. On 14 November the Australian service chiefs recommended to Cabinet that the 6th Division be sent to train in the Middle East and that another division also be raised and sent abroad. The timetable for the 6th's departure was tentatively set as December 1939 or January 1940. However, Menzies still demurred and deferred a decision on the issue to the full Cabinet meeting at the end of November. In the interim, he sought further British guarantees of security and received no shortage of promises in return.[23] In parliament, the government came under heated fire from, on the one side, those passionate that everything should be done to answer Britain's call, and on the other those still stressing the primacy of defending Australia. For the time being, political opposition and doubts about British honesty in its estimations of the Japanese threat, combined with the lack of land fighting in Europe, persuaded Menzies to continue to delay committing the 2nd AIF for overseas service.[24]

Once again, policy decisions taken across the Tasman helped force Menzies' hand. Seemingly far less concerned about Japanese intentions, on 20 November 1939 New Zealand announced its decision to send its own expeditionary force overseas. For a second time Menzies was subject to unfavourable press comparisons and he began to fall into step. Indeed, General Squires was advised that same evening by telephone from the Minister for Defence, Geoffrey Street, to begin preliminary planning for a possible despatch of the 6th Division.[25] Three days later, Casey again brought word from London urging an immediate commitment of troops, noting that German propaganda – suggesting that Australia was more interested in wool exports than fighting – was gaining traction in France.[26] A conversation between Menzies and Whiskard on the same day as Casey's cable, however, revealed that even at this late hour the prime minister still harboured considerable misgivings. There was little room left, however, in which he could manoeuvre. On 28 November, Cabinet at last decided that the 6th Division should be sent to Middle East in early 1940, as soon as it had reached a suitable stage in training. Although the decision was attacked vigorously by the Opposition on the grounds that the men were needed to defend Australia, continuing British promises of naval support to Singapore took much of the sting out of the Labor Party's position.[27] Menzies may have had lingering doubts, but under pressure from many fronts, the decision was finally made.

Controversy surrounding the commitment of the 6th Division to the Middle East did not melt away the moment the government made its announcement. Certainly the decision was sold to the public in terms of imperial safety in that Britain must hold the Mediterranean, not only for its own sake but because its loss would affect other theatres which would directly threaten Australia. Educated observers, however, knew that the situation was not so clear-cut. The battle for France would not be decided by a single Australian division, but at the same time the only full-time and trained formation in Australian might well be crucial in the Pacific. The fact was that the Middle East in the 1940s, despite imperial rhetoric, could only ever be of secondary strategic interest to Australia and there was never any agreement, then or since, on the importance of that theatre to overall Allied strategy.[28] Ironically, of all the voices raised against the despatch of the force, those from the army were the most consistent and sober. Squires, an Englishman, personally and consistently stressed the folly of assuming anything but a hostile Japan and the danger of sending troops abroad. As 1939 drew to a close, however, the line of thought he represented was undermined by the tranquillity of the Phoney War and by his replacement, General C.B.B. White, an Australian recently brought out of retirement and a staunch supporter of imperial defence. In any case, the government had made its decision and for the soldiers of the 6th Division, at least, there was no second guessing it.[29]

In mid-December 1939, with Britain still confident that Italy was not about to enter the war, a combined advance party of 47 officers and 57 men left Australia aboard the liner *Strathallan*, with a similar party of New Zealanders, to form an overseas base in Palestine.[30] This party was soon followed by the main body of the 6th Division. On 10 June 1940, as the Australians in Palestine trained and German columns pushed deep into France, Mussolini's declaration of war against Britain took effect. The next day

Australia declared itself also at war with Italy. At this point the strategic situation in the Middle East and the tactical situation of the 6th Division changed irrevocably. The 2nd AIF camps in Palestine and Egypt had suddenly fallen within a combat theatre. Instead of training, equipping and steaming to France to fight the Germans, the Australians now faced the very real likelihood of being caught in the middle of an Italian invasion from Libya and the inevitable British defence of Egypt.

A long string of decisions in Rome, London and Canberra had conspired to place Australian soldiers in the Middle East looking west across the desert towards their Italian counterparts now staring intently eastwards. For the Australians, this decision-making process was lengthy, fought out in parliament and in the press, and at no point was the eventual outcome a 'sure thing'. The machinations surrounding the commitment of the 6th Division were never as straightforward as proponents of the 'other people's war' idea might suggest. Blind loyalty to Britain certainly did not tip Menzies' hand. Rather, he was consistently suspicious of British assurances and unswayed by British efforts to shape his decision. The Australian government, on the advice of the Australian military, was also quite conscious of the potential risk posed by Japan. In the end the decision was made according to the established principles of imperial defence – itself a construct not of sentiment but a logical consequence of Australia's standing security dilemma. Australia policy-makers sent troops abroad in World War II with their eyes wide open. To commit to war in the Middle East on such a basis is simply incompatible with the notion of unwillingly, unwittingly or unnecessarily fighting 'other people's wars'.

The example set by the decision to commit the 6th Division to the Middle East in the early stages of World War II is representative of a consistent historical pattern. Australia's earliest (colonial) military expeditions to the Sudan (1885) and to South

Africa (1899–1902), for example, are cases in point. Proponents of the 'other people's war' myth describe such commitments as instances of Australia foolishly participating in, rather than avoiding, unnecessary foreign wars. In the case of the Boer War, instead of remaining neutral, the six Australian colonies and then the new Commonwealth government sent thousands of troops to fight alongside the British forces against the two Boer republics for no better reason than loyalty to the Queen and sentiment for the Empire – or so the story goes.[31] John Mordike goes as far as to suggest that the deployments were the consequence of conspiracies by British officers, in Australia and at home, to make use of expendable colonial manpower in pursuit of imperial policies.[32] Such an interpretation, of course, deliberately ignores the complicated reality of Australian rather than imperial identity in this period. In many ways, to suggest a commitment to Britain above and beyond a commitment to purely Australian interests is an entirely false construct. Most Australians at the turn of the century identified themselves not as Australians or subjects of Empire, but both: in Alfred Deakin's words as 'independent Australian Britons'. Any distinction between the two is the imposition of a contemporary worldview on an era which would have rejected it as foreign and inappropriate. Such an interpretation also conveniently ignores evidence of much more complex Australian motives, exhaustively researched and fully set out in rigorous works of real military history.[33]

In particular, to suggest an expedition to the Boer War was irrelevant to Australian security and strategic positioning is to demonstrate ignorance of the importance of the idea of imperial defence noted earlier in the minds of colonial and early Australian politicians and policy-makers. There was, of course, no chance that a newly federated Australia could defend itself from a large, aggressive foreign power. In this regard, it was entirely dependent on Britain. Imperial defence was an obvious solution. A commitment to assist the Empire wherever and whenever it should was required underwrote the defence of Australia should the day of crisis ever come. In the words of New South Wales political leader Sir John Robertson: 'if we expect England to stand by us in any trouble we ought to stand by England in her troubles'.[34] Put crudely, military expeditions like those despatched to the Boer War – a conflict which neither threatened Australia directly nor endangered the physical security of the Empire as a whole – were premiums on an insurance policy Australia could ill-afford to do without. Public fervour and sentimentality was an important part of Australia's Boer War, but not at all the essence of the governmental decision-making process. In Geoffrey Blainey's words: 'Loyalty to England was paralleled by loyalty to Australia and its own interests: the two loyalties ran side by side'.[35] This was our war by rational and calculating choice.

Many of the same arguments, both for and against the conception of Australia's participating in 'other people's wars' carry over into World War I. Was it, as some social and cultural historians have contended, more naive folly and blind loyalty to Britain that sent some 60 000 Australians to early graves on battlefields far distant from their homes? Frank Bongiorno and Grant Mansfield have noted how 'the "other people's wars" idea persists in popular thought in a way that suggests it speaks to a powerful contemporary sensibility about both war and Australia's place in the world'.[36] They go on to quote a letter-writer in the *Australian* newspaper, who contended after Anzac Day in 2006 that 'Gallipoli – like Vietnam, Afghanistan and Iraq – was an act of outright aggression, yet each year hushed schoolchildren are told the Anzacs fought for peace and the defence of Australia, as if Turkey was attacking us'.[37]

Again, however, quite apart from the continuing strategic

influence of the idea of imperial defence, careful distinction must be made between the flag-waving and emotional rhetoric that encouraged so many Australians to join the expeditions to Gallipoli and France willingly, and the motives and factors influencing their political elites to send them there. No doubt the idea of assisting Britain in an hour of real need – as opposed to the situations encountered in the colonial era and in South Africa – was an intellectual and emotional dynamic that cut across all sectors of the Australian community, but it was only one reason to raise and despatch the 1st AIF. There is no question that Australia had strong financial, trading and strategic reasons for allying itself with Britain in this war. In fact, the decision to support Britain should there be a general war in Europe was essentially made by a succession of Australian governments, of all political persuasions, years before 1914. Had the Allies lost this war, the balance of world power would have been radically altered – to the detriment of Britain and Australia. There is no reason at all to suspect that Australian politicians in the early twentieth century were any less shrewd than those a century later. They well knew the consequences should Britain face defeat, and chose accordingly. Moreover, those questioning the wisdom of committing Australian lives to war in 1914 unsurprisingly often neglect to acknowledge that Germany was, at the time, an emerging Pacific power with fortified harbours, modern wireless stations (including one at Rabaul in German New Guinea) and 'warships within steaming distance of Sydney, Perth and the crucial Torres Strait'.[38] Once again, there was always much more to it than thoughtless loyalty.

At the outset of World War II, in addition the decision to despatch another expeditionary force of Australians overseas to fight what appeared at the time to be another vast and costly European conflict, many Australians were also committed to the air war over Europe as part of the Empire Air Training Scheme, while the Royal Australian Navy placed as a more or less subordinate component of the Royal Navy. These air and sea commitments were justified under the same imperial defence rubric. Defeating Germany and the Axis powers most certainly did matter for Australia. Few would be so naive to suggest that a triumph of the Nazi worldview and polity would not have impacted Australians, for the worse. With the war so clearly seen, at the time and now, as a battle for the preservation of a liberal democratic values over an alternate an abhorrent alternative, in what way could this conflict be labelled 'someone else's war'?

All of this, of course, relates to the war in Europe and the Mediterranean. Those ascribing to the idea of habitual Australian involvement in wars better left alone often avoid a discussion of the Pacific War in its entirety. If it is acknowledged, then effort is usually made to artificially separate the Pacific from the wider conflict, as if they were not closely connected and integral aspects of the same war. The most obvious reason is that this aspect of World War II tends to contradict the 'other people's wars' paradigm. Certainly, for around six months in late 1941 and early 1942, the war was perceived by the Australian government and public as a battle for national survival. It is true, however, that the government, for pragmatic political reasons, declined to disavow the population of this idea for some time after it knew the real threat had passed. It is also true that historians are now well aware that Australia was never under threat of physical invasion: it was never an option that the Japanese government ever seriously considered and certainly not one they were ever going to be put into action.[39] Indeed, such an operation was always well beyond over-stretched Japanese logistic and operational capabilities so long as it remained in conflict with the United States. The point, however, is that for at least a short period the threat was perceived in Canberra as being immanent and dire. The Pacific theatre, by no stretch of the imagination, can not seriously be considered as anything but Australia's war.

The tradition of rational, cost-benefit calculations continued after 1945. There was no sudden lurch to uncritically and automatically accede to the demand of powerful allies in the face of 'real' Australian interests. The Korean War, for example, began on 25 June 1950 when North Korean forces launched an invasion of the South. Within 48 hours, the United States had offered air and sea support to South Korea, and the United Nations Security Council asked all its members to assist in repelling the North Korean attack. Twenty-one countries responded by providing troops, ships, aircraft and medical teams. Australia's contribution included an Air Force squadron and, initially, a battalion of infantry, both of which were already stationed in Japan as part of the British Commonwealth Occupation Force. As the Korean War progressed, while some countries were keen to extricate their troops, Australia increased its commitment, and the government sent a second battalion, which joined the Commonwealth Division on 1 June 1952. By the time the war ended in July 1953, total Australian casualties numbered more than 1500, with 339 killed.

Seemingly so far from Australia and Australian interests, Korea still fails to give substance to the 'other people's wars' contention. First, it is difficult to argue that blind sentiment and loyalty underwrote the deployment when the Australian public reaction to news of the war, and throughout its course, was distinctly subdued. Moreover, a military commitment had been requested by the United Nations, an organisation that Australia had had a substantial hand in establishing, and had a significant interest in strengthening. At its heart was the idea of 'collective security' – the concept in a military sense that an attack on one member was to be viewed as an attack on all members. This was seen as the time as a key answer to Australia's (post-imperial) strategic dilemma. Should the concept work in practice it would guarantee the security of this nation and other small-to-medium countries across the globe. It would certainly not succeed if, at its first test, nations like Australia failed to heed the call. A deployment to Korea was thus in every sense in line with Australian national interests. Not surprisingly, it received consistent bipartisan political support.

Throughout the same period, Australia also committed troops to the Malayan Emergency, declared in June 1948 after three British estate managers were murdered in Perak, northern Malaya, by guerrillas of the Malayan Communist Party. Following the murder of the British High Commissioner in October 1951, Whitehall's resolve was galvanised and the Malayan government stepped up counter-insurgency measures. Australia's involvement began in 1950 with the arrival of transport and bomber aircraft. By October 1955, an infantry battalion was sent to Penang, to participate in a lengthy 'mopping up' of guerrillas. By late 1959, operations against the communists were in their final phase and many had crossed Malaya's northern border into Thailand. As the threat continued to dissipate, the Malayan government officially declared the emergency over on 31 July 1960, although Australian soldiers remained until August 1963. Thirty-nine Australian servicemen were killed in Malaya – although only 15 of these occurred as a result of combat – and another 27 were wounded.

Australian forces in Malaya formed part of this nation's contribution to the Far East Strategic Reserve, which was set up in April 1955 primarily to deter external communist aggression (particularly from China) against countries in South-East Asia, including Malaya and Singapore.[40] Within a Cold War context, the emergency was in all aspects perceived at the time in Canberra and London as a struggle against the danger of Communist expansion in the region. Sensitive to a perceived Communist threat to its north, the Australian government was a willing participant. No wave of emotional delusion swept Australian policy-makers along. No British lies or coercion forced Australian hands. This was seen as a regional problem that demanded regional action.

The same may well be said of the Confrontation with Indonesia from 1962 to 1966. This small, undeclared war, which came to involve troops from Australia and Britain, was sparked by President Sukarno's conclusion that Malaysia – a nation born of a federation of Malaya, Sabah, Sarawak and Singapore in September 1963 – represented an attempt by Britain to maintain colonial rule in the region. The actual war began when Indonesia launched a series of cross-border raids into Malaysian territory in early 1963. Requests from both the British and Malaysian governments in 1963 and 1964 for the deployment of Australian troops in Borneo met with initial refusal, although the Australian government did agree that its troops could be used for the defence of the Malay Peninsula against external attack. Such attacks occurred twice in 1964 and Australian troops were used in mopping-up operations against the invading troops. Although these attacks were easily repelled, they did pose a serious risk of escalating the fighting. The Australian government thus relented in January 1965 and agreed to deploy a battalion in Borneo. Continuing negotiations between Indonesia and Malaysia ended the conflict, and the two sides signed a peace treaty in Bangkok in August 1966. Twenty-three Australians were killed during the Confrontation, seven of them on operations, and another eight wounded.

Australia's commitment to operations against Indonesia during the Confrontation in Borneo and West Malaysia again fell within the context of its membership in the Far East Strategic Reserve. Like the Malayan Emergency, it represented a regional crisis with clearly perceived security ramifications for Australia. It was certainly not sentimentality or blind loyalty which sent

Australian troops into harm's way. Nor was it public opinion: because of the sensitivity of the cross-border operations (which remained secret at the time), the Confrontation received very little coverage in the Australian press. Nor was it British pressure, for the Australian government turned down desperate pleas for help from both London and Kuala Lumpur for a considerable time. Shrewd calculation of Australian interests then, as always, steered the nation to war.

On a larger scale and much more controversial was the Australian military commitment to Vietnam from 1962 to 1973, in which almost 60 000 Australians served, including Air Force and Navy personnel. Some 521 died as a result of the war and over 3000 were wounded. It is well known that the Vietnam War was the cause of some of the most significant social and political dissent in Australia since the conscription referendums of the World War I. Much, subsequently, has been written about the decision to send troops, including conscripts, to fight in this war. Many in the anti-war movement at the time, along with a range of other commentators, have long signalled their moral and practical disquiet at Australia's participation in what has come to be seen in some quarters as an 'aggressive' war. As Garry Woodard, former Australian Ambassador to China and High Commissioner to Malaysia, pointed out in 2004 in *Asian Alternatives: Australia's Vietnam Decision and Lessons on Going to War*, the Australian government could have quite reasonably chosen a different path.[41] Moreover, even prominent Australian military figures like General Peter Cosgrove, former chief of the Australian Defence Force, have questioned the decision to go 'all the way with LBJ'. Cosgrove, who won the Military Cross in Vietnam, said in 2002 that the 'weight of history and analysis' was against the decision to commit troops. 'On reflection', he continued, 'I'd probably join the majority of Australians who thought in retrospect our involvement was not going to be successful ... we probably shouldn't have gone'.[42]

There are two typical elements to the 'other people's war' argument made by those set against the decision to commit troops to Vietnam. The first concerns how 'necessary' such a commitment really was; the second the degree of American pressure placed on Australia to do so. Were we, once again, dragged into a war that belonged to a great and powerful friend? In the first instance, while the long-running tradition of the public's acceptance of governmental decisions to commit to war was perhaps broken by Vietnam, the traditional pattern of rational, realist decision-making was not. Both Robert Menzies, once again prime minister as the Vietnam crisis escalated, and his government – and most of the Western world for that matter – subscribed to the 'Domino Theory' in South-East Asia. In a Cold War context, this theory seemed obvious at the time, even if historians have since come to accept that the domestic agendas behind the war between North and South Vietnam were more crucial than the overlay of 'great power' agendas placed upon it. The clear Australian government consensus at the time was that if the Vietnam War ended with an outcome that denied South Vietnam a real and protected independence, then Laos, Cambodia, Thailand, Malaysia, Singapore and Indonesia would find themselves 'vulnerable' to further Communist expansion. They would fall like dominoes up to Australia's very doorstep. This concept was a formidable reality to Australian policy-makers who were witnessing the boundaries of 'aggressive' Communism coming closer and closer. Paul Hasluck, Minister for Defence in 1963 and 1964, provided ample insight into governmental thinking at the time:

> I need not emphasise the importance to Australia of the outcome of events in South Vietnam. Our plain national

interest is to have a government there who will continue to fight the Viet Cong, to oppose North Vietnam, and to give some prospect to eventually unifying the country behind a stable anti-communist government which will still provide the local circumstances to enable the United States to keep a foothold in South-East Asia. Our second major interest is to retain an active United States presence in South Vietnam. Our third major interest is to prevent (not merely avoid) any major failure in South-East Asia of such a kind as to lead to a collapse of the will to resist in other countries.[43]

There is no case to be made that in this context, at that time, the Australian government – and Australians at large for that matter – saw the war as none of Australia's concern. That many sectors of the community changed their opinion as the war progressed, or that many Australians later came to doubt the legitimacy of the war as a whole, are important aspects of Australia's Vietnam experience. But they are largely beside the point insofar as the argument to commit Australian troops was concerned.

The Vietnam War raised a second issue regularly used by the proponents of the 'other people's wars' interpretation of Australian military history: that Australia was somehow forced into the war reluctantly by pressure from Washington. By this thinking the United States simply replaced Britain in the role of a bullying 'great power' ally, dragging Australia against its wishes and against its better judgement into conflicts better left alone. A cable sent, for example, by Alan Renouf, Australian Ambassador in Washington, on 11 May 1964 puts paid to this type of reasoning. Renouf explained:

Our objective should be ... to achieve such an habitual closeness of relations with the United States and sense of mutual alliance that in our time and need, after we have shown all reasonable restraint and good sense, the United States would have little option but to respond as we would want ... The problem of Vietnam is one, it seems, where we could ... pick up a lot of credit with the United States, for this problem is one to which the United States is deeply committed and in which it genuinely feels it is carrying too much of the load, not so much the physical load the bulk of which the United States is prepared to bear, as the moral load.[44]

The Australian government was forced into nothing as far as the Vietnam War was concerned. The commitment was willing and entered into with calculating clarity of purpose. In fact, as Gregory Pemberton has systematically demonstrated, it was the Australians who urged a hawkish policy on the Americans when they seemed to vacillate.[45] Far from being dragged into the Vietnam War, Australian diplomats and ministers actively encouraged the Americans to commit troops. This was done, however, not out of any misguided loyalty or foreign coercion, but as a consequence of cold self-interest.

The model established for Vietnam serves equally well when applied to the most recent Australian military commitments abroad. Serious and voluminous public debate surrounded (and continues to surround) decisions to commit Australian troops to the occupation of Iraq and subjugation of insurgents in Afghanistan. Again, the issue of the legitimacy or even morality of both conflicts has from time to time assumed centre stage. Equally, as important as these questions are, they are irrelevant to the question of 'other people's wars'. In years to come, Australian policymakers may well have difficult questions to answer regarding how much their decisions reflected public will and sentiment.

The more blood and treasure spent in such places might also, in time, encourage future generations to judge the practical utility of such deployments. Four decades on, Renouf's position still captures the essence of the matter. There was no blind loyalty to 'Uncle Sam'.[46] There is little evidence to suggest successful wholesale deception of the Australian government by Washington (although false American claims about the presence of 'weapons of mass destruction' in Iraq are, perhaps, a partial exception). Nor is there sufficient proof of external pressure as a decisive factor. These commitments were made to achieve perceived policy objectives.

There are many reasons for the genesis and perpetuation of the 'other people's wars' misconception in the military history of Australia. At one level, for example, it helps make more acceptable the monumental loss of life in conflicts like World War I, which in retrospect seem to many not to have been worth the river of blood spilled. It is comforting to shake our heads at the tragically sentimental attachment to the Empire and the horror it wrought upon our forebears. Alternatively, when the righteousness of the cause Australians have fought and died for appears open to dispute, from the Veldt to Vietnam, the 'other people's war' argument eases our collective conscience to suggest that we were somehow tricked or pressured into doing someone else's dirty-work. There remains a powerful temptation to believe in our enduring historic 'innocence' in this regard. At the other end of the spectrum, individuals and groups might find it convenient to push such a misconception to further their own agendas. In each and every case, however, the historical trail leads elsewhere. A myth is a myth. A half-truth is no truth at all. Australia's wars have been Australia's choices, or at least the consequence of the willing decisions of Australian politicians and policy-makers in pursuit of the perceived national interest. No enemy, apart from

Arthur Phillip, has yet to land on Australian shores. We have chosen when and where we fought. To students of politics and history, this should not be any great surprise. Long ago, Prussian military theorist Carl von Clausewitz defined war as an innately political act with distinctly political objectives. This is what differentiates it against murder and other forms of killing. That generations of Australian governments have followed Clausewitz's dictum is axiomatic. As noted at the very beginning of this chapter, none of this is at all a commentary on the 'correctness' of these wars in moral or practical terms, or of Australia's participation in them. Indeed, many such deployments, in the past and even the present, have much to answer for on both counts. Rather, the simple and singular point is that Australians have never, not once, nor by any stretch, fought 'other people's wars'.

Further reading

J. Beaumont et al., *Ministers, Mandarins and Diplomats: Australian Foreign Policy Making 1941–1969*, Melbourne University Press, Melbourne, 2003.

C. Bridge (ed.), *Munich to Vietnam: Australia's Relations with Britain and the United States since the 1930s*, Melbourne University Press, Melbourne, 1991.

D. Day, *Menzies and Churchill at War*, Oxford University Press, Melbourne, 1993.

P. Dennis & J. Grey, *Emergency and Confrontation: Australian Military Operations in Malaya and Borneo 1950–1966*, Official History of Australia's Involvement in Southeast Asian Conflicts 1948–1975, vol. 5, Allen & Unwin/Australian War Memorial, Sydney, 1996.

P. Dennis & J. Grey (eds.), *Serving Vital Interests: Australian Strategic Planning in Peace and War*, Army History Unit, Canberra, 1992.

J. Grey, *A Military History of Australia*, 3rd edn, Cambridge University Press, Melbourne, 2008.

D.M. Horner, *High Command: Australia and Allied Strategy 1939–1945*, Allen & Unwin, Sydney, 1982.

G. McCormack, *Cold War Hot War: An Australian Perspective on the Korean War*, Hale and Ironmonger, Sydney, 1983.

J. Robertson & J. McCarthy, *Australian War Strategy 1939–1945*, University of Queensland Press, St Lucia, 1985.

G. Sheridan, *The Partnership: The Inside Story of the US–Australian Alliance under Bush and Howard*, UNSW Press, Sydney, 2006.

R. Thompson, *Australian Imperialism in the Pacific: The Expansionist Era 1820–1920*, Melbourne University Press, Melbourne, 1980.

C. Wilcox, *Australia's Boer War: The War in South Africa 1899–1902*, Oxford University Press, Melbourne, 2002.

[5]

'THEY ALSO SERVED': EXAGGERATING WOMEN'S ROLE IN AUSTRALIA'S WARS

Eleanor Hancock

Anzac Day is becoming Australia's *de facto* national day, and Anzac our national story. Yet despite well-meaning claims to the contrary, the Anzac myth does not include all Australians. It cannot include those who have migrated here recently, for example, or those whose ancestors fought on the 'enemy' side. Unlike the Indigenous critique of Australia Day as a national day, this inconvenient truth about Anzac Day has not had the impact one might expect, presumably because those excluded are not in a position to criticise the mythology or the new centrality of Anzac Day out of fear of being labelled un-Australian. It is for this reason, perhaps, that those who commented favourably online on Marilyn Lake's critical article on the Anzac myth in *The Age* were so careful to point out their own family links to Australian military service.[1]

One response to the seeming Anglo-Celtic dominance of Anzac is a process we might call the 'they also served' phenomenon, exemplified by the appearance of books on German Anzacs, Russian Anzacs, and the desire for groups that were previously marginalised to have their own war memorials. Yet even with the national myth's exclusion of Australians whose ancestors arrived after the two World Wars or those who descend from the populations of nations that fought on the other side, the greatest apparent problem for Anzac as a national mythology is its exclusion of half of Australia's population – women.

In the twentieth century and beyond, Australia has fought its wars as expeditionary wars. Except for nurses, such expeditions excluded women until 1985, when the few and relatively small women's services were disbanded and their personnel integrated into the regular armed services. Only in 1990 were a number of combat-related duties opened to women, and only very recently, in 2011, were more direct combat-oriented occupations opened to both sexes.[2] But these are all relatively modern developments. How is the wholesale exclusion of Australian women from the Anzac story prior to 1985 to be reconciled? One way has been the development of the notion that Australian women somehow managed to make an important contribution to the Australian war effort in the two World Wars. As appealing as the idea might appear, and as useful a way as it might be to avoid Anzac friction along gendered lines, it is nonetheless a lingering and powerful myth.

Readers of this and *Zombie Myths* will be aware of the role that academic military historians play in correcting distortions in the Australian military fable, such as those that have been created for Australian women's participation in war. Yet there is a common misconception, even on the part of some fellow historians, that academic historians of Australian military history serve as high priests at the temple of Anzac. They do not. Instead they tend to be the most rigorous and well-informed critics of the Anzac mythology. Why then have these growing myths about the role of Australian women in war not been demolished? There are a number of possible explanations. One is this gap between military historians and the wider profession.³ The history of Australian military nurses, for example, falls between the stools. For historians of gender, it seems to be military history; for military historians, it may not appear to be military history proper. This gap results in an unsophisticated historiography about women's participation in the war effort. Moreover, male military historians may hold back from expressing their critiques of such works from a concern that they could be misinterpreted as a sexist form of gate-keeping. Finally, while some aspects of women's wartime participation in the World Wars in other countries have at times been seen as an advance in women's opportunities and/or their emancipation, Australia does not fit this model. The silence of general historians may reflect a certain avoidance of this discomfiting aspect of gender relations and women's history in this country.

In any case, Australia's tradition of expeditionary wars has meant that – aside from the bombing of Darwin and Broome in 1942 – Australians at home have never known the modern civilian experience of war, such as the horrors of deliberate civilian bombing and the difficulties of occupation by hostile foreign troops.⁴ This has allowed a strict separation to exist between the military experience of war and the civilian experience in most Australian minds. This division was broken down as a result of the World Wars in nations such as Britain and Germany, but not in Australia. Its continuation in Australia has allowed many Australians to assume that civilian or non-combatant status will protect women from war's violence, and for a long time it has allowed Australians, including Australian feminists, to conceive of war as 'secret men's business'. The 530-page Oxford *Australian Feminism: A Companion* – which defines feminism as including 'a concern about women's claims to full citizenship and to recognition of their social, economic, cultural, and political participation' – has, for example, no entry on war.⁵

In the past, when women were expected to identify vicariously with men's heroism, the absence of female heroines from the national story would not have been surprising or questioned. In the twenty-first century, however, a national myth that involves only half the population should be more problematic. How can women be encompassed within the Anzac paradigm? This is an issue that is important both to those who support the emerging focus on Anzac as the formative national experience and – for different reasons and motives – to historians who want to shift the focus to, or heighten the attention given to, women's own experiences.

This difficulty has been overcome to some degree by artificially extending Anzac to encompass women by exaggerating, wherever possible, their role and contributions to Australia's twentieth-century wars. This has often originated from a well-intentioned desire to 'wish away' the exclusivity of the original concept of Anzac.[6] It has resulted, for example, in a major focus on the experience of Australian military nurses. These formed the one group of Australian women to serve overseas in all major twentieth-century Australian conflicts, the only group of Australian women in a military capacity to be permitted to serve near the front until 1985, and also the only group of Australian women in a military capacity to become prisoners of war. The 38 Australian members of the Australian Army Nursing Service (AANS) who were imprisoned by the Japanese in World War II were the only Australian women normally resident in Australia to have an experience of danger, suffering and death equivalent to that of thousands of women in other countries during the same war.[7] A wide-ranging hagiography of Australian military nurses has developed as a result, according to which Australian nurses were 'gallant, unsung heroines' and 'heroic women'.[8]

Importantly, nurses do not challenge traditional concepts of gender roles in that they have often been historically perceived as embodying 'female' characteristics through their selflessness, nurturing, caring and perhaps subservience to male authority figures like doctors.[9] The resulting ambivalence this creates can be seen in Kirsty Harris's startling suggestion that the history of World War I nurses 'contains pertinent lessons for today's military strategists, not least of which is that the presence of Australian women in a war zone can have immense benefits for Australian men away from home'.[10] By this bizarre assertion, she suggests that Australian soldiers recover more readily when nursed by their own compatriots. Alternatively, nurses in casualty clearing stations occupied, in Ruth Rae's opinion, frontline positions. Exaggerated claims for the comparative role of nurses versus serving soldiers flow from this, including Rae's incredible conclusion that 'the nurses were not combatants but they were witnesses and in many ways that can be a harder role. To endure pain is sometimes easier than to continually observe the suffering of others.'[11] This sentiment is unlikely to have been shared by those actually suffering from war wounds. Such studies demonstrate a lack of realistic judgment and knowledge of the wider context of the war. Harris also claims, for example, that the execution of nurse Edith Cavell 'highlights sharply the distinct differences in the scope of civilian and military nursing'.[12] It does not. Cavell was a matron in a Belgian civilian hospital, who was executed not because she was a nurse but because she 'was involved in resistance activities that no occupying power would tolerate'.[13]

The comparatively small numbers of Australian military nurses employed in overseas combat zones have been the subject of multiple detailed (although uncritical) studies. Yet at the same time exaggerated claims about their neglect by historians abound. It is a surprising kind of neglect since nursing is included, for example, in the medical history volumes of the official history of World War I. Such claims are still, however, made by historians of nursing, by popular historians and in the general literature aimed at schools and the public by the Department of Veterans' Affairs.[14] Jan Bassett, for one, suggested that army nurses have been neglected or idealised by historians.[15] To Rae they are 'forgotten'; Harris considers them marginalised by historians; and to Rees they are 'the other Anzacs'.[16] As late as 2005, Rae argued that 'there is an almost total absence of information about the role of the Australian nurse during WWI'[17] – yet there are at least eight specialist studies of them.[18] Why are these claims both exaggerated and repeated? Why, no matter how much is written about Australian military nurses, is this never enough? Nurses' role in the Anzac myth, despite the best efforts of these authors, is and will necessarily remain marginal. It is marginal because their numbers, when set against the numbers of Australian soldiers who fought overseas, are minuscule. The more marginal the claim, the more, perhaps, it needs to be repeated.

For the record, the contribution of Australian nurses in World War I, and of Australian women in the women's services in World War II for that matter, was minor. This can only be concealed by over-claiming – and indeed the numbers involved seem to climb steadily, based on generous interpretations of service.[19] Harris reaches a maximal number of 3199 Australian nurses who served in World War I by counting nurses who served with any Allied military unit, not just Australian organisations.[20] If Rae's figure of 416 000 Australians who enlisted and served overseas in the first AIF is accepted, then these nurses would be some 0.76 per cent of the total (and even less, if Australian men who served in other Allies' services were also counted).[21] Various authors give different figures for the number of men who served overseas in the first AIF – alternatively 324 000 and 416 000. Making some rough calculations, this was either 14 or 17 per cent of the Australian male population at the time. Using Harris's generous figures for the number of female nurses serving overseas (3199), they represent just 0.14 per cent of the female Australian population at the time.

In World War II, 726 543 men enlisted in the 2nd AIF, comprising 21.57 per cent of the Australian male population. Taking Patsy Adam-Smith's figure of 66 718 women in the women's services and military nursing services, this was 2.04 per cent of the Australian female population.[22] The Department of Veterans' Affairs' own figures for male and female service in World War II indicate that 66 160 women served in all the women's services, while 926 500 men served in the three armed services: giving women 6.6 per cent of the total Australians in military service.[23] These figures are based on crude computations and need to be refined by closer statistical analysis, but they do give a sense of the relative insignificance of the role permitted to Australian women in both wars. Comparatively and proportionately, women's service was unimportant. It has gained disproportionate historical attention because nurses and other medical staff were the only Australian women allowed to serve near the front line.[24] It is therefore, for most of the twentieth-century military history of Australia, the only way that Australian women could claim some of the aura or lustre of Anzac. The exaggerated service of Australian nurses thus served to prove that 'Australian women were just as capable as Australian men of meeting the challenge of war'.[25]

Equally, the various cliches of popular belief about a distinctively Australian military ethos —usually differentiated from that of the British – are replicated for Australian women in war. A.G. Butler, author of the World War I official medical history, claimed that 'Australian nurses, wherever they went, were courageous and tactful standard bearers of Australian democracy'.[26] Other historians depict Australian nurses as similar to the 'digger' in their civilian ethos, their differences from the British, their bravery, their mateship, their egalitarianism and their loss of life.[27] Harris even claims 'a uniquely Australian set of practices for military nursing'. It is not clear what she considers these to be, although earlier in the book – based solely on the claims of Australian nurses themselves, and on one report of an Australian medical services' director – she asserts that Australian nurses were used to more responsibility and displayed more initiative than their British counterparts. She does not make any comparison to the military nurses of other Dominions. Here is a case of the Anzac myth influencing the interpretation of historical evidence. The information Harris herself provides also contains examples from which it might equally be concluded that British and American nurses had superior experience, training or were permitted to undertake responsibilities from which Australian nurses were excluded.[28]

Overall, the history of Australian women's involvement in Australia's wars is the history of an absence, but an absence which needs to be explained. In both World Wars, there was a clear gap between women's desire to participate actively in the war effort and the lack of wider social and political support for them to do so.[29] What remains then to be investigated is the reluctance to use Australia's woman-power more extensively in the period 1941 to 1943, when the nation appeared to be facing a crisis of national survival. Contemporaries expected a Japanese invasion, yet the Australian War Cabinet ruled in 1943 that no servicewomen were to be sent overseas except in the medical services. More than 24 000 women joined the Australian Women's Army Service (AWAS) and over 400 eventually served overseas – mainly in New Guinea in clerical and signalling positions – but only after New Guinea was no longer judged to be a combat zone.[30] Women's Auxiliary Australian Air Force (WAAAF) personnel employed in the Allied Intelligence Centre at Air Force Command in Brisbane were not permitted to go outside Australia when the centre moved off-shore: instead US Women's Army Air Corps' staff had to be trained to replace the Australian servicewomen overseas.[31] Equally, the most senior officer of the AWAS, Colonel Sybil Irving, claimed that she refused permission for AWAS to fire anti-aircraft guns, because 'they will be the future mothers of Australia and one would not wish them to have the spilling of the blood of other mothers' sons on their hands'.[32]

It is also important to note that while Australian women may have felt they had possibilities for emancipation during World War II, what is striking is how narrow these possibilities actually were when contrasted to those of women in other nations, such as Britain or Germany. Comparative studies would highlight how minor the roles permitted to women in Australia actually were, which may be one reason such studies have not been done. The reasons for these restrictions are historically understandable in context. The gendered Federation settlement that had protected the interests of men as wage-earners meant that Australia was always 'one conflict behind' in war's effect on opportunities for women.[33] In World War I, the Australian Army Nursing Service was separate from the armed forces, while its British equivalent, the Queen Alexandra's Imperial Military Nursing Service, was incorporated within the British military medicine structure. While women's service units were already formed in Britain in World War I, it was not until World War II that similar units were formed in Australia.[34] In 1938, Britain formed the Auxiliary Territorial Service, and the Women's Auxiliary Air Force in June 1939. The WAAAF was the first such service formed in Australia, but not until February 1941.[35] Sir Percy Spender claimed to Gavin Long that the army was responsible for this delay because of its strong hostility to the concept of women's services: 'Women's Services were ridiculed at the outset, and strongly opposed by the [Australian] Army. This was in spite of the fact that they were being built up in England.'[36]

Even in World War II, Australian gender attitudes remained conservative. The editors of the most recent significant study of gender and war in Australia (published some 16 years ago), Joy Damousi and Marilyn Lake, recognise that the war raised the issue of women's right to paid work symbolically rather than numerically, and they can only claim that women were enlisted and conscripted into employment on 'a large scale'.[37] Equally, Pat Grimshaw and her fellow authors claim that 'large numbers' of women were drafted into the metal trades and munitions (50 per cent of munitions workers by 1943).[38] And Kate Darian-Smith reports that in 1944, when female paid employment was at its peak, 'women constituted almost 25 per cent of the total workforce, and almost one third of all women aged fifteen to sixty-five years were in paid labour'.[39] However, more accurate figures reveal that 'almost 25 per cent' is, in fact, 24.1 per cent, while 'almost one third' is more accurately 31.6 per cent.[40] Rounding these numbers up makes them seem greater. The percentages of women described as 'munitions workers' obviously depend on the historian's definition of munitions. Using figures provided in the official history of the war economy, women workers made up 41.15 per cent of those employed in government munitions factories, and 24.88 per cent of those employed by private contractors, making women overall 26.73 per cent of the combined workforce in munitions.[41]

Australia went into World War II with large-scale male unemployment and under-employment. Women's employment expanded not because attitudes to gender roles changed, but because the wartime economy soaked up the male unemployed and the number of women of working age also increased. In July

1939, women in paid employment were 23.4 per cent of the work force and 27.6 per cent of women aged between 15 and 65; in June 1943 women in paid employment were 24.3 per cent of the work force and 31.9 per cent of women aged between 15 and 65.[42] These are modest increases. The percentage of women employed at this time was comparable to that in the United States (32 per cent), but lower than that in Britain (37 per cent). Australian conservatism at a time of national crisis can be further illustrated by a comparison to the employment of women in Nazi Germany. In 1939 women made up 38 per cent of the German civilian workforce; by September 1944 they were 52.5 per cent. While Germany's changing boundaries make it hard to compute women employed as a percentage of total German women, the percentage of German women in employment during the war ranged between 50.4 and 55.6 per cent. German women served not just as civilian auxiliaries to the armed forces but in anti-aircraft batteries and ultimately in combat.[43]

Combat and war need not necessarily be male-only experiences, and have not been so historically or in other societies. Yet twentieth-century government policy and social attitudes made them so in Australian. A desire to claim the equivalence of women's sacrifice or of the significance of their contribution must always be strained when women were excluded from the front line and from most dangers. Historians need to avoid devaluing what women were excluded from. One can certainly understand the dismay at the absence of heroines in our national mythology and culture, but nothing is gained by creating their existence through falsification or exaggeration. The historical gendered division of labour in warfare by Australians is a reality. It cannot be wished away just because it causes modern discomfort.[44] One may wish that women's role had not been so marginal, but one must also recognise that it was.

Further reading

J. Beaumont, 'Whatever happened to patriotic women 1914–1918?', *Australian Historical Studies*, October 2000, pp. 273–86.

J. Beaumont (ed.), *Australian Defence: Sources and Statistics*, The Australian Centenary History of Defence, vol. 6, Oxford University Press, Melbourne, 2001.

J. Damousi & M. Lake (eds), *Gender and War: Australians at War in the Twentieth Century*, University of Cambridge Press, New York, 1995.

M. Lake et al., *What's Wrong with ANZAC?: The Militarisation of Australian History*, UNSW Press, Sydney, 2010.

M. McKernan, *The Australian People and the Great War*, Nelson, Melbourne, 1980.

R. White, 'War and Australian society', in M. McKernan & M. Browne (eds), *Australia: Two Centuries of War & Peace*, Australian War Memorial, Canberra, 1988.

[6]

THE NONSENSE OF UNIVERSAL AUSTRALIAN 'FAIR PLAY' IN WAR

Dale Blair

'Australian soldiers are nothing if not sportsmen, and no case ever came under my notice of brutality or inhumanity to prisoners.'[1] So wrote General Sir John Monash soon after World War I. There is no doubt a great many Australian servicemen in this and other conflicts, when called to the service of their country, have indeed attempted to uphold such chivalrous and sporting notions, and to act fairly and within the bounds of existing conventions or rules of war. However, the universality of this ideal, the suggestion that somehow Australian troops are unique and that all have unwaveringly applied their 'digger-ethic' of fair play on the battlefield, is simply untrue. It is an Anzac myth of the first order. The historical record in this regard is clear. The sporting attitude of fair play implied by Monash has not always been evident in the Australian conduct of war. This has been most often exhibited through behaviour such as killing prisoners or through a refusal to take prisoners at all. Regardless of how uncomfortable an acceptance of such actions on the part of a minority of Australian servicemen might be, or how awkwardly it might sit within the contemporary public Anzac paradigm of unquestioning veneration of the deeds

The nonsense of universal Australian 'fair play' in war

of past servicemen, such acts are also part of this nation's military past and must be honestly acknowledged.

The brutal nature of war, conducted by humans with all their frailty and flaws, does not by any means guarantee chivalric attitudes and action by soldiers dragged into its violent sphere. Atrocities occur. Yet war crimes are things Australians prefer not to associate with the Australian military. Such things belong to the stories of Nazi Germany, Imperial Japan, and the Taliban – not Australia. It is important, however, to accept and confront instances where transgressions of international law and the rules of war have occurred if we are to ensure that the historical record and memory of the nation's conduct in war retains objectivity and accuracy in this regard. Historical records show, unequivocally, that Australian soldiers in wartime have, at times, overstepped the mark and not played 'fair'.

Given this, what is remarkable is that when presented with the facts, or even possibility, of such behaviour, some Australians stridently decry those who dare suggest that improprieties or poor judgement by Australian servicemen have occurred. A recent case in point was referred to the Director of Military Prosecutions (DMP), Brigadier Lyn McDade. Supposed supporters of Australian troops went into paroxysms because Australian commandos were to be charged with a variety of offences including manslaughter, failing to obey a lawful order, and dangerous conduct as a consequence of a series of events which unfolded in Afghanistan. In the action subject to enquiry, six Afghan civilians, including five children, were killed in a compound during a search for a Taliban leader. The case was referred to McDade only after it had been reviewed twice by army investigating officers. Doubts as to the legitimate conduct of these Australian soldiers were clearly at the forefront of the decision to pass the case on to the DMP. Yet McDade was subsequently subjected to a torrent of abuse, in print, online and on the radio. She was attacked as being a grand-standing meddler seeking to further her career, and of being out of touch with the pressures facing combat troops. Federal Opposition leader Tony Abbott weighed in to the debate (if it could be called that) and suggested the troops had been betrayed and were being sent into action with one hand tied behind their backs. The tone of this vindictive campaign, as journalist Tom Hyland commented in the *Sunday Age*, suggested that 'until now, we have sent troops to war unrestrained by the rule of law'.[2] Since Federation, however, international law has always governed Australian troops in battle, and these laws have also always been incorporated into the military manuals used to train Australian soldiers. The extent to which those laws have been obeyed and, when found to have been breached, the offenders prosecuted, is another matter.

The best-known of transgressions by Australian servicemen in killing enemy prisoners is that of 'Breaker' Morant during the Boer War. Lieutenants Harry Morant and Peter Handcock of the Bushveldt Carbineers were executed after being found guilty by a British court martial for having killed eight Boer prisoners. Morant and Handcock's guilt in this matter is undeniable. Boer War historian Craig Wilcox declared that they were engaged in 'cold blooded slaughter' and that they, having been implicated in four other deaths, were 'closer to serial killers than soldiers'.[3] Morant and company were not alone in engaging in such behaviour, but nor was it a particular Australian transgression: the majority of Australian servicemen in South Africa did not kill prisoners. Furthermore, underpinning the Morant story is the assertion that he was acting in accordance with verbal orders issued from above to take no prisoners. This was refuted by the British in court but has remained a point of contention. If it were true, the order would have been an unlawful act by those higher authorities that contravened existing rules of war and compromised the behaviour of both British and Empire soldiers. The Morant case only received much public attention in Australia after the event. Yet it was the perceived injustice of British military law, rather than the murder of enemy prisoners, upon which focus centred. One result was that the Australian government refused to allow the death penalty to be carried out against Australian soldiers in World War I.

World War I threw up numerous examples of Australian soldiers showing no quarter to the enemy and killing enemy prisoners. Incidents can be found in Charles Bean's volumes of the official history, in more detailed battalion histories, and in soldiers' personal letters and diaries. As such, the Morant case cannot be viewed as an aberration. In fact, one is left to surmise that the killing of prisoners was tacitly if not directly approved by higher command and systemic throughout the Australian Army during this conflict and again, in particular, against the Japanese in World War II. Killing enemy prisoners appears in some instances to have been viewed as acceptable and that enemy soldiers so disposed of were fair game.

Charles Bean, war correspondent and official historian, was forced to confront the existence of this attitude and behaviour soon after stepping ashore at Gallipoli. He was told by Australian and New Zealand soldiers 'that they had orders from their subordinate officers in some cases to take no prisoners, in the first rush at any rate, and whilst things were bad'.[4] Bean added, 'I don't believe this ... though it may be true'.[5] Although Bean's disapproval was evident, it sat incongruously against his celebration of the spirit of the Australian soldier. In the same diary entry he compared the Australian soldier with his New Zealand counterpart. He quoted an Australian soldier as saying 'Kind hearted beggars, the N. Zealanders, a Turk snipes them and then they catch the beggar and take him by the hand and lead him down to the beach'.⁶ The imputation was clear: the Australians would have shown no such clemency. Bean took the opportunity to point out a fundamental difference in national character as he saw it: 'undoubtedly the N.Z. fights more with his gloves on than the Australian: the Australian when he fights, fights all in'.⁷

Bean's description of the process of 'ratting' at Pozieres in 1916 may be another prime example of fighting 'all in':

> Throughout the village could be seen isolated Australians 'ratting' occasional fugitives from the rubble heaps, chasing terrified and shrieking Germans and killing them with the bayonet, or shooting from the shoulder at those who got away, and then sitting on the door-steps to smoke and wait for others to bolt from the cellars.⁸

Are we being invited to share a pride in the nonchalant ruthlessness of the Australian soldier? Are we being asked to accept that such sport, of killing men who are clearly no longer a danger, was acceptable in the 'fury of war'? To be fair, some prisoners were taken in this engagement, so we know 'ratting' was not practised by all Australians at Pozieres. In this account, Bean also provided a context of extenuating circumstances: having taken the village and begun digging in, the Australians had become targets of some enemy snipers who had taken refuge in or survived in the rubble and cellars of the village during the bombardment and the initial Australian attack. It was this, Bean insinuated, that justified the merciless efficacy of some of the Australians on that occasion, the fact that they had been 'stung by the killing of mates beside them'.⁹ One can certainly understand soldiers being inspired by a thirst for revenge. That in itself, however, does not provide justification for killing men who are clearly placed in a situation where they are incapable of resistance or no longer have a desire to resist.

Throughout his volumes of the official histories, Bean refrained from seriously judging or questioning Australian attitudes to killing in this manner. His uncritical approach has not always been accepted. The British historian John Keegan considered Bean's treatment of Australians involved in killing prisoners at Passchendaele in 1917 as platitudinous.[10] The incident Keegan referred to was that involving the death of Captain F. L. Moore of the 5th Battalion. When a German pillbox garrison signalled their intent to surrender, Moore moved forward to accept their capitulation, but was shot down. Moore's men immediately killed the perpetrator and others. The garrison's total extermination was only prevented by the interposition of other officers.[11]

In a footnote about this action Bean recounted what he considered a 'terrible' incident, recorded by Captain W. D. Joynt, 8th Battalion, which took place about the same time in his brigade. Joynt admitted to seeing a group of Australians accepting the surrender of the defenders of the lower level of a double-storey pillbox. As the Germans emerged, a shot was fired from the upper level – where the defenders were unaware of the surrender below – and an Australian was killed. Considering this the 'vilest treachery', the Australians commenced to bayonet all the surrendering Germans. Although Bean described the men as being 'too heated' to realise the facts, it was obvious that, for some, the action was cold and calculated and far from frenzied. Bean included a description of how one Australian who, on preparing to bayonet a German, found his bayonet unattached, so he proceeded to attach it while his imminent victim begged for his life. With his bayonet eventually fixed, the Australian then killed the defenceless soldier.[12] The calm detachment displayed was hardly indicative of someone 'too heated' to act otherwise. It was a cruel, cynical and deliberate act of vengeance. In this instance, Bean's argument does not sit comfortably with the facts. Joynt, too, although he knew the truth of the situation, was far from sympathetic in his post-war account. He voiced a widely held and subsequently entrenched view that Germans defending blockhouses and displaying the 'bad sporting spirit of shooting as long as they were safe and then rushing out expecting mercy' were entitled to none.[13] For Keegan, the Australian behaviour here was an example of 'improper violence'.[14]

How should we interpret the behaviour of these Australian soldiers? Their actions suggest a group mindset that legitimised their actions even though in doing so they were contravening the rules of warfare. That the unfortunate Germans were 'entirely innocent' was patently obvious, yet Bean was still unable to condemn the actions of the Australians. Instead he adopted a general and passive view that accepted the inevitability of such incidents, the blame for which he claimed lay with 'those who make wars, not those who fight them'.[15] In the broadest sense, one can hardly argue with such a contention. Simply put, if there were no war there would be no killing of men – either legitimately or illegitimately. Yet by applying such a viewpoint, Bean was avoiding the immorality of such particular actions and, by extension, acting as an apologist for the Australian soldiers involved. Keegan's more objective chagrin is easily shared, as such actions raise fundamental questions about the morality underpinning the Australian conduct in this theatre. One must ask whether there are any circumstances at all that justify the practice of 'no quarter', either through the killing of surrendered soldiers or through the refusal to take prisoners.

The rules of war to which Australian soldiers were supposed to adhere in World War I were embodied in the 'Hague Rules'. These conventions, set down in 1899 and revised in 1907, moved toward more explicitly guaranteeing the humane treatment of prisoners and gave extensive consideration to the obligations of governments and armies in the treatment of prisoners of war. Of specific pertinence to the conduct of the individual in combat was Article 23. Under this clause it was especially forbidden to kill or wound treacherously individuals belonging to the hostile nation or army; to kill or wound an enemy who, having laid down his arms, or having no longer means of defense, has surrendered at discretion; or to declare that no quarter will be given.[16] Britain incorporated the Hague Convention in its *Manual of Military Law* published in 1914 and again in 1916. Chapter XIV, paragraph 50, reiterated that the act of killing prisoners who had laid down their arms was forbidden. Furthermore, in the next paragraph the British manual stated that:

> This prohibition is clear and distinct; there is no question
> of the moment up to which acts of violence may be
> continued without disentitling the enemy to being ultimately
> admitted to the benefit of quarter. War is for the purpose
> of overcoming armed resistance, and no vengeance can be
> taken because an individual has done his duty to the last but
> escaped injury.[17]

Acceptance of the rights of surrendered enemies was also unequivocal. So, too, was the undertaking in the following paragraph: 'Care must therefore be taken that all ranks are acquainted with the laws of war and that they endeavour to observe them'.[18]

As members of the British Expeditionary Force in France fully conversant with the *Manual of Military Law*, there can be no doubt that Australian officers were aware of their obligations in this respect. Moreover, given the large portion of Australian officers drawn from the legal fraternity, there exist few reasons to suggest they did not comprehend their responsibilities toward ensuring the prevention of such treachery. The degree to which the rank-and-file understood their responsibilities is perhaps less certain. Nevertheless, it was the responsibility of officers to instruct them in such matters if they did not already know. Another important aspect of the *Manual of Military Law* was contained in paragraph 433, which required combatants to obey all commands issued by a superior officer. This, as Joanna Bourke points out, ran counter to the prevailing custom that soldiers were only compelled to obey 'lawful orders', or those they considered appropriate to the moment.[19]

The British Army during World War I certainly endeavored to make these rules understood. Treatment of enemy prisoners was one of the many topics taught to officers and non-commissioned officers in the schools of instruction behind the lines during the war. Circulars, too, were distributed. These included details on how to conduct prisoners to the rear with specific instructions on what could and could not be taken from them.[20] Of particular interest was a circular issued and titled 'The Soldiers' Don'ts of International Law'. This document was clearly designed as a ready-reckoner for soldiers to know and apply their and their enemy's rights in battle. It concluded with commendable legal and Christian intent: 'Don't go beyond your rights, and Do as you would be done by'. A close reading reveals some odd inconsistencies of intent and admiration. With quirky British grace, it suggested: 'Don't shoot a spy off hand; he is doing a very plucky thing, and deserves a trial'. It preceded this with a stern and unsympathetic warning: 'Don't rub or file your bullets; if you are caught with such bullets on you, you will be shot, and serve you right'. Yet in regard to the act of killing surrendering soldiers, the circular was ambivalent. What interpretation would a soldier put on the advice, 'Don't kill a man who has thrown his arms down as a sign that he has ceased to resist', when it was followed by

'DON'T be heartbroken if you kill such a one by mistake – it is his fault for having resisted up till too late'?[21]

Australian soldiers in World War I were undoubtedly aware of the basic rights of the individual in battle. Generally speaking, it is difficult to see how they cannot have had some understanding of how to act toward the surrendering or captured enemy, given the British Army's obvious – even if ambiguous – commitment to upholding international law. Translating these understandings from the manuals and applying them under the duress of combat was, however, often a process tinged with uncertainty. Such application of the laws (as they were understood) would vary with the emotional intelligence of the individual as well as the discipline and leadership within the units to which soldiers belonged. It is apparent that some Australian officers harboured an uncompromising attitude toward the enemy from the outset that was clearly communicated to their soldiers. For example, one can only surmise at what attitudes were fomenting within the Victorian-raised 22nd Battalion prior to its arrival at the Western Front. At its first battalion parade, the unit was addressed by its Commanding Officer, who pronounced the regimental motto to be 'Wipe out the bloody Germans'. Despite criticisms from prominent clerics and some newspaper discussion, the motto stuck in abbreviated form – W.O.T.B.G – and formed part of a chorus in the regimental song.[22]

An unsigned and undated letter held by the Australian War Memorial reveals the abhorrence of one person, at least, over alleged atrocities committed by Australian soldiers during this conflict.[23] The letter was sent to Australian Administrative Headquarters in London and is worth quoting in full, not only because of the extraordinary claims it makes but also because of the principled (if occasionally misspelled) position that the writer adopts:

Dear Sirs,

I have been told by wounded soldiers in hospitals and walking cases storeys [of] cruelty and murder of German wounded and prisoners committed by Australian soldiers. From the evidence I have, there can be no doubt.

I asked a soldier in Kings College Hospital if [he] had seen any German prisoners he said Yes – he saw some been brought in by English Tommies and when they got near the Australians the Australians told the English Tommies to clear or they would kill both of them. The Australians killed the whole of the German prisoners – now this was simply cold blooded murder. Another Australian told me he and another was coming back after a trench raid, the other fellow had two German prisoners and they could not get along as fast as they would like so he killed the two German prisoners. Brave men these, where they not – A Canadian told me he (an officer) had seen the Australians jump on the wounded Germans as they lay on the field of battle and told German prisoners to go back [as] they did not want them and when they turned to go back they turned the machine guns on them and mowed them down – A A.M.C.A. [medical corps soldier] told me one of his stretcher-bearers carried a razor in his pocket and when he came to a wounded German he would finish him off by cutting his throat and he is still doing it – all these and other men have signed their statements. Disc nos given and names of places where these events took place – I am engaged in collecting evidence from all classes of soldiers both sides not from Govt. statements. I have seen some of these and even these prove that the British Army and the Allies are [far] from been saints or even civilized.

Facts are stubborn things and this book will not be plesent

The nonsense of universal Australian 'fair play' in war

reading for young Australians or cover those [who] fought in this war with glorey – I thought if your attention [is drawn] to this matter you might be able to do something to stop the crulity and murder. For two wrongs don't make a right. We ought to show the Germans we are far above this kind of work. If the men saw the officers were determined to put a stop to it, they would [not] do that wich spoils the fine work they have done during the war. At present the officers only wink at it the men say and take no steps to stop it.

Yours trully[24]

Unfortunately, the statements that the writer mentioned do not accompany the letter. They have either been lost, destroyed or are still to be discovered. Nonetheless, the commandant of the Australian Administrative Headquarters kept the letter for posterity's sake and after the war forwarded it to the Australian War Museum section for preservation – an indication, perhaps, that he did not reject the claims out of hand. It would be easy to dismiss such claims as outrageous. The thought that a stretcher-bearer was engaged in slashing the throats of German prisoners seems highly unlikely given the compassion generally understood to have been extended by such men collecting the wounded of friend and foe alike. One is certainly less sanguine, however, about dismissing the possibility that Australian soldiers could act in such a manner given the incidents Bean portrayed with regard to 'ratting' at Pozieres and the events which followed Captain Moore's death at Passchendaele.

It is also clear that, despite Bean's willingness (albeit somewhat guardedly) to address the issue officially, some senior officers of the Australian Imperial Force (AIF) wished to avoid any controversy that might besmirch the name of Australian soldiers. Brigadier General 'Pompey' Elliot, for example, was keen to distance his soldiers from allegations of unseemly behaviour. In the New South Wales Returned Sailors' and Soldiers' Imperial League of Australia journal *Reveille,* he penned a rebuttal to a claim by Robert Graves that Australian troops had murdered German prisoners at Mourlancourt.[25]

In a similar vein, the correspondence generated between Brigadier General John Gellibrand and Bean, in response to an article published in the *Sydney Sun* by the recently repatriated commander of the 9th Brigade, Brigadier General Alexander Jobson, is also of special interest. Jobson claimed that troops under his command had openly and deliberately ignored the rules of war and given 'no quarter' to enemy troops. An outraged Gellibrand wrote to Bean expressing his doubt as to the veracity of such claims, stating he had only heard of two cases in the whole war and that both were hearsay. He suggested Jobson had been 'gulled' or was suffering battle strain. 'If it is true', Gellibrand wrote, 'it is not typical of our men or officers and it is an abortion of spirit if it is false'. Gellibrand urged Bean to publish a letter celebrating 'the Australian as a fighter, with clean hands and a clean record'.[26] Yet Bean did not provide the unequivocal response that Gellibrand was looking for. Instead he replied:

> Candidly I don't know what to do in that case. I am up against this, that one has so constantly heard our men and officers talk as if these things did happen, and laugh about them, that I am half inclined to think they must have happened more often than we would like to believe. I have never had any first hand evidence of this on either side except in one or two cases; but if the rumour does get round that it happened, at least our men and officers have done nothing to stop the rumour being spread ... Whether these things are done or not, one hates the attitude which approves of them,

and the publication of them could only excuse the German for refusing to take prisoners from amongst our own men ... You see I cannot well come out and say I don't believe that this is done, because I have heard so many wild stories which I don't know the truth of.[27]

The stories were not so wild. In another incident an officer of the 27th Battalion shot seven prisoners with his revolver after a corporal, commendably, had refused to do so.[28] Such episodes were far more widespread than senior commanders wished to acknowledge. Australians, too, were sometimes on the receiving end of unlawful treatment when captured by the Germans. Australian wounded were killed and Australian prisoners shot down for no apparent reason. Whether this was a response to Australian indiscretions, as Bean had feared, cannot be determined.[29] More likely the incidents were examples of the same brand of spontaneous unregulated violence.

Bean argued that a 'primitive bloodthirstiness' took possession of most men, particularly in close-quarter fighting. He accepted its presence as inevitable on both sides because men were 'wrought up by the strain to an intense desire to strike' with orders 'to inflict as much loss as possible'. In trench raids in particular their duty required that 'they spend the few allotted minutes in striking at everything around them, killing, wounding, or capturing'. The introduction of such trench raids as an Allied tactic on the Western Front, born of frustration at the usual stalemate, undoubtedly compromised a soldier's ability to act lawfully: such raiders operated with time limits, had to look to their own safety, and were ordered specifically – in contravention of existing rules of war – to kill the enemy as opposed to taking a position. In any case, Bean admitted that the details of the actions of some Australians did not make pleasant reading, and in another footnote cited the case of a German sergeant who was hauled from a dug-out and shot several times after showing plucky resistance. The German was described as sinking helplessly to the ground, although Bean does not state whether he was dead or not, and the 'brave man' was later 'brained by the knobkerry of some soldier whose lust for blood was not yet satisfied'. Bean was not condoning such behaviour. Yet he reconciled his disappointment against the argument that such an act was 'inseparable from the exercise of the primitive instincts'.[30] The wider question for us is whether we should accept such a premise or is it at its heart incompatible with understanding humans as rational and moral beings?

The history of the 3rd Battalion provides one of the most illuminating examples of the idea of 'no quarter' and how it was enacted. Its account of the unit's part of an attack on Bayonet Trench, on 5 November 1916, raises a number of issues. The bomb and bayonet work that was proudly described shows that giving quarter was simply not countenanced. Privates Weger and Meaker were the first two bayonet men in this encounter and were instructed to 'start the dirty work' – the killing of the unlucky German survivors in the dug-outs after a bomb had been thrown in. The pressure on inexperienced men to engage in this 'standard' practice was immense. One soldier reported to his sergeant that he had found a German in a shelter. He was told to 'fix' the German, but he replied that he could not kill a man that way. The sergeant's reply was devoid of morality and compassion: 'Go on, you haven't killed one yet; I'll give you one more chance and then I'll fix him myself'. To his credit the soldier in question did not compromise his stand and it was left to the sergeant to kill the hapless German. The victim was clearly beyond the point of being a threat. In all likelihood he would have attempted to convey some sign that he wished to surrender and to plead for mercy. There was no justifiable legal or even military reason to kill him. However, the men had been addressed prior to the fight by a Lieutenant Loveday and told that the upcoming battle was 'an excellent opportunity to avenge the death of their colonel', who had been mortally wounded a few days beforehand.[31] Killing as retribution was something that was specifically outlawed in the Hague Rules.

During the 3rd Battalion's assault, some Germans were actually taken prisoner. One was described as 'smaller than the others' and able to speak some English. His diminutive stature (and possibly youth), along with the fact that he could speak English, appear to have contributed to his survival. He was one of two unwounded Germans captured during the action, but the Australians proceeded to slaughter the wounded prisoners in their care. One Sergeant Yorke, who was asked to take a message back to headquarters, agreed, then added laconically: 'All right, I'll go back through the trench and fix up those —— Huns, their moaning has been getting on my nerves'. When the order finally came to retire, the small German prisoner was carried back but other prisoners were euphemistically noted to have gone 'for a stroll'.[32] The incident is corroborated in the diary of Sergeant A. E. Matthews:

> Orders came through from Brigade for us to evacuate our position and to leave no live Germans behind. Guessing that there would be dirty work for somebody killing the wounded prisoners, I and a Lance Corporal volunteered to escort the two unwounded prisoners back to Battn Hqrs and we had just got away when we heard the awful screams of the men who were being slaughtered through military necessity.[33]

For their heroic conduct in this attack, Weger and Meaker received the Distinguished Conduct Medal, Loveday the Military

Cross, and Yorke was recommended for an award by his brigade commander.³⁴ If, as Matthews states, the orders to kill the enemy wounded emanated from brigade headquarters, then the Australian commander, Brigadier General James Heane, is deserving of condemnation, the more so because as a senior officer there could have been no question as to his misunderstanding the rules of war.

The same patterns of behaviour were again evident in World War II and, if anything, they were more openly admitted. Ivor Hele, an official Australian war artist, actually produced a sketch entitled: 'Shooting wounded Japanese prisoners, Timbered Knoll'. It was dated 30 July 1943. By that time, if any doubt had existed previously, the war against the Japanese had assumed the ugly face of a race war – most certainly from the Australian perspective. Each side depicted the other as barbarians and non-human. In this context little empathy was cultivated and an uncompromising ruthlessness imposed itself: the rules of war were flagrantly disregarded by officers and men of both sides. In an address to his soldiers General Sir Thomas Blamey, Australia's Commander in Chief, referred to the Japanese as an 'inhuman foe … a curious race – a cross between the human being and the ape'. They were 'vermin' to be exterminated.³⁵ General Paul Cullen, whose men were known to have bayoneted Japanese prisoners, found himself unable to condemn his soldiers, 'It was my battalion and I felt guilty', he reflected, 'but it was understandable. I'm not critical of the soldiers.'³⁶

The range of incidents of such atrocities was wide and evidence of them is easy to uncover. Charles Lindbergh, the famous American aviator, spent four months with the Americans in mid-1944 and kept a journal in which he documented numerous acts of barbarity toward the Japanese. Mentioned among the incidents he described was the Australian practice of throwing prisoners from airplanes and then reporting that they had committed *hara-kiri* (suicide).³⁷ How true this was is open to debate in the face of no obvious admissions by Australian troops. It cannot be discounted, however, and given the openly expressed desire of officers and men to annihilate the Japanese, as Paul Ham has suggested, the victors can be relied upon not to leave records of their wartime disgraces.³⁸

In another noteworthy display of a singular lack of any sense of 'fair play' in this conflict, on 29 December 1944, during operations at Bougainville, Brigadier R.F. Monaghan signalled to men of the 42nd Battalion: 'For the present we have enough information to require no further prisoners. For now slaughter will commence and every Jap seen will be promptly and ruthlessly killed. Information all ranks.'³⁹ A week later Monaghan chose to revisit his order in rather more civil tones. (It is likely that superiors felt his language had been too blatant and that if such uncompromising actions were to be advocated they should at least be veiled, if only thinly, with a modicum of decency.) The new message hardly hid the original intent and was well short of being a *mea culpa*:

> Further to my 0241. This instruction should not be in any way interpreted to infringe the Hague convention laws and usages of war. Enemy prisoners who fall into our hands alive must be treated with the greatest humanity and will be of value but the painstaking special efforts in setting traps are no longer for the present required. They may, however, be necessary again. Further it is asked that the killing urge be maintained in troops and the trapping urge no longer predominant. Pamphlets have been dropped promising immunity to the enemy who must repeat must be given safe conduct. Read to all ranks and certify completion of promulgation.⁴⁰

Treating prisoners with 'the greatest humanity' was commendable and the right thing to do. They had to be allowed the opportunity to surrender, of course, but this was a courtesy rarely extended to the Japanese. When they were captured – usually in an emaciated and exhausted state – there was no guarantee of safe passage. The number of references in Australian battalion histories of captured Japanese being shot while 'trying to escape' defies belief, given their generally chronically weak condition at the moment of capture. The truth of the following 42nd Battalion account, for example, given the attitude being cultivated by Monaghan, is open to question:

> A Jap armed with a bayonet and carrying some Australian biscuits gave himself up. He was worn out and seemed unable to fight any more against hunger and exposure. Afterwards when he had rested and fed, he must have repented his action, for when he was being escorted back to the Battalion Headquarters he attempted an escape and was shot.[41]

The discovery of dead Australian soldiers mutilated by the Japanese during the fighting at Milne Bay in August 1942 is often cited as a turning point in Australian attitudes toward their enemy in this theatre. Any thought of giving quarter was cast from the men's minds. Although the post-war period would reveal the extent of Japanese atrocities, there had really been little opportunity for such knowledge to reach the men in the front line up until late 1942. It is important to note, however, that those discoveries were fuelled by a long history of 'white supremacy' and fear of the 'yellow peril' that made it easier for uncompromising attitudes to foment. One cannot discount the possibility that the celebration of a national 'hardness' evident in World War I reportage and folklore also created a standard of ruthlessness to which some men aspired in battle and so acted out when given the opportunity.

The same level of hostility was not evident between Australians and European enemies in other theatres of war. In stark contrast to the propaganda-influenced views of the bestial 'Hun' of World War I, the Germans and the Vichy French of World War II were generally seen by the Australians as civilised, worthy and respected opponents (even if the Italians, whose fighting ability was much maligned, were largely seen as a joke).[42] These were not feelings that easily engendered the necessary malevolence to engage in atrocities. That is not to say that such things did not occur. Margaret Barter in her book about 2/2nd Battalion cites a story, which had gained currency as a factual heinous act, of Australians throwing grenades into compounds of Italian prisoners. It appears, however, that the incident derived more from a bad practical joke in which an Italian grenade, rated no better than a basket bomb on cracker night, was rolled in at the feet of some sleeping prisoners. Five Italians were wounded and a digger found guilty over the incident.[43] Worse, however, was an incident in which a member of an Australian patrol machine-gunned 20 Germans captured at Tobruk for no apparent reason. His act was viewed as 'treacherous and brutal' by the rest of the patrol.[44] Nonetheless, Australian higher commanders were, as in World War I and in the Pacific, implicated in deliberately advocating conduct that sat outside the rules of war. During the German invasion of Crete, soldiers of the 2/11th Battalion were told not to take prisoners, and at Alamein fighting patrols had limits placed on the number of prisoners they could take.[45]

The vast majority of illegal incidents perpetrated by Australian soldiers has occurred in land operations. Two actions involving Australian airmen, however, ought to be included in this discussion. In World War I, Australian airmen from No. 1 Squadron participated in an attack on a retreating Turkish column at Wady Fara in Palestine on 21 September 1918. The gorge through which the Turks were attempting to retreat became blocked through the destruction of vehicles and transports which were abandoned by their drivers. Turkish infantry scattered and tried to find alternative means of escape, but their efforts were hampered as they were continually strafed by British and Australian planes. According to the Australian official history the attack began with a sortie by two Australian planes which fired off '600 machine gun rounds into the confusion. That was the beginning of a massacre ... the panic and slaughter beggared all description.'[46] Throughout the course of the day, a further 44 000 machine gun rounds were fired and six tons of bombs dropped upon the trapped and fleeing Turkish infantry. By day's end the airmen had given up estimating the losses inflicted and 'were sickened by the slaughter'.[47] At question here is whether excessive force was used. This is a central philosophical consideration of both just war theory and the rules of war. Having disrupted the Turkish column and put it to flight was it necessary to return again and again to attack a retreating column, to attack men who no longer presented any immediate threat?

Similarly, after the Battle of the Bismarck Sea, in which eight Japanese transport ships carrying approximately 6400 soldiers and marines were sunk, Australian and American fighter squadrons spent several days strafing survivors stranded in barges and life boats. The official history regarded this work as a 'terrible yet essential finale', one for which it admitted the air crews 'had little stomach' and some of whom suffered 'acute nausea' as a result.[48] Such reactions were understandable in those being asked to kill essentially defenceless men. The argument in favour of the action was that these survivors would ultimately reinforce the Japanese land garrisons, and that it was better to kill them while the opportunity allowed than at a later time when they would be fortified and more difficult to overcome. This is a dangerous line of logic and might equally be used to justify the execution of prisoners, for example, in a wide range of circumstances. Certainly, however, the Australian public appeared to hold few misgivings about the attack. Cinesound cameras accompanied the fighters, and film of the strafing run featured in a newsreel that was screened at cinemas. The commentary, which can only be described as gleeful, described the Japanese as getting what they deserved and being sent back to their ancestors. A direct hit on a defenceless lifeboat was acclaimed as excellent shooting.[49]

One would have thought that the racism exhibited toward the Japanese during World War II would have carried through into the Korean and Vietnam conflicts. The outright hatered that was mustered against the Japanese, however, was notably lacking against North Korean, Chinese and Vietnamese soldiers. To be sure, racist comment still informed the soldiers' private writings, but as Richard Trembath has argued in his study of Australia's Korean War soldiers, those diggers made a genuine effort to 'understand' their enemy and this lack of hostility was 'evidence of how the camaraderie of war can mediate traditional lines of prejudice'.[50] Only one of the veterans interviewed by Trembath alluded to the adoption of past practices: 'N. Koreans had a reputation as cruel to extreme', he reported, 'they received short shrift from us ... few prisoners were taken.'[51]

The wars mentioned thus far were fought on traditional lines in so far as it was one military force pitted squarely against another. Vietnam changed that paradigm. The way the Viet Cong exploited the civilian population meant that distinguishing friend from foe became an increasingly difficult and stressful aspect of war. Booby traps and mines were used on a previously unimagined scale. One incident that shaped many people's perceptions about how the war in Vietnam was being fought was the massacre of civilians at Mai Lai by American soldiers in March 1968. The methodical barbarity of this atrocity, carried out against women, children and old men, in many ways heralded the collapse of support for the war amongst the Australian and American public. Australian soldiers did not commit any atrocities on an equivalent quantitative scale, but as allies of the perpetrators they were tarred with its dirty brush.

Certainly civilians were killed as a consequence of Australian actions in Vietnam. The most well-known incident occurred at Binh Bah, a village occupied by the Viet Cong and large numbers of civilians. Australian infantry and armour attacked on 6 and 7 June 1969 and, according to Paul Ham, they went to great lengths to avoid civilian casualties, trying to evacuate terrified villagers and refraining from firing indiscriminately during the fighting. Nevertheless a number of innocent villagers were killed, causing the action to be remembered – inexplicably to Ham – as a civilian bloodbath by some soldiers. Ham argues that such memory reflects 'the play of guilt and trauma on the mind' of some of the soldiers present.[52] Perhaps some of these men of the 5th Battalion believed that not enough was done to protect the civilians. One can only sympathise with their plight in being placed in the situation of an engagement in a populated zone.

One's empathy might be tested, however, by an incident recounted by an Australian soldier in Michael Caulfield's *The Vietnam Years*:

> Anyhow, somebody had walked on a mine or whatever ... we still think that somebody set it off, he didn't actually walk on a mine and it went boom. Because there was a woman and a couple of kids or a child I think just quite close by. And – anyway, it didn't kill him, it blew his leg off. But things like

that, you didn't trust them ... The woman was shot. And it would never have hit the Australian news for obvious reasons. I mean there was an instinct in guys – they didn't take her away and shoot her, not like a firing squad. The guys at the scene just swung around and mowed her down. First reaction. She's standing there and this bloke just got blown up, whether she was guilty or innocent, you know ... There was more of that sort of stuff happens than you will ever hear about for obvious reasons ... I think the child was shot too of course and imagine the uproar, 'Australians mowing down innocent civilians – blah blah blah'.[53]

It is difficult to reconcile the killing of this woman and child as unavoidable, or that the soldiers' reaction was so instinctive that they could no longer discern their status as civilians. Caulfield alludes to the application of 'the forgiving haze' to justify such acts, and he points out that despite the appalling nature of such crimes one must still accept that the lot of the soldiers was that of 'a halfway decent bloke in a very bad place who made a decision he still cannot explain or forget'.[54] Overall Caulfield argues that at Nui Dat and Phuoc Tuy Province, the Australians tried to uphold their humanity and that, while ugly incidents occurred, they were not reflective of the general behaviour or attitude of Australian troops.

Aside from the problematic nature of civilian casualties, it is evident that the practice of killing wounded enemy, as had occurred in the World Wars, also happened in Vietnam. Terry Burstall, a veteran of the Battle of Long Tan, recalled the shooting of two wounded Viet Cong soldiers after that battle. He quotes a colleague as describing them, prior to their murder, as 'just sitting there looking pretty helpless'.[55] Burstall revisited the theme of killing prisoners in an article in *The Age* marking the twentieth anniversary of the battle: 'There must have been 20 blokes alive there when we went back through them in the morning. I'd say we killed about 17, murdered them. We murdered those poor bastards and then we started to clean up.'[56] Bob Buick took particular exception to Burstall's revelations, claiming it was not true and stating 'Our commanders and I mean at all levels would not permit such an atrocity'. Buick admitted that the shooting of wounded enemy soldiers did occur, but argued they were mercy killings since the victims were mortally wounded.[57] One might counter that it is not the role of soldiers to make that judgement.

Caulfield's observation about the Vietnam experience of Australian soldiers is applicable to diggers who have fought in all wars: that the 'memories of lives taken wrongly, bad deeds done' was 'the lot of the men we send to war, the burden we demand they carry but never want to know'.[58] Since the Vietnam War, Australia has deployed troops in numerous peace-keeping exercises and in combat roles in Iraq and Afghanistan. These actions have been conducted with much smaller forces than the armies of the World Wars and Vietnam. In that time, the professionalism of the Australian armed forces has increased markedly, as has international scrutiny of soldiers' behaviour in combat, certainly those from Western nations. More recently still, social media has meant that unofficial records of soldiers in action and in war zones have created a broader public arena in which infractions might become known. This may act as a further deterrent for soldiers to act illegally. Modern-day soldiers enter combat well instructed about the rules of engagement and are even provided with rules of engagement cards. However, no amount of training will ever overcome the fraying effects that combat can have on soldiers. They are under immense psychological stress and one cannot say with any certainty that atrocities will not be committed in the future by Australian service personnel. We can say that the vast majority of Australian soldiers have not committed atrocities. We can also say that the chances of such incidences occurring are much reduced through better training and scrutiny. It can only be hoped that the blatant killing of prisoners and wounded men that was tacitly approved by higher commanders in the World Wars, and overtly so in the war in the Pacific, will not be practised by Australia's military forces of the future.

Further reading

D. Blair, *No Quarter: Unlawful Killing and Surrender in the Australian War Experience 1915–1918*, Ginninderra Press, Canberra, 2005.

J. Bourke, *An Intimate History of Killing: Face-to-Face Killing in Twentieth Century Warfare*, Granta Books, London, 1999.

M. Caulfield, *The Vietnam Years: From the Jungle to the Australian Suburbs*, Hachette Australia, Sydney, 2007.

J. Dower, *War without Mercy: Race and Power in the Pacific War*, Faber & Faber, London, 1986.

B. Gammage, *The Broken Years: Australian Soldiers in the Great War*, Penguin, Melbourne, 1975.

D. Grossman, *On Killing: The Psychological Cost of Learning to Kill in War and Society*, Little Brown, New York, 1996.

P. Ham, *Kokoda*, HarperCollins, Sydney, 2010.

——, *Vietnam: The Australian War ~ The Illustrated Edition*, HarperCollins, Sydney, 2010.

International Committee of the Red Cross, *International Law Concerning the Conduct of Hostilities: Collection of Hague Conventions and Some Other Treaties*, Geneva, 1989.

M. Johnston, *Fighting the Enemy: Australian Soldiers and their Adversaries in World War II*, Cambridge University Press, Melbourne, 2000.

J. Keegan, *The Face of Battle*, Jonathan Cape, London, 1976.

G. Kewley, *Humanitarian Law in Armed Conflicts*, VCTA, Melbourne, 1994.

R. Trembath, *A Different Sort of War: Australians in Korea 1950–1953*, Australian Scholarly Publishing, Melbourne, 2005.

[7]

THE UNNECESSARY WASTE: AUSTRALIANS IN THE LATE PACIFIC CAMPAIGNS

Karl James

Prime Minister John Curtin began in his 1943 Australia Day broadcast with 'Australia is the bulwark of civilization south of the Equator. It is the rampart of freedom against barbarism.' Speaking to the nation, with additional listeners in Britain and the United States, Curtin set out Australia's ongoing contribution to and the sacrifices already made in World War II. The Royal Australian Navy's (RAN) warships and the airmen of the Royal Australian Air Force (RAAF) were serving all over the world. Australian soldiers had endured bitter retreats in Greece and Crete, but had won glory at Tobruk and had been at the spearhead of Allied troops at El Alamein. In the Pacific, Curtin pledged, those Australians taken prisoner by the Japanese would be 'revenged thrice over'. In Papua, Australians had fought in some of the worst conditions of the war to wrestle Kokoda, Buna, Gona and Sanananda from the Japanese. American soldiers and airmen fought 'knee to knee' alongside the Australians. This, Curtin concluded, was 'Australia's fighting record'.[1]

It was an impressive record. Between 1940 and 1942, Australian forces were prominent in the Mediterranean and North Africa fighting the Italians and Germans. Closer to home, Australian forces had helped stem Japan's southern-most thrust in desperate battles in Papua during 1942, with the last shots having only been fired days before Curtin's broadcast. In the coming year, Australians and Americans would continue to fight 'knee to knee', advancing along New Guinea's north-east coast. American forces also conducted a series of amphibious operations in the Solomon Islands and New Britain that, together with the New Guinea offensive, successfully encircled and isolated Rabaul, the main Japanese base in the south Pacific. During 1944, General Douglas MacArthur's 'island hopping' campaign took Americans into Dutch New Guinea and on to the Philippines. By year's end, Japanese cities were subjected to a terrifying bombing campaign, first from American long-range bombers flying from China and Saipan, in the Central Pacific, and from April 1945 by carrier-borne aircraft. Planning was well underway for an American-led invasion of the Japanese home islands when the war came to a devastating end in August 1945. Until that point the war in the Pacific had been expected to continue at least until 1946.

During the later phases of the Pacific War, however, Australia was left far behind. The Australian Army was excluded from operations in the Philippines and beyond. Instead, Australians fought on 'mopping-up' Japanese troops in Australia's Mandated Territories of New Guinea and Bougainville, and on Borneo. Australian forces were, in fact, more heavily engaged during 1945 than at any other time in the war, but it was at the same time a period of disagreement and disappointment – and has remained so ever since. In early 1945, for example, an Opposition Senator asserted that Australian forces were being 'whittled away on a more or less "face-saving" task' in New Guinea and Bougainville.[2] Such sentiments were widely echoed in the press, debated in Parliament and discussed by the soldiers themselves. Brigadier

Heathcoat 'Tack' Hammer, an infantry commander on Bougainville, later commented:

> Every man knew, as well as I knew, that the Operations were mopping-up and that they were *not* vital to the winning of the war. So they ignored the Australian papers, their relatives' letters of caution, and got on with the job in hand, fighting & dying as if it was the battle for final victory.[3]

Sergeant S. E. Benson, of the 42nd Battalion, was more blunt, writing bitterly that it had been 'a purely political decision' to fight an aggressive campaign on Bougainville in what was obviously a 'strategic backwater'.[4]

From 1945 to the present, veterans, journalists and writers have repeated this notion, almost as a mantra, of Australia's final campaigns in the Pacific as an 'unnecessary war' – where men's lives were wasted needlessly for political rather than strategic reasons. Others, most notably journalist Peter Charlton, have argued that the campaigns were fought for the self-aggrandisement of old generals. War correspondent-cum-historian Max Hastings has even more recently alleged that Australian forces were 'bludging' in the islands rather than fighting elsewhere in the Pacific.[5] Such orthodoxy, such a consistent stream of complaint over time, however, does not make it true. The idea of an 'unnecessary waste' in the late Pacific campaigns is an inaccurate and misleading interpretation.

The main villain in the myth of wasted Australian lives is usually General Sir Thomas Blamey. He is an easy target. Landing at Gallipoli on 25 April 1915, Blamey served with distinction during World War I to become Lieutenant General Sir John Monash's chief of staff in 1918. Blamey soldiered on during the interwar period, but his time as Victorian police commissioner during the 1930s attracted scandal. When war was declared in 1939, Blamey was appointed to command the newly formed 6th Division when the second Australian Imperial Force was raised, and he subsequently commanded the 1st Australian Corps in the Middle East. Short and rotund, Blamey was a skilled staff officer with a cutting intellect and forceful personality. He was also tactless and attracted controversy. But as Curtin once told a group of newspapermen, in 1939 the government 'was seeking a military leader not a Sunday school teacher'.[6] Blamey returned to Australia on 26 March 1942 with the 1st Australian Corps where he received the news that he had been appointed Commander-in-Chief, Australian Military Forces. There was no fanfare.

Nine days before Blamey's appointment, on 17 March, General Douglas MacArthur arrived in Australia with his family after escaping from the disastrous campaign in the Philippines. 'I have come through', MacArthur pledged famously, 'I shall return'. Tall and slim, a West Point graduate, highly decorated, a former US Army Chief of Staff, and a Republican, MacArthur cut an imposing figure. When he arrived in Australia, he was publicly celebrated as a hero. Only a month earlier, Singapore had fallen to the Japanese in the worst defeat in British military history and Darwin had been bombed. Many Australians feared a Japanese invasion. MacArthur's arrival and the accompanying promise of military support from the United States meant that Australia would not have to face its darkest hour alone.

As men, Curtin and MacArthur could not be more different, but they formed a firm bond nonetheless. When the two first met, MacArthur told Curtin: 'We two, you and I, will see this thing through together ... You take care of the rear and I will handle the front.'[7] This approach suited both men well and played to their strengths. Unlike other Allied leaders, such as Churchill and Stalin, Curtin did not pretend to be militarily minded, and he was content to leave the fighting to MacArthur and his generals. Curtin, who was also the Minister for Defence, had been a journalist, trade union leader, a prominent anti-conscription campaigner and a former alcoholic. He had been prime minister for less than six months after the Australian Labor Party came to power in October 1941. Curtin supported MacArthur's appointment as Supreme Commander, South West Pacific Area (SWPA) and essentially assigned Australia's forces to MacArthur's command. Blamey was appointed Commander, Allied Land Forces, but he had little practical control over American troops.

MacArthur's area of responsibility was vast. The SWPA included Australia, New Guinea, New Britain and Bougainville – the territories mandated to Australia from Germany by the League of Nations after World War I – as well as the Netherlands East Indies (modern Indonesia) and the Philippines. The directive that established SWPA provided that the Combined Chiefs of Staff from the United States and Britain would determine grand strategy, including the allocation of forces. MacArthur received his orders from the US Joint Chiefs of Staff. Australia had no real say, therefore, in deciding Allied strategy. Curtin's inexperienced government has been criticised for surrendering Australian sovereignty to the United States in this regard, but it is difficult to imagine what else it might have done.[8] Yet the Australian government had an escape clause. The directive establishing the SWPA included the rider that each nation retained the right to 'refuse the use of its forces for any project which it considers inadvisable'.[9]

As the war unfolded in the SWPA, Australian troops in New Guinea and elsewhere bore the brunt of fighting in 1942 and 1943, but these two long years of jungle warfare were exhausting. As the Americans began taking a more prominent role, in December 1943 Blamey directed that the Australian Army be 'totally with withdrawn from an active operational role in New Guinea'.¹⁰ All but two of the six Australian divisions in New Guinea would return home for training and rehabilitation on the Atherton Tablelands in south-east Queensland.¹¹ MacArthur afterwards stated that it had been the Australian success in Papua 'that turned the tide of battle and on which all future success [had] hinged' and that Australia's 'brilliant' campaign helped 'speed the Japanese defeat in New Guinea'.¹²

There was never any doubt that Australia would return to the field; it was only a matter of where, when, and in what strength. Curtin was determined Australia would remain fighting. In November 1943, the prime minister told MacArthur that he wanted Australian forces involved in the liberation of Australian mandated territory. Australia 'has a special interest', Curtin noted, 'in the employment of its own forces in the operations for the ejectment of the enemy from territory under its administration'.¹³ It seemed logical to Curtin that Australian troops should be used in Australia territory. A month earlier, in October 1943, the Australian War Cabinet deemed it of 'vital importance' to Australia that its role in future operations be sufficient 'to guarantee us an effective voice in the peace settlement'.¹⁴ Curtin personally reiterated this point to senior Allied leaders and commanders in London and Washington during an overseas trip in mid-1944. Curtin realised that no matter how much wheat, meat and material Australia supplied to rationed-starved Britain and to the American forces in SWPA, Australia's real post-war influence in the Pacific would be in proportion to the amount of fighting it undertook.¹⁵

Looking towards the future, however, Curtin's immediate concern was manpower. This issue dominated the government's decisions regarding the later stages of the war effort. Nearly a million Australians served in the armed forces, more than half of them overseas. Along with the three services, Australian society and industry had also been rapidly mobilised for war. There was a tremendous strain on resources. The services had to compete for manpower with the industrial sector that was already struggling to meet the demands of the Australian and American military, and beginning to anticipate the need for peacetime commodities. Adding to these pressures was the need to begin preparing for the arrival of a British fleet that was to deploy in the Pacific and join in operations against Japan. Just as the Americans had used Australia for logistical support and as a staging area, so too now would the British — and this meant base installations, ship repairs, storage, hospitals and fleet air arm facilities across the country. The first British warships were expected in late 1944, and by mid-1945 the fleet was to include four battleships, ten aircraft carriers and sixteen cruisers.

Australia's population, especially the male labour force, was not large enough to meet these combined demands. The government's attempt to balance the war effort against the need for labour thus began in earnest in late 1943 when the War Cabinet decided the army needed to be reduced by 20 000 men by mid-1944. This figure was in addition to those normally discharged for age, discipline or medical reasons. After additional reviews, the War Cabinet decided in August 1944 that another 45 000 men — 30 000 from the army, the rest from the air force — would need to be released by June 1945. The navy's strength was capped at 38 000.[16]

Blamey was very much aware of the government's contrasting manpower pressures against the need to maintain the army as an offensive force. He had also been anticipating from early 1944 that Australian troops would be used to relieve the more than six American divisions garrisoning New Guinea. 'I think it obvious', Blamey wrote in March, 'that the operational role of the Australian Forces in New Guinea itself has practically terminated, and therefore any excessive number retained there will be wasted'.[17] MacArthur agreed. The US general's major objective – and personal crusade – was the liberation of the Philippines; New Guinea was but an obstacle that had to be overcome. Rather than grinding down the enemy's strength directly, MacArthur adopted the strategy of 'island hopping', making amphibious landings on suitable islands and areas that could be developed into bases to isolate and block the Japanese, leaving them to 'wither on the vine'. This allowed for a speedy advance, but also required leaving large numbers of Japanese troops behind the 'front'.

As MacArthur began preparations to return to the Philippines, on 12 July 1944 he sent Blamey a memorandum asking for Australian forces to take over 'responsibility for the continued neutralization of the Japanese in Australian and British territory and Mandates in the Southwest Pacific Area'. MacArthur also mentioned that in 'the advance to the Philippines it is desired to use Australian Ground Forces and it is contemplated employing initially two AIF Divisions': one division would be used in November 1944 and the other in January 1945.[18] To replace the American garrisons Blamey decided to use seven Australian Militia brigades consisting of conscripts, who by law could only serve in Australian territory, as well as men too young for the AIF and volunteers. This would leave Australia's preferred sword arm – the 1st Australia Corps, consisting of the veteran 6th, 7th and 9th Divisions (all volunteer members of the AIF who could serve anywhere in the world) – available for future operations.

MacArthur, however, did not agree with Blamey's plan. He considered the prospect of seven Australian brigades, equal to about a third of the American forces currently employed in the area, as 'totally inadequate'. After serious discussions, on 2 August 1944, MacArthur issued another directive stating that the minimum forces to be employed were four brigades on Bougainville;

one brigade to cover Emirau, Green, Treasury and New Georgia Islands; three brigades to New Britain; and four brigades to the New Guinea mainland. The Australian forces were to take over the outer islands and New Guinea by October, and Bougainville and New Britain by November 1944. At this time the Japanese were thought to number 24 000 around Wewak in New Guinea; 13 400 on Bougainville; and 38 000 on New Britain.[19] Because an Australian division consisted of three brigades, MacArthur's insistence at this point – that the equivalent of four divisions be deployed to cover the withdrawal of US troops – meant the AIF's 6th Division had to be used in the islands alongside Militia formations.

Why the discrepancy? Gavin Long, Australia's official historian of World War II, argued that it was probably a matter of pride: MacArthur did not want it recorded that six American divisions were replaced by just six or so Australian brigades. It could not be shown that Australian troops were capable of the same job as the Americans, but with only a third of the numbers. Blamey, on the other hand, appeared at ease with the idea that an Australian brigade was the equivalent of an American division.[20] Alternatively, historian David Horner has suggested that MacArthur may have wanted to keep the Australians occupied in New Guinea, thus meaning fewer AIF divisions available for use in the Philippines, or in case a new British command was formed in SWPA.[21]

Whatever the reason, Blamey could neither challenge nor change the situation, and he took no pleasure in having to reduce the 1st Australian Corps from three to two divisions. Blamey was not happy, later writing privately to Robert Menzies, the leader of the Opposition, that: 'The allocation of Australian troops to operations is entirely the responsibility of General MacArthur, and I have no real say in the matter beyond carrying out the orders of

I receive. While I have pretty strong feelings ... I have no right to criticise them.'[22] From September 1944, Australian troops thus began moving to the islands. The 6th Division went to Aitape, on New Guinea's north coast; the 2nd Australian Corps, consisting of the 3rd Division and two independent brigades, took over in Bougainville and the Solomon Islands; the 5th Division moved to New Britain; while the 8th Brigade, already in New Guinea, remained around Madang.

Blamey was in a difficult position. His government wanted to use Australia forces in Australian territory (New Guinea) but MacArthur insisted on nearly twice the number that Blamey thought necessary, and for an indefinite length of time. Blamey was also expected to release 30 000 men from the army, roughly equivalent to two infantry divisions, by mid-1945, all the while maintaining the 1st Australia Corps' capabilities for an assumed future role in the Philippines.[23] Blamey had previously only been thinking in terms of containing the Japanese, but MacArthur's insistence on deploying large numbers of Australian troops made some form of aggressive action possible. MacArthur had not specified how to neutralise the Japanese, and Blamey had a degree of latitude to undertake an offensive. The Australians were fresh, well supplied, and – in New Guinea and Bougainville at least – were thought to outnumber the supposedly sick and starving Japanese. Blamey could either submissively employ his 12 brigades on a task he thought seven were capable of doing, or he could go on the attack with the intention of weakening or destroying the enemy and with a view to reducing the required size of his own forces in the future.

In the end, Blamey decided on a limited offensive in areas where it could be conducted successfully and cheaply. On 18 October 1944, he ordered 'offensive action to destroy enemy resistance as opportunity offers without committing major forces'.[24]

On 7 November, he elaborated on his earlier orders, explaining that 'action must be of a gradual nature', to 'locate the enemy and continually harass him, and, ultimately, prepare plans to destroy him'.[25] Blamey was ordering limited aggressive action – not an all-out offensive. The idea was to wear down the Japanese in short, sporadic engagements. What was of overriding importance, however, was keeping Australian casualties to a minimum, and this consideration always set the context for these campaigns. While Blamey clarified his orders for his commanders, he did not inform the Australian War Cabinet. This was an oversight that would return to haunt him months later.

The subsequent Australian campaigns in New Guinea and Bougainville were both slow, grinding affairs, fought through swamps, along jungle tracks, and across river crossings and mountain spurs. Air support was minimal, while naval involvement was modest and sporadic. Lieutenant Colin Salmon later described the Bougainville campaign as 'one long bloody hard slog'.[26] Relieving the American corps at Aitape on New Guinea's north coast in September 1944, the 6th Division began a creeping advance eastwards towards Wewak, the last Japanese stronghold in New Guinea. The advance followed two parallel axes: one along the coast and the other through the mountains. Wewak was captured in May 1945 but resistance in the area continued until the end of the war. In total, 442 Australians were killed retaking Wewak, with 1141 more wounded. On Bougainville, the 2nd Australian Corps took over from the Americans at Torokina, on Bougainville's west coast, in October 1944. From here, the Australian campaign followed three axes: one ran across Bougainville's mountain spine to the east coast, another followed the coast to the island's northern tip, while the main push was to the south, towards the main Japanese concentration around Buin. When the war's sudden end brought this campaign to a close, the Australians controlled about two thirds of the island. Casualties on Bougainville were heavier than Aitape–Wewak, with 516 Australian dead and 1572 wounded.

The 5th Division's approach on New Britain was quite different. Rather than going on the offensive, here the Australians were limited to patrolling and confining the Japanese to the Gazelle Peninsula and Rabaul. The Japanese were content to remain where they were and did not try to break out. The Australian casualties in this sector were far lighter when compared to the other areas, with 74 men who were killed or died, and 140 wounded. Critics have argued the New Britain approach should have also been applied to New Guinea and Bougainville. This would have saved lives – but it would have also committed the Australian garrisons to these islands for an indeterminate length of time.

Meanwhile, as the war had moved further from Australia, so too had MacArthur. At the start of September 1944, his Advance General Headquarters began moving from Port Moresby, Papua, to Hollandia in Dutch New Guinea. A week later, the Americans were joined by a small group of Australian staff officers led by Lieutenant General Frank Berryman, Blamey's trusted Chief of Staff. Berryman's role was to assist with plans for the future employment of the 1st Australian Corps, and to safeguard Australian interests. Berryman kept Blamey informed of the mood in MacArthur's headquarters, observing firsthand the ever-increasing marginalisation of Australian forces. Throughout September and into early October 1944, the Americans speculated that the Australians would be used in the Philippines, but Berryman could not get a definite decision. Proposed operations involving Australian troops ranged from participating in the invasion of Luzon, or landing on Mindanao for a future advance to Borneo or Java.[27] Importantly, when MacArthur had met Curtin for the final time on 30 September 1944, the general repeated his promise that in the future, along with 'the garrison role for the neutralization of Japanese pockets of the various islands', the AIF would 'accompany the United States Forces in the advance against the Japanese'.[28] A week later, however, MacArthur's Chief of Staff, Lieutenant General Richard Sutherland, told Blamey and Berryman it was 'not politically expedient for the AIF to be amongst the first troops into the Philippines'.[29] The liberation of the Philippines began shortly afterwards with MacArthur wading ashore on Leyte on 20 October 1944.

In late November 1944, MacArthur's Advance Headquarters left Hollandia for Leyte. It was about this time, as Berryman was forced to insist his small headquarters be allowed to follow, that Berryman realised that the Americans were losing interest in the Australians. For the rest of the year, Berryman had almost daily battles with MacArthur's headquarters over the future use of the 1st Australian Corps. The hope of its employment in the Philippines was finally dashed on 5 January 1945, when Sutherland told Berryman that ten American divisions were sufficient to recapture Luzon, and Australian forces would instead concentrate on Borneo and the Netherlands East Indies.[30] A month later, an end to the major campaign in the Philippines was in sight. There were even plans for a victory parade in Manila. On 4 February 1945, Berryman wrote in his diary that MacArthur was:

> now busy staging his triumphant entry and to date no senior Australian officer has been invited to participate – one would think the AMF are not part of SWPA or that we did not do the bulk of the fighting in the critical stages of the campaign when our resources were so limited.

Still smarting a week later, he continued:

MacArthur more than once said he would take [the] AIF to Manila with him but now in his hour [of] victory he has not even invited one [Australian] representative to be present – a lack of courtesy to say the least ... I have not even hinted that we should be represented as our dignity & pride is proof against inclusion in a flamboyant Hollywood spectacle ... In his hour [of] victory his ego allows him to forget his former dependence on the AMF & is in keeping with GHQ policy to minimise the efforts of Australia in SWPA.[31]

Although the fighting in the Philippines continued until the end of the war, the AIF took no part in what where tough, hard-fought ground battles. Australia's contribution to the liberation of the Philippines was limited to the RAAF and the RAN. Australian warships participated in the major naval battles of Leyte Gulf in October 1944 (with the heavy cruiser HMAS *Australia* badly damaged by Japanese kamikazes), and Lingayen Gulf in January 1945. A small number of Australians with the Central Bureau signals intelligence also went to the Philippines. Integrated into the larger air and sea operations, it is difficult to easily recognise the RAAF's and RAN's contribution in this campaign as a distinctly Australian national force. After months of 'toing and froing', Berryman expressed his frustrations in a letter to the Secretary of the Department of Defence and War Cabinet secretary, Sir Frederick Shedden, in April 1945: 'I shall feel relieved when I Aust Corps is concentrated in a forward area ... I have worked on so many plans within the last few months that nothing will surprise me but it will be a relief when something is decided definitely.'[32] Shedden wrote to MacArthur that 'Australian opinion considered it a point of honour to be associated with operations in the Philippines as an acknowledgement of American assistance to Australia'.[33] Shedden's plea fell on deaf ears.

As the saga of the AIF's employment in the SWPA was being played out, the Australian press was wondering about the army's whereabouts. There had been no official reports about its activities since the second half of 1944. MacArthur's headquarters had not released any information concerning the Australian takeover in the Mandated Territories or of offensive operations in New Guinea and Bougainville. There were only vague statements that the AIF would be deployed in the 'future'. Newspapers, meanwhile, ran stories on the successful D-Day landings in France and the fighting in north-west Europe; the Red Army's staggering advance towards Germany; and the bloody American victories in the Central Pacific and the Philippines. It seemed that, while an eventual Allied victory was in sight, Australia's 'diggers' had been removed from the picture. In late 1944, the *Sydney Morning Herald*'s editor, for example, described the army as a 'fighting army held in leash'. Australians are a spirited people, the editor continued, and they do not desire their army be 'relegated to a secondary role or left indefinitely in reserve while the Pacific war marches to its climax'.[34] The editor of the *Canberra Times* wrote sarcastically: 'Will anyone knowing the whereabouts of Australian soldiers in action in the South-West Pacific please communicate at once with the Australian Government'.[35]

On 9 January 1945, MacArthur's communiques finally mentioned that Australian forces had relieved American forces in New Guinea, the Solomons and New Britain, and that 'Continuous actions of attrition at all points of contact have been in progress'. With these few sentences, the press was able to publish reports and photographs that had been accumulating for weeks. In Long's opinion, 'never in the history of modern war had so large a force, although in action, been hidden from public knowledge for so long'.[36] Despite this initial flurry of stories, the press's interest quickly waned, and by February 1945 the ongoing campaigns in the Mandated Territories were already beginning to be described as 'mopping-up operations'.

This was a period of intense frustration for Blamey, who was becoming increasingly concerned with a 'feeling that we are being side-tracked' that was 'growing strong throughout the country'.[37] The government shared this sentiment. After meeting with Curtin, who had himself been sidelined through illness for two months, on 13 February 1945 Blamey sent the prime minister a draft letter reminding him that elements of the 1st Australian Corps had been back in Australia for periods of up to 18 months and had taken no part in the war since 1943. He argued it was 'not desirable to retain so many Australian troops in an ineffective role'. Two days later Curtin sent an expanded version of Blamey's draft to MacArthur, stressing that the government considered it a 'matter of vital importance to the future of Australia and her status at the peace table in regard to the Pacific that her military effort should ... be on a scale to guarantee her an effective voice'.[38]

The 1st Australian Corps, meanwhile, continued to languish on the Atherton Tablelands. Things were getting boring, wrote Sergeant Les Clothier in his diary. 'Everyone, including the officers, is well and truly fed up.'[39] Many other Australian soldiers recalled this as a dreary and monotonous period. Trooper Ossie Osborne remembered it as:

> the worst period of my time in the army ... It was totally boring. There we were, we were well trained, well experienced, fit as fiddles. There was a war going on all over the Pacific and here we were spending our time running around on the Tablelands playing soldiers or playing cricket or football and getting into trouble.[40]

By early 1945 MacArthur was at last willing to give the AIF a definite role as his eye turned to liberating Borneo and the Netherlands East Indies. 'My purpose', MacArthur told Curtin in March, 'is to restore the Netherlands East Indies authorities to the seat of government as has been done within Australian and United States territory'.[41] MacArthur continued that this would be his final task before reporting to the Joint Chiefs of Staff that he had accomplished his purpose in SWPA. The exiled Dutch authorities in Washington had long been urging the Americans to expel the Japanese from their territory.[42] MacArthur similarly felt that re-establishing the Dutch colonial government in Batavia would enhance America's status in the region. Not to do so, he told General George Marshall, the US Army Chief of Staff, 'would represent a failure on the part of the United States to keep the faith'.[43] MacArthur also noted that he had made a commitment to the Australian government to make use of their troops, who were becoming restless.

Most recently, historian Peter Dean has pointed out that the strategic justifications put forward by MacArthur and others for the Borneo operations (codenamed 'OBOE') were 'tenuous'. By early 1945, the US Navy's blockade of the Japanese home islands was already preventing them from receiving oil from Borneo, while the oilfields and refineries were so badly damaged that even if the Allies captured Borneo they would take months if not years to be repaired. The final claim, pushed by the US Navy's Admiral Ernest King – that Brunei Bay in British North Borneo was needed as a base for the British Pacific Fleet – was dismissed when the Admiralty rejected its usefulness.[44] Marshall himself noted that the Borneo 'would have little immediate effect on the war against Japan'.[45] It is difficult in such context to avoid the impression that the OBOE operations were motivated as much by MacArthur's ambition to see himself in his final act as the liberator of SWPA as by his sense of obligation to the Dutch. This was also an opportunity to silence Australia's growing agitation by allocating the AIF something of a consolation prize after being excluded from the Philippines.

The OBOE operation was to have been a series of six amphibious operations with the 6th, 7th and 9th Divisions landings down Borneo's east coast and moving on into Java, where MacArthur hoped the Japanese would be crushed by early August 1945.[46] Curtin, however, supporting Blamey's recommendation, refused to release the 6th Division prematurely from its campaign in New Guinea.[47] Ultimately, only three of the six proposed OBOE operations went ahead. During April 1945, the first units from the 1st Australian Corps began moving from Australia to Morotai, in the Halmahera islands group, north of Ambon. Morotai became the staging area for an invasion of Borneo. Also based on Morotai was the RAAF's 1st Tactical Air Force, whose fighter and bomber aircraft had become responsible for air operations south of the Philippines.

Meanwhile, criticism and discontent in Parliament and the press continued to grow. Blamey's enemies – and there were many – attacked his leadership and credibility, and called for him to resign. The 'general public has very little faith in him as the Commander-in-Chief', claimed Senator Hattil Foll, while the army was 'seething with dissatisfaction'.[48] The Opposition used this as an opportunity to attack the government's handling of the war effort, criticising the quality and quantity of the army's equipment. Although his health was failing, Curtin staunchly defended Blamey, but after a particularly heated debate in Parliament he sent Senator James Fraser, the Acting Minister for the Army, on a 12-day inspection of New Guinea, Bougainville and New Britain to investigate the quality of the army's equipment. Privately though, Curtin's doubts about Blamey's ongoing conduct of the war were growing. He admitted, for example, that it had been his 'assumption' that the operations being carried out in the islands were in accordance with MacArthur's earlier July 1944 directive, and that they had met with MacArthur's approval.[49]

Senator Fraser's inspection was a whirlwind and carefully choreographed tour. For example, when on 9 April 1945 his entourage arrived at Torokina, the main Australian base on Bougainville, it only stayed two days. The Australian commander, Lieutenant General Stan Savige, a loyal friend and supporter of Blamey, arranged for a demonstration of infantry weapons and live ammunition under jungle conditions before taking Fraser to a battalion in a forward area for a brief visit. As Fraser left, he told Savige that he was leaving with confidence in both their efforts and equipment.[50] Curtin tabled Fraser's report in late April, telling parliament that the government accepted 'full responsibility' for the operations being carried out. The campaigns were being conducted successfully and with few casualties. The prime minister also pointed out that the Americans were conducting similar operations in the Philippines. Fraser thought that while some equipment had been delayed for the 6th Division, Savige and the commander on New Britain were happy with the quality of the engineering and fighting equipment available.[51] Curtin, however, was not a well man. At the end of month he was hospitalised as his health failed again. After several weeks in a hospital, Curtin insisted on returning to the Lodge. 'I'm not worth two bob', he told his driver on the way back to his residence.[52]

Blamey's time came in May 1945 when Treasurer and Acting Prime Minister Ben Chifley requested his attendance at the War Cabinet to explain his policy in the Mandated Territories.[53] Blamey offered the Cabinet a clear and well-reasoned appreciation of his strategy on 22 May 1945. His policy, he explained, had been adopted to destroy the enemy where this could be done with relatively light casualties, thus freeing Australian territory and liberating the 'native population', and thereby progressively reducing the military's commitments and freeing up personnel for release from the army. This was the approach that had been implemented in New Guinea and on Bougainville. On New Britain, where the Japanese at Rabaul were known to be well entrenched and to outnumber the Australians, Blamey's directive was to contain the Japanese on the Gazelle Peninsula and not go on the offensive. He went on to point out that the American policy of letting the Japanese 'wither on the vine' was not working: it tied down large forces in passive roles and was 'a colossal waste of manpower, material and money'. 'We are well into the second year of this policy', Blamey argued, and 'the enemy remains a strong, well organised fighting force' (the Japanese had become largely self-sufficient with gardens cultivated by New Guineans and Bougainvilleans). Blamey pointed out that once the Americans reached the Philippines, MacArthur himself had changed his by-passing strategy and sought the complete destruction of the Japanese. Blamey hoped that by the end of 1945, the twelve brigades in the area could be reduced to five; with a division of two brigades on New Britain, one brigade in the Aitape–Wewak area in New Guinea, and one brigade on Bougainville – leaving a brigade in reserve. In these last two areas, he intended for the Papuan and the New Guinea Infantry Battalions and small guerrilla groups to finish destroying the remaining Japanese.[54]

Just before Blamey attended the War Cabinet meeting, MacArthur wrote to the Australian government with a submission that could have been damning if Blamey's policy had not been explained so thoroughly. MacArthur, aware of the criticism surrounding the campaigns in the Mandated Territories, tried to distance himself from the controversy: 'I and my headquarters have never favored it, and while its execution has been successful and efficient in every way and worthy of praise, I regard its initiation as having been unnecessary and inadvisable'.[55] Chifley was no fan of Blamey and questioned him closely. Blamey should have reminded the government earlier and often that his policy was in keeping with the government's own long-standing policies and priorities, and that the practical considerations were justifiable. But the general nonetheless made his point. Shedden was convinced, commenting to Chifley that 'so far as the general question of strategy is concerned ... Blamey had made a very sound case in justification of the operations which he has been carrying out'.[56] Blamey's line of argument was presented to the Advisory War Cabinet on 6 June 1945 and it was formally approved at the end of July.[57]

Another topic discussed by Blamey and the War Cabinet was an American plan to use the 7th Division for the invasion of Balikpapan, codenamed OBOE Two, scheduled for 1 July 1945. The War Cabinet had previously supported the use of the 9th Division to capture Tarakan Island (OBOE One), on Borneo's north-east coast, as well as the area around Brunei and Labuan in north Borneo (OBOE Six), as this would increase Allied control of the sea between Malaya and Japan: but there was real cause for doubt over Balikpapan. Blamey had recommended the 7th Division be withdrawn from the operation, describing Balikpapan as 'a derelict Dutch oilfield'. Indeed all the Australian senior officers who would become involved with the landing – be they army, air force or navy – thought the operation lacked 'any real object'.[58] The American Chiefs of Staff were also sceptical, with Admiral King describing the operation as 'unnecessary'. MacArthur, however, would not be denied. He explained to General Marshall that the operation would not affect preparations for the invasion of Japan, and that all the ground troops involved would be Australians who had been out of action for more than a year. 'I believe', MacArthur wrote, that if the operation were cancelled or postponed it would produce 'grave repercussions with the Australian government and people'.[59] The Joint Chiefs thus approved the plan. MacArthur similarly manipulated the Australian government with a heavy-handed response at the suggestion of withdrawing the 7th Division:

> The Borneo campaign in all its phases has been ordered by the Joint Chiefs of Staff who were charged by the Combined Chiefs of Staff with the responsibility for strategy in the Pacific. I am responsible for execution of their directives ... I am loath to believe that your Government contemplates such action at this time when withdrawal would disorganise completely not only the immediate campaign but also the strategic plan of the Joint Chiefs of Staff.[60]

Following MacArthur's stern – even intimidating – reply, the Australian War Cabinet and Curtin (who was consulted in hospital) endorsed the Balikpapan operation. As Horner has shown, MacArthur's threat that the Joint Chiefs' strategy would be completely disorganised with the withdrawal of the 7th Division was a bluff. But it worked. The Joint Chiefs had approved Balikpapan because they thought the Australian's wanted the operation, while the Australian government only agreed to MacArthur's plan out of obligation to the 'grand strategy' of the Joint Chiefs.[61]

When they were launched, the OBOE operations themselves were spectacular and more lavishly supported than any other Australian operation of the war. The AIF was at the peak of its efficiency. The 7th and 9th Divisions were experienced, its soldiers well trained and drilled in their tasks, and its young leaders battle hardened. The RAN and RAAF were also prominent in each operation, with minesweepers through to heavy cruisers participating in the invasion while Australian fighters and bombers, including four-engine heavy bombers, were constantly overhead. Each operation was conducted successfully with skill and bravery.

OBOE One took place on 1 May 1945 when the 9th Division's 26th Brigade landed on Tarakan. Despite the copious quantity of firepower available, tough fighting took place in the hills and jungles around the township. Lieutenant Tom 'Diver' Derrick was mortally wounded during one such action on 22 May. Enlisting in 1940, he had served in Tobruk during the siege and had been decorated at El Alamein in 1942. He went one better a year later, awarded a Victoria Cross for an action in New Guinea, and he was subsequently commissioned. For many people, the death of Derrick, a brave, well-respected and much loved soldier, epitomises the futility of the Borneo campaign. Worse, Tarakan had been invaded in the first place so its airfields could be used to support later operations – but when taken they could not be made ready in time for this. Serious fighting on the small island went on until mid-June, with skirmishes continuing afterwards. Altogether, 225 Australians were killed on Tarakan and 669 were wounded.

The rest of the 9th Division landed in Brunei Bay and Labuan Island in north Borneo on 10 June with the task of securing the bay and surrounding area. This was accomplished by mid-July and for the rest of the war most of the division's efforts were taken up with civic action, administering and caring for the nearly 70 000 civilians in the area. During this operation, 114 Australians were killed or died of wounds, while 221 were wounded.

Made a reality at his own insistence, and possibly in acknowledgment of the controversy it sparked, MacArthur allocated the 7th Division's Balikpapan operation an unprecedented amount of air and naval support. Surprise was not an issue. Balikpapan was pounded for nearly three weeks in what was the longest pre-landing bombardment for any amphibious operation of the war. The invasion armada numbered over 250 vessels. On the pre-dawn eve of the invasion, Balikpapan appeared as a dull red glow on the horizon. Dawn on 1 July 1945 revealed what veterans described as a 'terrifying scene'.[62] Clouds of black, oily smoke from the bombed refineries blanketed the beach, buildings lay in rubble, and fires burnt all along the coast. In the short but sharp fighting that followed, the Japanese resisted fiercely where they could, but by 25 July 1945 the town, harbor and surrounding territory were secured, and the Australians were carrying out deep patrols beyond Balikpapan. When the war came to an end a few weeks later, 229 Australians had been killed during this campaign, and 634 more were wounded.

Having worked so hard to support Australia's war effort, it was a cruel twist that Curtin did not live to see Japan's ultimate defeat. He died at the Lodge on 5 July 1945. In the two and half years since his 1943 Australia Day broadcast, Australian and American forces had become increasingly separated, and by the war's end could no longer be described as being 'knee to knee'. When MacArthur, Curtin and Blamey had the same objectives during 1942 and 1943, the partnership in SWPA was outstandingly successful. But the Australian and American alliance was a marriage of convenience, and Australia was always going to be the minor partner. This was most obvious in the late Pacific war, with MacArthur's insistence on using twice the number of troops that Blamey thought necessary when relieving the American bases in New Guinea and the islands, and with MacArthur's excluding the AIF from action in the Philippines.

Required to commit large forces in the Mandated Territories, Blamey decided on an offensive approach in New Guinea and Bougainville that would potentially free up Australian troops for discharge from the army or subsequent operations by the end of 1945. The Australians only attacked where they thought they outnumbered the Japanese and where they thought they could be successful with minimum casualties. The merit of the New Guinea and Bougainville campaigns will always be debated, but there is no dispute that the approach to New Britain was correct, and that any attempt to attack Rabaul would have incurred heavy casualties for no real return. The conduct of each campaign also fulfilled the spirit of the government's long-stated policy of using Australian forces in Australian territory, and its perceived need to be seen as contributing to the fight in order to secure a voice in the peace that followed. Yet, with these operations being fought for practical as much as political reasons, Blamey should have been more forthcoming with Curtin and the War Cabinet about his aggressive policy from the outset. Likewise, the politicians should have paid closer attention to the rationale and conduct of the campaigns. If this had happened, Curtin could have immediately countered criticisms of Blamey and his strategy. Instead, it appeared as though Blamey had been caught out. His motives were seen to be suspect and questionable, with the government only retrospectively rubberstamping his decisions for offensive actions. The criticisms and justifications for the later OBOE operations are similar to those for the Mandated Territories, with the Borneo campaign taking place, perhaps more than any other, for political rather strategic reasons. Yet even with the Balikpapan campaign, the government demonstrated Australia's commitment to MacArthur and honoured the original directive that had established the SWPA.

There is no question that in 1944 and 1945 Australian soldiers were fighting and dying in areas where their blood and sweat could do nothing to hasten Japan's surrender. But this does not equate to a conclusion that such campaigns were an 'unnecessary waste'. They were fought by Blamey in an aggressive manner in order to shorten the campaigns and free up Australian manpower, as he had been directed. They were also fought in accordance with the Australian government's clear desire and intention to see Australian servicemen shouldering such a burden of the fighting as would ensure favourable post-war political positioning. It is worth remembering in this regard that armies exist not to win glory in what might later be seen as watershed battles but rather to act as instruments of national policy. A political objective can never be the 'wrong' reasons for soldiers to die – it is, in fact, the only good reason. Blamey may well be criticised for not keeping open a good line of communication with Curtin, but he cannot be damned for carrying out his government's wishes. Nor was it Blamey's fault that Australians did not participate in operations more ostensibly relevant to the outcome of the Pacific War. It was MacArthur, Blamey's senior officer, who kept the 1st Australian Corps from action in the Philippines, and it was MacArthur who effectively sent the 7th Division to Balikpapan – again for his own reasons – against Blamey' advice.

Further reading

P. Charlton, *The Unnecessary War: Island Campaigns of the South-West Pacific 1944–1945*, Macmillan, Melbourne, 1983.

P.J. Dean, *The Architect of Victory: The Military Career of Lieutenant-General Sir Frank Horton Berryman*, Cambridge University Press, Melbourne, 2011.

P. Hasluck, *The Government and the People 1942–1945*, Australian War Memorial, Canberra, 1970.

M. Hastings, *Nemesis: The Battle for Japan 1944–1945*, Harper Press, London, 2007.

J. Hetherington, *Blamey, Controversial Soldier: A Biography of Field Marshal Sir Thomas Blamey, GBE, KCB, CMG, DSO, ED*, Australian War Memorial/Australian Government Publishing Service, Canberra, 1973.

D. Horner, *Blamey, the Commander-in-Chief*, Allen and Unwin, Sydney, 1998.

——, *High Command: Australia and Allied Strategy 1939–1945*, George Allen & Unwin/Australian War Memorial, Sydney and Canberra, 1982.

K. James, 'The final campaigns: Bougainville 1944–1945', PhD thesis, University of Wollongong, Wollongong, 2005.

G. Long, *The Final Campaigns*, Australian War Memorial, Canberra, 1963.

P. Stanley, *Tarakan: An Australian Tragedy*, Allen & Unwin, 1997.

S.R. Taaffe, *MacArthur's Jungle War: The 1944 New Guinea Campaign*, University of Kansas Press, Kansas, 1998.

[8]

LOST AT SEA: MISSING OUT ON AUSTRALIA'S NAVAL HISTORY

Alastair Cooper

It is a bit strange that a country like Australia – where the overwhelming majority live on the coastal margins of an island continent, whose modern incarnation was founded by a navy, and which is as deeply dependent on maritime trade and industry as any country – should have so little public appreciation of its long naval history. Contemporary public understanding of Australian naval history is highly variable, with some aspects known very well, while others are not well recognised at all. While Australian military history is for good reason dominated by the 'Anzac' tradition and army or land-based narratives, the Royal Australian Navy (RAN) as an institution has consistently failed to overcome the 'silent service' approach. This may have been fitting up until the middle of the twentieth century, but is certainly no longer appropriate. This chapter examines the state of naval history in this country, investigates some of the key reasons that such a situation has come about, and suggests some topics of Australian naval history worthy of much greater attention. Australia is missing out on its naval history, and it is time for a change.

Certainly, when considering what parts of a nation's history receive the most attention or largest volume of published outputs, it is very easy for historians or devotees of a particular subject to claim that their subject of interest is unloved or under-appreciated. Moreover, stirrings of jealously might encourage a lament that there ought to be much less of 'this' and much more of 'that'. This chapter explicitly rejects such sentiments. History should not and does not have to be a zero sum game. A greater breadth and depth to Australian naval history, for example, does not have to come at the expense of that of the other armed services. In part this is because the development of the field can come from the Australian Navy as an organisation better understanding the importance of its own history, both for itself and as a part of Australia's national heritage. It is also in part because it would be both improbable and perhaps undesirable to attempt to recast the dominant Anzac land-based tradition. Yet there are many subjects, people and events in Australian naval history that are worthy of greater attention. One subject, HMAS *Murchison*'s operations in the Han River in Korea in 1951, will be examined later in this chapter in some detail. It is not that *Murchison*'s operations have never been recorded or that there are not other subjects of equal or even greater merit: what is significant is that her operations are an amazing story of skill, determination and bravery, but one which is completely absent from the public mind. It is a case of 'prime' historical material that has never been offered for wider public consumption and it is an example of the type of missed opportunity which pervades Australian naval history as a subject area.

There is a 'negative' version of this type of discussion: that some aspect of history is over-represented. The most common recent iteration of this argument is that Australian military history occupies a predominant position in the national psyche and that this is undesirable, if only because it excludes other aspects of the national heritage. Perhaps unsurprisingly, this is most commonly observed in the lead up to Anzac Day. This 'beggar thy neighbour' approach is unproductive at best: watching historians fight is, with only one exception this author can think of, very unlikely to generate a broader interest in any aspect of the subject.[1] The only productive way to achieve balance, if indeed an imbalance exists, is for historians and devotees of a particular subject to do the research, give the lectures, and write the books that meet the demands of varying audiences. In so doing they expand the contribution of history to Australia's heritage and public discourse, as well as advancing the subjects and causes that they care about. This is a much more positive method of contribution.

In any case, the fact is that the public does not have a very good understanding of Australian naval history. Certainly there are well-known battles, such as the first HMAS *Sydney*'s sinking of the German cruiser *Emden* in November 1914, or the second *Sydney*'s sinking of the Italian cruiser *Bartolomeo Colleoni* in July 1940. Some other well-known episodes in Australian naval history focus on the sinking of ships and other more difficult issues: the loss of the second HMAS *Sydney* in November 1941 (when all 645 crew died), of her sister ship HMAS *Perth* in February 1942 (353 crew died, over half the ship's company), and that of HMAS *Canberra* at Savo Island in August 1942 are cases in point during the World Wars. A little later, the sinking of HMAS *Voyager* in 1964 and USS *Frank E Evans* in 1969 in collisions with the carrier HMAS *Melbourne* – and the subsequent Royal Commissions – managed to capture public attention for a time. In more recent times, the treatment of servicewomen in the Navy in general, and in ships at sea in particular, has generated a great deal of print.

The history of the Australian Navy and its contribution to Australia, however, is much more than these discrete and often painful events. From escorting and carrying troops in wartime to surveying the harbours and sea routes that support much of Australia's economic prosperity; from conducting rescues at sea in the most difficult of circumstances to contributing to Allied intelligence breakthroughs, the Royal Australian Navy has a broad and rich history that is worthy of better understanding. The problem is that it has been a history that has never been well publicised, or well received by the wider community.

Even for those events that are well known, what is often lacking from the public discourse is the context for these events and the conduct of the naval personnel. It is not that naval history should only deal with its positive aspects, but that the successes and the disasters, the defining events and the broader context, the ships and the people, should all be understood in something approaching equal measure. The sinking of many Australian ships in war, for example, often occurred in the course of transporting or escorting troops, so although there may be controversial aspects to each individual event, the ships and their crews were contributing to a worthwhile objective in a risky environment. In this context Piers Macksey's criticism of histories covering British leadership in the American War of Independence is also appropriate to an assessment of the operational history of the Royal Australian Navy:

> The men who conduct a war are more intemperately and uncharitably criticised than those who run an administrative machine in peacetime. Statesmen and commanders are equally victims; for in war the results are swift, harsh and measurable, and censure readily precedes understanding … To understand the war, one must view it with sympathy for ministers in their difficulties, and not with the arrogant assumption that because they were defeated they were incompetent, and that all their actions proceeded from folly.[2]

This is not an argument for the idealisation of the Navy as an institution. In addition to the public discussion of naval history, including an understanding of the objectives and risks of naval operations, the Navy also needs to understand where and how its people and procedures have succeeded and where they have been found wanting. In many ways, people within the Navy have made strides to address this, particularly in the last twenty or thirty years, but it is questionable whether the Navy has truly institutionalised a commitment to its own history as a guide to its future. There is much to be learnt not only from operational history, but in the study of the organisation, the people within it, and its relationships with other institutions in Australia. The history of women in the Navy, for instance, and the extent to which that experience has mirrored Australian society, certainly deserves further study: it is also likely that the contemporary Navy would learn much of use from such work. Simply to know whether contemporary problems are enduring themes or exceptional events in naval history would be valuable information. To know to what degree the Navy's problems were its own or part of larger issues in Australian society would be even more important. Similar arguments can be advanced for understanding the Navy's relationship with other institutions, particularly its industrial suppliers and its political leadership.

There are two main reasons why public knowledge of Australian naval history is patchy: the dominance of the army in the Anzac tradition; and the lack of long-term interest by the Navy in its own history. The starting point to understanding the dominance of army history is that size matters. While the writings of Charles Bean and the widespread resonance of the Anzac tradition with the public are inextricably linked with army history, they are in some ways simple reflections of the numbers involved. Although the RAN Bridging Train served throughout the Gallipoli campaign, for example, it was numerically a much smaller organisation than the army units. During World War I, almost 417 000 men – over half of the eligible white male population – enlisted in the Australian armed forces, the overwhelming majority in the army.[3] The Navy had 3800 personnel at the start of this war, and over 5000 at the end. Of the 55 306 Australians who died in the conflict of 1914–1918, only 108 served in the RAN.[4] This theme of relative size is consistent throughout the twentieth century: in World War II the Navy was much larger, peaking at about 40 413 personnel in June 1945, but the peak size of the army was around 542 000 in August 1943 and the Royal Australian Air Force's reached close to 182 000 people in August 1944.[5] As a result, through the last century of Australian history the pool of people with direct experience of the Navy is relatively small and this has mattered as far as historical attention is concerned.

This issue of relative size is given further emphasis if the Navy's history is narrowly cast on operational subjects, because it leaves out so many parts of the service's history. For example, navies are capital- and technology-intensive organisations and their operational effectiveness is directly related to the efficiency and appropriateness of their industrial support base. But the understanding of the impact of industrial and dockyard activities on the effectiveness of the Australian Navy has never been systematically studied. Another example is the extent to which the Navy has mirrored Australian national priorities: ships are discrete units and their location and employment quickly and directly reflect the priorities of the government. The Australian Navy is no different to other navies in this respect but – in an echo of the 'other people's wars' myth discussed by Craig Stockings in Chapter 4 – the prevailing impression is that the Royal Navy and British associations have predominated to the detriment of Australian interests. This impression is not accurate, but a broader study, assessing Australian national interests and how the Navy has supported them, is another important area of investigation which has never been studied consistently, let alone comprehensively.

Furthermore, the location of naval operations has tended to diminish public knowledge and awareness of them, as they usually occur out of sight, often far from Australia. The Japanese submarine attacks in Sydney Harbour, for example, are an exception not the rule. Those parts of naval operations that do occur where they can be observed, such as harbour defences and minesweeping, are performed by small, slow and outwardly unimpressive vessels, while the conduct of the operations themselves is painstaking and focused below the water. As a consequence, these tend not to be parts of naval history that capture much attention from naval historians, let alone the broader public.

A second aspect of the location of maritime operations that tends to militate against broad public engagement is the ephemeral nature of the naval battlefield. It is possible to visit many terrestrial battlefields, and the topography and features of those battlefields are often still visible, can be photographed and disseminated broadly. An interested person can start to appreciate what the battle might have been like. The naval battlefield by contrast is much more difficult to visit. Even to a trained eye, one patch of ocean is much like another and the battle is defined by the presence of the warships, most of which have moved on after the battle and left few traces behind. Even the warship crews present at such battles have greatly differing perspectives, each of which are equally valid, but incomplete. The majority would have served below decks and may have heard a great deal, but not seen anything beyond the next bulkhead, let alone their enemy. Even those on the upper decks may have seen little. The resulting fragmentary stories are not easy to collect and piece together, making it difficult for historians to construct engaging, broadly appealing narratives.

How naval ships operate also contributes to the relative paucity of naval history and its understanding. Simply put, not many people know what goes on in the different parts of ships and how each contributes to the effectiveness of the vessel overall; and very few of those who do have recorded their experiences. While it is self-evident that naval, army and air force units are quite different, these differences have a real impact on the ease of transmission of history. Aircraft and air bases are quite similar to their commercial counterparts and are relatively accessible; army units, battlefields and bases are to varying degrees readily accessible and can be observed by both contemporary and later visitors. In combination with the twentieth-century Australian Navy's relatively parsimonious approach to the award of medals, the simple difficulty for a naval officer to observe bravery by a sailor in a different part of a ship goes a long way to explaining the relative lack of official acknowledgement and publicity regarding meritorious service by many naval personnel. Indeed, the Commanding Officer of HMAS *Murchison* during the Korean War (a subject to which this chapter will return) observed in later years that he wished he had pushed harder for greater recognition of bravery for his crew.[6] It is not unreasonable that the broader public does not seek to know more about actions that the Navy itself has hardly acknowledged.

How navies view the relationship between a ship and the vessel's commanding officer is another factor that reinforces the relative invisibility of the remainder of the crew. While the 'great men' of the Navy are undoubtedly worth studying, it is not possible to fully appreciate their accomplishments, decisions and failings, without also understanding the roles of those who served under them. The World War II losses of the cruisers *Sydney* and

Perth, and the *Voyager–Melbourne* collisions are all examples where the responsibility for the loss of the ship, which resides with the commanding officer, can be confused with explaining and understanding how and why these ships were lost. In all three cases, to understand the reason for the loss it is necessary (although not always sufficient) to understand the operation of the ships' bridge watchkeeping teams. The actions of the German ship *Kormoran* probably deceived not only Captain J. Burnett, but some or all of the other officers and sailors on *Sydney*'s bridge before that engagement began. While the decision-making process in this case will never be known with certainty, it is possible to construct hypotheses about how it occurred by understanding how the ship operated.[7] But this is seldom done. How many know, for instance, who else was on the bridge with Burnett?

The fact that ships are discrete units also tends to act against a well-rounded understanding of events when they are lost, as the unit records are often destroyed or lost with the sinking of the vessel. As a result, significant parts of an account of a vessel's final hours, days and weeks are based on incomplete, circumstantial and inferred evidence. In the absence of specific information it is easy for others to assume the worst, whether justified or not.

Importantly, while understanding of Australian naval history is patchy, it is not always for a lack of source material. A quick examination of the number of records available to anyone who is interested shows that Navy source material is voluminous and increasingly easily available, even online. The number of records available is in roughly equal proportion to the relative size of each of the armed services. In the National Archives of Australia in January 2011, there were about 19 151 records brought up by a search for 'navy'; 19 692 for 'air force' and almost 400 000 for 'army', the last figure reflecting the number and method of storage of individual service records. A similar broad catalogue search at the Australian War Memorial returned 12 987 'navy' records, 41 908 'army' records and 22 558 'air force' records: numbers that are broadly consistent with the sizes of each service referred to earlier. Similar proportional search results are returned from sources such as Wikipedia (5587 from 'Australian naval history', 8281 'Australian air force history', and 11 330 'Australian army history').[8]

The situation is not all bad news. Since the late 1980s, Australian naval history has received greater sustained attention than at any other stage in its existence. Starting with the work of some eminent naval historians, the Navy has put an increasing effort into the research and publication of its history. In large part this has been achieved through the work of authors such as Tom Frame, James Goldrick, David Stevens, Ian Pfennigwerth and others who have been associated with the Navy's historical studies. The appointment of Dr John Reeve as the Osborne Fellow in Naval History at the University of New South Wales campus at the Australian Defence Force Academy, supported by the Navy, has reinforced this work. This is an appropriate level of support by the Navy, because no other organisation has the level of motivation or the depth of institutional knowledge to be able to promote this field of study. Yet the Navy also needs to assimilate the idea that to fight and win at sea requires an intimate understanding of all the facets that create naval capability. Not everything of importance occurs on the water, and those things that do occur at sea need careful patient explanation to the public. These are considerations that the Navy has over its long history generally failed to grasp and they contribute directly to the current state of naval history.

Despite this greater recent attention by the Navy and an undoubted increase in the number and quality of publications on Australian naval history, there remains an undercurrent of disquiet amongst naval historians. Often this is expressed as a wish for greater attention to navy history, yet quantity is not really the issue. Our concern arises because those events that are traditionally taken as defining moments in naval affairs often attract a generally negative tone: they become stories of loss without understanding why. The contrast with army history is stark. At Gallipoli, the Australian army took part in a long, drawn out defeat; but it is remembered positively as the exemplification of so many positive attributes of Australia and Australians. When the World War II losses of *Sydney*, *Perth* or *Canberra* are remembered, the tone is much different.

So what is to be done? More resources for the study of naval history alone are not enough, although they would not hurt. Nor will greater attention from the broader public be garnered simply by decrying its lack. The single most important factor is for naval historians to describe the history of the Royal Australian Navy in a way that acknowledges the gap between subject and audience – and to appreciate that the subject must first be brought to the audience, not vice versa.

Having described some of the problems and difficulties of naval history, the remainder of this chapter will show how those problems might be remedied.[9] This will be done through a re-examination of the truly remarkable operations of HMAS *Murchison* on the Han River during the Korean War, including an account of what action within the ship was required to undertake these operations. HMAS *Murchison* was a 'Modified Bay' class frigate, built in Australia at the Evans, Deakin and Company dockyard in Brisbane. A product of the demand for more capable antisubmarine convoy escorts, *Murchison* was built during World War II but not completed until late 1945, after the war ended. *Murchison* was in the waters off Tasmania, conducting routine peacetime training, when on 10 March 1950 she was directed to return to

Sydney to prepare for a deployment to Korea.[10] Although destroyers were preferred for Korean operations, the Navy's new 'Battle' class destroyers were not fully operational and frigates were all that were available to replace the destroyers already deployed. *Murchison* was chosen because she had the best radar equipment of the available frigates.

In the aftermath of the World War II, the Navy had insufficient personnel to provide a full crew for all ships and the requirement to provide two vessels for service in Korea was a strain. Just to get *Murchison* to a point where she could deploy was an exceptional effort. At the time the decision was made, *Murchison* had a crew of between 60 and 80, instead of the full compliment of 180 needed for operations. The training of radar operators that the ship had been engaged in practised a much narrower range of skills than that required of a ship in a combat zone. The ship also needed a period of maintenance to remedy defects that could be tolerated in peacetime running but not in a war zone.

Murchison was brought up to near her full complement by the blunt but effective method of requiring other ships in the fleet to provide a specified number of sailors. Rather than sending their best sailors, the providing ships took the chance to rid themselves of men with poor disciplinary records. While not the most promising start, *Murchison*'s Executive Officer, Lieutenant Commander W.O.C. Roberts observed:

> this unlikely group developed into the liveliest and most efficient ship's company ... in their former ships they were the above average intelligence type of sailor who found themselves bored rigid with peacetime routine. In an operational situation they found a meaning in the drills and discipline and responded accordingly.[11]

The process of forming an 'unlikely group' into a lively and 'most efficient ship's company' is something that is passed over quickly in all existing accounts of *Murchison* in Korea. As the distinguished historian Paul Kennedy has argued in the wider context of World War II, the historical accounts 'may be lacking a fuller appreciation of that trickier level of "History in the Middle"'.[12] So too in naval history, the process of making a ship's company work well deserves greater attention, for it is this aspect that enables the technological capabilities of the ship (the characteristics on which most naval historians tend to concentrate) to be utilised to their full potential. In *Murchison*'s case, there were several remarkable aspects. The ship's mess decks – the crew's living quarters – had to be largely refitted, as they had been reconfigured, probably without authorisation, to be more comfortable for the ship's smaller peacetime complement. With the influx of about 120 people, former storage and sleeping spaces had to be reinstated.

Then the new arrivals needed to be fitted into the ship's organisation. Every warship has at least three basic modes of operation – cruising watches, defence watches and action stations – and a variety of special purpose modes, such as emergency stations, leaving ships stations, underway replenishment and entering or leaving harbour stations. For each of these modes of operation, each person onboard has a specific task and location, and sometimes a different one for each. These different stations are usually recorded on the ship's watch and station bill, forming a living document that must be updated with the coming and going of each sailor, whether the movement is permanent or temporary. The sailors have to know not only where to go for each mode of operation, but what they have to do when they get there, day and night, good weather and foul. Speed of action, reliability and the capacity to cope with the stress of injuries to others or damage to ship systems are also required. This kind of highpitched capability is achieved through constant drills, pushed to an even higher tempo in a 'work-up' process for deployment. *Murchison* must have achieved most of this during the passage north to Korea, which included a port visit and associated training in Hong Kong.

The work-up period which *Murchison* completed en route to Korea applied not only for the experienced crew, but also for the ten junior sailors who joined the ship direct from the Flinders Naval Depot. These sailors would have experienced the steepest learning curve of any in the ship. One of them, Stephen Joyce, who served as part of the gun crew for *Murchison*'s forward twin four-inch 'A' gun, thought that: 'having the senior crew, and also having new crew on board we were lucky that we had changeover RN [Royal Navy] sailors that had served during the war in the RN and then signed on in the RAN, we had excellent teachers'.[13]

The efficacy of the work-up process can be judged in hindsight from the success *Murchison* achieved during her Korean deployment, which was acknowledged both by the allied naval commanders and by the Australian Navy, with the award of the Gloucester Cup – an award made annually to the ship judged to have been the best and most efficient in the preceding year – on her return to Australia. The success reflects very well on two aspects of the Navy. The first is *Murchison*'s officers and senior sailors who scheduled and conducted the multitude of training drills that brought the ship up to such a high standard in a relatively short period. The second is the Navy's institutional culture which would have guided the officers and senior sailors and which, despite the massive reduction in numbers of people and ships, seems to have retained the lessons from World War II.

Notwithstanding the apparent success of this training, the start of the deployment was not all straightforward. *Murchison* had a major engineering failure during her first patrol in Korean waters when both fuel pumps failed, dramatically reducing speed to about 4 knots – little more than a crawl. The ships engineers were unable to fashion replacement parts onboard and no replacement could be found in Korea or Japan. As a result, *Murchison* spent over a week waiting for spares to be flown from Australia. The inability to source them locally is interesting, because there were several current and former US Navy 'Tacoma' class frigates operating in the Korean theatre (operated by the United States, Colombian and Korean navies) that were built to a very similar design to the Australian 'Modified River' class. It is possible that the actual fuel pumps fitted differed greatly between the Australian and US built ships. If this was the case, the difference must have been considerable, as *Murchison*'s engineers could probably have adapted equipment, particularly with assistance from a dockyard or support ship. An alternative explanation is that the Australian and US naval supply systems were not very well integrated, and the Australian ships were either unaware of, or unable to source, the required spare parts from the US Navy logistics organisation.

Once *Murchison* actually commenced operational patrols, she spent all of her time deployed to the western coast of Korea, generally a shallow and challenging navigational environment for a warship. The area of operations for which *Murchison* is best known, and should be much better known, is the Han River estuary. Several frigates spent long periods operating in the Han River estuary to enable them to bombard North Korean positions in the vicinity of the armistice negotiations at Kaesong, the idea being that this would put pressure on the North Korean negotiators. To achieve this, the frigates had to operate in a poorly charted area, with massive 10-metre tidal ranges and associated currents, shifting channels, sandbars and mudflats. All of this was very close to a hostile shore from where North Korean ground forces could fire on the frigates from concealed positions. The combination of marine navigational and war-fighting challenges at the same time, in littoral waters where a ship's sensors had to cope with two vastly different environments, is one of the most difficult for any ship. It was no different for *Murchison.*

The lack of complete charts meant that the first task for *Murchison* and the other frigates operating with her was to survey the area. In part this was accomplished by small boats taking depth soundings throughout the estuary, gradually expanding the area in which the frigates could operate. At other times, it required the use of a leadsman; a sailor who stood in the bows of the ship and measured the depth of the water with a lead line. The leadsman was unprotected from enemy fire and the weather, and also had no individual means to fight back if required. So the task required great courage, physical endurance and concentration. This is one key instance of the individual roles that must be performed well to enable a ship to operate well. It is also an example of those aspects of Australia's naval history that have not been well recorded or frequently described in the existing historical record.

The challenge of navigating a ship in waters like the Han River estuary is difficult to underestimate. One analogy is that it is a bit like rally car driving for ships. The margin for error is very small, so a ship's most experienced sailors would normally be operating all the critical functions, from the engine room throttles and communication telegraphs to the ship's wheel and bridge watch-keeping team. This mode of operation is known as 'Special Sea Dutymen' and is intended to ensure a ship can respond to any navigational or other contingency. *Murchison*'s Commanding Officer, Commander Allen Dollard, recalled that one of these key sailors was the Coxswain, Warwick Rowel, who was:

> absolutely immaculate. When you are travelling in these channels ... you are steering to half a degree, and he would

steer exact, he was never flustered. But apart from that, his general conduct – he was one of the oldest hands on the ship – his influence on the ship's company was terrific. He had young helmsmen in the wheelhouse with him, in action, and he was very calm and doing exactly right. I relied one hundred per cent on him. If he made a mistake, we were up on the mud.[14]

At some points in the estuary, the navigable waters were so tight *Murchison* had to perform the equivalent of a handbrake turn to reverse course: the ship drops its anchor and uses it to keep the bow in place while it changed direction, before raising the anchor and proceeding again. To do such an action well required close co-ordination. High levels of endurance were required of *Murchison*'s crew, as many hours were spent in these confined waters performing such movements, during day and night patrols. The tasks each person performed all required high levels of concentration and some would have been physically demanding.

Close inshore operations like those conducted by *Murchison* had a high degree of risk and were a subject of continual discussion between US and Royal Navy commanders, who disagreed on whether the risks were worth the possible influence on the North Korean negotiators. Certainly the possibility of a vessel grounding was ever-present. On top of the navigation risks, *Murchison* and the other frigates in the area faced the continual threat of enemy fire which could have disabled them, leading to even greater chance of grounding and possible destruction by enemy ground forces.

The weather also had a massive impact on a ship like *Murchison* in Korea. Many of the crew's tasks performed on the upper decks – the ship had an open bridge and all its guns were open mountings – and the temperatures were so cold that exposed skin could stick to metal and the grease for gun mountings could freeze. The Australian Navy did not have enough suitable cold-weather clothing, so sailors often relied on civilian clothing to keep themselves warm. *Murchison* had also been built for operations in warmer waters, so the ship did not have the heating systems built into the original British design. Even inside the ship, temperatures were so low that condensation froze on the bulkheads and the crew used layers of brown paper to help stay warm. Stephen Joyce recalled:

> when we were on shore leave you bought brown paper, and you used to wrap the brown paper round your body, then put your – of course, the singlets in those days, they were like a thermal type thing – then pull your singlet down over that, then your jumper over that, and then you used to cut the brown paper in strips and wrap it round your legs, and the brown paper would act as an insulation against the cold.[15]

The truly amazing thing here is that *Murchison* still reached such high operational standards. The ship overcame immense difficulties of weather, operating conditions and crew training. This success enabled the ship to operate safely and consistently in the Han River estuary, prepared to conduct not only the naval gunfire bombardment tasks, but also to respond the North Korean ground force attacks in response.

In September 1951, *Murchison* was involved in several close-range battles with North Korean forces that had concealed positions on the northern shore of the estuary. The ranges were very short, around 1800 metres (or one nautical mile) and on some occasions much less. This was point blank range for *Murchison*'s main armament of two twin 4-inch guns, and not much more than that for its secondary armament of 40-millimetre Bofors guns.

The Australian ship returned fire, but the results were inconclusive and the incidents demonstrated the risks of such operations by large ships. The restricted waters meant the initiative lay with the North Koreans, who could chose if and when to engage from ashore. *Murchison* was hit numerous times by machine-gun fire and occasionally by some larger shells, but no serious damage was done, nor were there any deaths. The engagements did, however, reflect very well on the tactical and operational standards that the vessel had achieved, and this had a widespread positive effect on the Australian Navy's reputation as a fighting service, particularly because on the first occasion she was so engaged *Murchison* had a senior US Admiral on board to observe the bombardment operations. *Murchison* spent more time in the Han estuary than any other ship and was light-heartedly dubbed the 'Baron of the Han' at the end of her deployment in February 1952, indicative of the esteem in which she was held by Allied forces.

Sadly, on 2 February 1952, while en route to the naval base at Sasebo in Japan, *Murchison* collided at night in rough weather with an unlit South Korean motorised fishing junk, with the loss of several of the junk's crew. In the course of the rescue operation, the ship's Chief Bosun's Mate, Petty Officer Reg Farrington, jumped into the water to help save the fishermen. Farrington had also been responsible for much of the training of the *Murchison*'s junior seamen, and as the captain of the after 4-inch gun mount had played a crucial role first in forming them into a highly skilled gun crew and then leading them in the ship's numerous close actions in the Han River. His courage in action and in the rescue at sea was enormous. While this was never formally recognised by any award, there is no doubt that Farrington is yet another small portion of Australia's naval history that is worth the public knowing much, much better.

The purpose of tracing *Murchison*'s time in Korea is two-fold.

The fact that its remarkable story, replete with drama, danger and bravery, is unknown outside specialist circles is testament to the traditional inability for naval history to find resonance with the general public, in stark contrast to the land-based military history. It is in this regard but one vignette of a vast trove of under-appreciated stories. At the same time, *Murchison*'s adventure in Korea is a story of a crew and its achievements under very difficult and dangerous circumstances, not an account of the type of singular spectacular and climactic engagement resulting in sunken vessels that has so often dominated what is known of naval history in this country. *Murchison* is an example of what can and should be done to help rectify the silence that pervades far too much of Australia's naval history.

Further reading

The Naval Historical Society of Australia, <www.navyhistory.org.au>.
The Sea Power Centre – Australia, <www.navy.gov.au/Sea_Power_Centre_-_Australia>.
T.R. Frame, *Where Fate Calls: The HMAS* Voyager *Tragedy*, Hodder and Stoughton, Sydney, 1992.
T.R. Frame, J.V.P. Goldrick & P.D. Jones, *Reflections on the Royal Australian Navy*, Kangaroo Press, Sydney, 1991.
J. Grey, *Up Top: The Royal Australian Navy and Southeast Asian Conflicts 1955–1972*, Allen & Unwin, Sydney, 1998.
N. Lambert, *Australia's Naval Inheritance: Imperial Maritime Strategy and the Australia Station 1880–1909*, Papers in Australian Maritime Affairs, Maritime Studies Program, Canberra, 1998.
I. Pfennigwerth, *Tiger Territory: The Untold Story of the Royal Australian Navy in Southeast Asia from 1948 to 1971*, Rosenburg Publishing, Sydney, 2008.
——, *A Man of Intelligence: The Life of Captain Theodore Eric Nave, Australian Codebreaker Extraordinary*, Rosenburg Publishing, Sydney, 2006.
D. Stevens (ed.), *The Royal Australian Navy*, Australian Centenary History of Defence, vol. 3, Oxford University Press, Melbourne, 2001.

On HMAS *Murchison*:

V. Fazio, *River Class Frigates of the Royal Australian Navy: A Story of Ships Built in Australia*, Slipway Publications, Sydney, 2003.

R. O'Neill, *Australia in the Korean War: Combat Operations*, vol. 2, Australian Government Printing Service, Canberra, 1985.

W.O.C. Roberts, 'Gun battle on the Han', *Naval Historical Review*, 1(2), September 1976.

[9]

'LANDMARK' BATTLES AND THE MYTHS OF VIETNAM

Bob Hall and Andrew Ross

Like all wars, the 'American War' in Vietnam is shrouded in myth and fabrication. From an Australian perspective, many of these concern the diplomatic and political processes leading to our involvement in the war, or the after-effects of the conflict on those who served there. This chapter focuses more specifically on the myths arising from the combat operations of the 1st Australian Task Force (1ATF). Many of these legends and folklore of combat were inherited from the 'American War' as a whole, and in popular and academic imagination alike have often been applied to 1ATF combat operations. The first of these myths is that the 1ATF combat experience in South Vietnam consisted of a series of major 'landmark' battles with the Viet Cong (VC) and the People's Army of Vietnam (PAVN).[1] Australian military historiography of the war tends to concentrate on these landmark battles to the exclusion of smaller, but far more numerous 'contacts'.[2] It also tends to see these battles in terms of conventional war: as simple contests of military power stripped of their political import. The focus on such landmark battles, and the failure to see them in their political and diplomatic contexts, distorts our understanding of the war.

'Landmark' battles and the myths of Vietnam

Another common myth of combat in the Vietnam War is that the enemy controlled the jungle and dominated the night, while the forces of the United States and its allies – including 1ATF – flailed ineptly because they lacked the enemy's superior local knowledge and were unused to operating in these conditions. These popular imaginings are also incorrect, and possibly arise from the failure of Australian military historiography to address the full spectrum of Australian operations including the minor contacts. Finally, this chapter examines the iconic weapons of the war: the AK47 favoured by the enemy forces and the M16 issued to Australian troops. The former took on an almost mythical status and rapidly developed a reputation as vastly superior to anything the United States and its allies could field. In particular it was seen as a vastly more capable and effective weapon than the M16. There is no doubt that the AK47 was robust and effective but it by no means deserves the elevated reputation it seems to have acquired in comparison with the M16.

As the Australian historian Jeff Grey has made clear, like other conflicts the war in Vietnam was not of uniform intensity throughout the country.[3] The northern provinces of the Republic of Vietnam, which made up 1 Corps Tactical Zone (CTZ, or I Corps), and the western provinces of 3 CTZ near the Cambodian border, were the sites of numerous large-scale battles slightly similar to the battles of a conventional war. They sometimes involved divisional or regimental-sized forces – thousands of men – and the application of heavy firepower – tanks, artillery and air strikes. Enemy casualties were often very high.

However, the Australian area of operations in Vietnam was well away from these hot-spots of activity. The Australians focused their combat effort on Phuoc Tuy Province, on the east coast of Vietnam. In this province and its surrounds, the war predominantly took the form of a classic counterinsurgency, characterised by thousands of small, often inconclusive fire-fights. These were so fleeting, involved so few participants on either side, and were so open to doubt as to which side might have 'won' them that to describe them as 'battles' would be inappropriate. Instead, they were known as 'contacts', the term nicely conveying the implication of the fleeting, often chance encounter which, in nearly all cases, they were. The Australian Task Force experienced about 3900 such contacts.

Nor was the war uniform over time. There were, for example, peaks of VC and PAVN activity that took the form of general offensives, and from 1969 onwards what might be called 'high points'. These were often followed by a lull in the fighting while both sides regrouped. During enemy offensives or 'high points', the general pattern of small contacts was interrupted by 'landmark' battles. These engagements had their own distinct characteristics. They involved a 1ATF force greater than a rifle company (about 120 men) engaged in combat against a larger – sometimes much larger – VC or PAVN force. They were all initiated by the enemy, often after a long period of planning. They often involved a ruse, by which the enemy drew a force out of the 1ATF base into ground that had been selected and prepared – 'luring the tiger from the jungle' as the enemy called it. These landmark battles were always characterised by a strong tendency on the enemy's part to stay and fight. Unlike the fleeting contacts, which usually lasted just minutes, some of these battles lasted for several hours. They often resulted in high enemy casualties. Usually, the enemy sought a political as well as a military outcome. Consequently, these battles were few in number – only about 16 in total. Such engagements include the battles of Long Tan (18 August 1966), Operation Bribie (17 February 1967), Baria, Long Dien and Fire Support Base Anderson during the Tet Offensive of 1968 (in the period 1–19 February 1968), Fire Support Bases Coral (13 and

'Landmark' battles and the myths of Vietnam

16 May 1968) and Balmoral (24 and 28 May 1968), Long Dien (22–23 August 1968), Binh Ba (6–7 June 1969) and Nui Le (21 September 1971). Despite their small number, these battles, and the battle of Long Tan in particular, have tended to influence the public conception of the Vietnam War.

The largest and most iconic of the landmark battles for Australia was the battle of Long Tan. It is often depicted as an heroic struggle by an under-strength D Company, 6th Battalion, Royal Australian Regiment (6RAR), of just 108 men against the combined enemy forces of the 275th VC Regiment and D445 Local Force Battalion, numbering about 2500 troops. Over a period of more than three hours, D Company was subjected to wave after wave of enemy assault, taking many casualties in the process. Pinned by overwhelming enemy small arms fire, with accumulating wounded and ammunition running low, the company faced annihilation. But in a display of immense courage, determination and outstanding tactical skill, it survived the enemy onslaught.

What is often overlooked, however, is that the Australian company was supported by a regiment of 105-millimetre artillery, a battery of medium artillery, air support in the form of airstrikes, an emergency resupply of ammunition by airdrop from helicopters of the 9th Squadron, Royal Australian Air Force, and in the closing stages of the battle by the timely arrival of an armoured personnel carrier squadron carrying another company of reinforcements from 6RAR.[4] Elements of a third company from 6RAR also soon arrived on the battlefield. The Australians then, formed what would later be termed a 'combined arms team': a balanced force of infantry, armour, artillery and air power all linked together under a single command and co-ordinated using radio communications. By contrast, the enemy force at Long Tan (and the other landmark battles) consisted only of light infantry troops with no armour or air support, poor communications below battalion level, and with no capacity to resupply themselves with ammunition mid-battle. The VC and PAVN troops at Long Tan also lacked indirect fire support. The field artillery supporting the Australians at Long Tan fired over 3100 rounds, while another 242 rounds of medium artillery were fired by supporting US Army artillery units. In contrast, the enemy force managed only a few mortar rounds in support of their troops.

Without effective indirect fire support, the enemy forces at Long Tan (and other such battles) relied on other factors to achieve success. Since they held the initiative, they could determine, within certain limits, where and when the battle would take place. While we do not know the details of enemy planning for the battle of Long Tan, we do know that typically these major battles were very carefully designed, the ground carefully selected and prepared, with soldiers briefed and thoroughly rehearsed.[5] Again, however, once battle began, VC/PAVN forces relied above all on massed infantry and the acceptance of high casualties in pursuit of carefully considered political and tactical objectives.

Holding the initiative gave the enemy in Phuoc Tuy considerable advantages, but once battle was joined these advantages were soon lost in the face of the flexibility, heavy firepower and armoured mobility usually found in the combined arms team. It is no surprise then, that the 'butcher's bill' at Long Tan dramatically favoured the Australians: 245 enemy dead were found on the battlefield and another three were taken prisoner, with an unknown but probably large number of dead and wounded carried away by their comrades. In contrast, 17 Australians were killed in action at Long Tan, one died of wounds and 24 were wounded.

The casualties incurred in other landmark battles were similarly one-sided. At the battle in Baria, over 1–2 February 1968, an Australian rifle company mounted in armoured personnel carriers lost seven men killed, to the enemy's 42 killed. At the battle of Long Dien, on 22 August 1968, a 1ATF force including tanks and armoured personnel carriers killed 40 enemy for the price of 12 Australians wounded. At Binh Ba, on 6–7 June 1969, an Australian rifle company in armoured personnel carriers with four Centurion tanks in support killed 99 enemy for the loss of one Australian killed and 10 wounded. Such was the power of the combined arms team.

But the 1ATF 'victories' in these battles were curious because they appear to have had little impact on the enemy's ability to continue combat operations for the duration of the 1ATF tour of duty (from May 1966 to September 1971). These more usual operations were of a much lower intensity, taking the form of the thousands of fleeting contacts in which the average enemy strength was just six. Heavy firepower such as the artillery or air-delivered weapons, which had such decisive effect in the landmark battles, had little effect in these smaller contacts. Artillery and mortar 'blocking' or 'channeling' fire was sometimes applied with the aim of causing enemy casualties as they withdrew from the contact, but it is unlikely that this had any significant effect.

There were about 3900 such contacts between 1ATF and VC/PAVN troops over the period of the Australian presence in Phuoc Tuy. If we consider the sixteen landmark battles as a group, they resulted in 4075 Australian troops in combat with a total of about 8180 enemy soldiers, and they resulted in 287 Australian compared with 1010 enemy casualties. When we consider the 3900 contacts as a group, however, they collectively involved 82 700 Australians in combat against 20 980 VC/PAVN soldiers, and resulted in 1147 Australian and 4480 enemy casualties.[6] In terms of both effort and losses to both sides, therefore, such contacts far surpassed the landmark battles. Collectively, the contacts had a greater destructive effect on the VC/PAVN forces operating in

Phuoc Tuy than did the much more famous battles. Clearly then, the battle of the contacts was the real war that Australians fought in the province, the landmark battles were aberrations.

There is no question that VC/PAVN commanders in Phuoc Tuy were highly experienced and competent. Many had been fighting for many years before the Australians arrived. They must have known that large-scale battles would lead to military defeat at a high cost in terms of casualties. Then why did the enemy initiate the 'landmark' battles?

The answer is that these battles do not represent simply a string of outstanding Australian military successes. The enemy fought them not to defeat the Australians on the battlefield, but primarily for political purposes. Speaking years later about the Tet Offensive of 1968, General Vo Nguyen Giap, North Vietnam's chief strategist and Minister for Defence, acknowledged the importance of political and diplomatic objectives in large-scale VC/PAVN battles. He said 'for us, you know, there is no such thing as a single strategy. Ours is always a synthesis, simultaneously military, political and diplomatic.'[7] Those Australian Army officers responsible for formulating doctrine for the conduct of 'Counter Revolutionary Warfare' – a term then regarded as interchangeable with counterinsurgency – would have agreed. Australian doctrine stated that 'counter insurgency operations are simultaneously political and military in their nature. There is no purely military solution.'[8] Both sides then, understood that the combat had a political as well as military purpose. Yet in our subsequent thinking about the war, we have all but lost touch with the possible political and diplomatic objectives that the enemy may have had. Seeing these landmark battles only in their conventional military terms – as purely military contests – absolves us from wondering whether the enemy achieved their political and diplomatic aims. What is more, if they did achieve them, then we may be forced to reconsider whether they 'lost' these battles at all, at least in these wider terms.

In *To Long Tan*, Ian McNeill advances several military and political aims that the VC may have had as they prepared for the battle: to recover the two liberated villages of Long Phuoc and Long Tan; to inflict casualties on the Australians and encourage the Australian public to demand their recall from Vietnam; and to reconnect the revolutionary forces with the people.[9] These are no doubt broadly correct, although one could quibble about particular aspects. It is doubtful, for example, whether by August 1966 the Australians had in fact 'broken' the connection between the revolutionary forces and the people in Phuoc Tuy. But perhaps there were other political aims. We may not know precisely what combination of military, political and diplomatic purposes each of these battles was intended to serve, nor the weight given to each factor, until the archives of the Democratic Republic of Vietnam (DRV, commonly known as North Vietnam), the National Liberation Front (NLF), and the Provisional Revolutionary Government are open to examination. We can, however, speculate.

To return to the example of the battle of Long Tan, it is a fact seldom acknowledged that the battle took place in the middle of an election campaign in the Republic of Vietnam (the South). And this was not just any election campaign. It was a campaign for the election of a National Constituent Assembly which was to draw up a new constitution and electoral laws for a democratic South Vietnam. The election was a major step by the South towards establishing its political legitimacy. As such, it cut across everything the NLF – a communist-led coalition of nationalist and communist individuals and groups opposed to government of the Republic of Vietnam – and the government of the DRV stood for. From mid-July 1966, the NLF and the DRV mounted a campaign throughout South Vietnam of steadily increasing violence, intimidation and propaganda against candidates for the election, polling stations, voters and government officials. Electors were warned not to participate under pain of death. The battle of Long Tan unfolded three weeks before polling day, and underscored the power of the NLF and DRV to carry through with their threats.

As the battle in the rubber plantation at Long Tan ended, a new psychological and propaganda struggle for the way the battle was to be perceived began in the villages of Phuoc Tuy. Almost immediately, NLF supporters in the province claimed the battle had been a defeat for the Australians. Two weeks before polling day, Radio Hanoi and Radio Peking broadcast lurid accounts of the battle claiming an overwhelming victory for PAVN forces.[10] This psychological struggle was a part of the battle that the NLF and DRV seem to have unreservedly won, for there was no comparable Australian psychological operations effort. The battle for the Vietnamese people's political allegiance in this regard – the much-vaunted 'hearts and minds' – was never contested. Although their doctrine for counter-revolutionary warfare explicitly stated that psychological warfare played a 'vital role' in counter-insurgency, the Australians deployed to Vietnam without any such capability.[11] A psychological warfare capability only gradually built up within 1ATF, based on scratch groups of enthusiastic amateurs with little or no training, equipment pulled together from wherever it could be found, and with poor support from within the Task Force. It was not until April 1970, four years into the war, that a properly staffed and resourced 1st Australian Psychological Operations Unit was created, and even then it seemed to be an afterthought.

The scale of the psychological warfare effort on the other side and its rapid deployment suggest that, for the enemy, the political aims of the battle were at least as important as the military objectives.¹² Yet if the battle of Long Tan was an enemy attempt to adversely influence the vote for the National Constituent Assembly on 11 September 1966, it failed. Throughout the Republic of Vietnam, over 80 per cent of registered voters turned out to vote despite 210 VC-conducted anti-election incidents. In Phuoc Tuy Province, the turnout was even higher: 89.4 per cent of the province's 36 700 voters cast their ballot in the election.[13]

While the enemy's aims in some of the landmark battles remain unclear, in others these aims can be linked to political or diplomatic developments. The battles of 'mini-Tet' in May 1968 were timed to maximise the DRV bargaining position at the beginning of the Paris Peace talks. The battle of Binh Ba on 6–7 June 1969 was linked closely to the meeting of US President Richard Nixon and President Nguyen Van Thieu of the Republic of Vietnam at Midway Island on 8 June 1969. Similarly, the battle of Nui Le on 20–22 September 1971 was connected with the Republic of Vietnam presidential election less than two weeks later. Although specific political or diplomatic outcomes may or may not have been achieved through these battles, the socialist revolution survived in the South, despite allied efforts, to ultimately achieve victory.

At a meeting in Hanoi on 25 April 1975, Colonel Harry Summers, chief negotiator for a US delegation, was in conversation with Colonel Tu, his opposite number from the DRV. 'You know you never defeated us on the battlefield', said Summers. Tu replied 'That may be so, but it is also irrelevant'.[14] Military defeat at the hands of the American or Australian forces did not matter. What was necessary, but never fully achieved by the United States and its allies, was the political defeat of the enemy.

Beyond the prevailing misconceptions of the true nature of combat operations for Australians in Vietnam, other myths persist. There is no doubt, for example, that the VC had a well-merited reputation for excellence in jungle warfare throughout South Vietnam. The US Army and the Army of the Republic of Vietnam (ARVN) were rarely able to find the enemy in their search-and-destroy operations unless the enemy decided to ambush or attack isolated allied units. VC/PAVN ambushes, in particular, regularly inflicted heavy casualties on allied forces before the enemy broke contact and slipped away to fight another day. But again, this was not the pattern in Phuoc Tuy Province. A projection of this experience onto Australian servicemen in Vietnam is not at all accurate.

Through its operations in the Malayan Emergency and Confrontation, especially in North Borneo, the Australian Army had developed considerable experience in counter-insurgency warfare. It had developed high levels of skill at small group patrolling and ambushing at platoon, half-platoon and section levels. In Vietnam, it quickly applied these skills. Soon after the establishment of the 1ATF base at Nui Dat, reconnaissance, fighting and ambush patrols were deployed, and an intensive program of operations involving patrolling and ambushing was maintained until the withdrawal of the Task Force in late 1971. Of the 3909 Australian contacts in Phuoc Tuy, about one third (1300) were planned ambushes and another third were patrol encounters. Such ambushes involved Australians lying in wait for a group of enemy to enter a pre-selected 'killing ground'. At the optimum moment the ambush was sprung by bursts of machine-gun and rifle fire, and most often the detonation of claymore mines. Ambushes were highly effective ways of contacting the enemy because they conferred on the Australian patrol the benefits of having selected and prepared the ground. This enabled mines to be positioned, machine guns to be sited to achieve maximum effect, flanks to be protected, camouflage checked and orders issued. In prepared Australian ambushes, patrols saw the enemy and opened fire first in 96 per cent of contacts. Opening fire first not only achieved surprise, it confered significant advantages in lethality. In Australian ambushes, for every friendly soldier who was killed or wounded, there were ten enemy casualties.

The VC/PAVN in Phouc Tuy were much less successful at ambushing than the Australians. Such enemy ambushes were conducted on only 103 occasions, ten times less often than Australian patrols mounted. Not only did such ambushes occur less often, when they were executed they were less effective. Despite having the advantages of having selected and prepared ground, for every one VC/PAVN casualty suffered in their own ambushes, there were only 2.7 Australian casualties.[15] The 'ambush battle' in Phuoc Tuy Province was not a success for the VC/PAVN.

There were several reasons for this outcome. First, VC/PAVN troops lacked the cross-country navigation skills possessed by Australian patrols. Using map and compass, the Australians moved through the jungle without relying on the network of tracks that criss-crossed it. The VC/PAVN, however, tended to depend upon these marked routes. They knew the track system well and used it to move swiftly between their jungle bases, but sometimes they were over-confident and moved along these tracks while talking and with weapons slung. Although the track network provided a means of rapid movement to the enemy, it also presented ideal opportunities for ambush. Australian patrols seldom used the tracks and were therefore much more difficult to ambush. Second, Australian patrols were highly skilled at what was called 'bush craft' – the techniques of silently moving through the jungle, stopping to listen and observe, and maintaining high levels of security through the use of sentries and scouts. Third, whereas VC/PAVN units had few opportunities to practise their marksmanship skills, the Australians had regular practice. Through good bush-craft, excellent tactical drills, sound marksmanship, high levels of self-discipline and effective junior leadership – all of which were the results of thorough training – the troops of 1ATF out-matched the VC/PAVN in this important counter-insurgency skill.

Patrol contacts, which made up one third of all Australian contacts in Phouc Tuy, occurred when a moving Australian patrol bumped into a moving VC/PAVN patrol and a fire-fight ensued. Unlike ambushes, in patrol encounters neither side had selected the ground in advance, and to that extent they represent a form of contact in which the ground played little part and the contest was determined by the battle skills, resources and determination of the two sides. Of these contacts, the Australians saw the enemy and opened fire first in 78 per cent of cases.[16] Once again, 1ATF patrols reaped the benefits of most often initiating the contact: for every Australian casualty in such contacts there were nine enemy casualties. In the remaining 22 per cent of cases the enemy fired first, but even then they regularly failed to maximise this advantage: for every enemy casualty in patrol encounters where the Australians were caught unawares, there were only 1.4 casualties from 1ATF. The cause of this imbalance was, once again, the superior bush-craft of the 1ATF patrols.

A third enduring myth concerning the Australian experience in Vietnam – or rather another inappropriate imposition of the wider American experience on to the Australians in Phuoc Tuy Province – was the idea that the VC ruled the night. The VC/PAVN certainly dominated the province in the night hours before the arrival of 1ATF in May 1966, but over subsequent years this nocturnal superiority was wrestled away. Although the enemy used the hours of darkness to redeploy and resupply its forces unseen, the most significant night-time activity was the penetration of the villages of the province. Until late 1968 the VC/PAVN had virtually unimpeded night-time access to all villages and towns for food collection, intelligence gathering, taxation, recruitment, proselytising and socialising.

Australian doctrine for counter-revolutionary warfare recognised the importance of isolating the insurgents physically and psychologically from the population.[17] It advocated that this process should begin early in the struggle. Deficiencies or vulnerabilities in the insurgent organisation were to be identified and exploited. One of these vulnerabilities was the insurgents' reliance upon access to the villages for food. By cutting off VC/PAVN access, the Australians knew that they could bring pressure on the large enemy forces without engaging them in direct battle. Most enemy penetrations into villages occurred at night when, under cover of darkness, enemy patrols could cross the open rice paddies and enter the villages without being seen and prevented by counter-insurgent forces. Soon after their arrival, Australian units therefore began to increase their ambush patrols close to the civilian settlements that gave support to the VC. In 1968, 1ATF initiated 123 successful ambushes within 2.5 kilometres of Phuoc Tuy villages. This figure fell to 113 in 1969 due to Australian 'out of province' operations, but rose again to 132 in 1970, indicating the steadily increasing pressure that 1ATF applied.[18]

By itself, 1ATF never had enough troops to clamp a permanent military cordon around all the villages of Phuoc Tuy Province. Inevitably there would be gaps in any protective screen that the Australians attempted to establish. The building of the ill-fated barrier minefield was an attempt to overcome this deficiency. In any case, providing security around the villages did not become the top priority for 1ATF until General Creighton Abrams, Commander, United States Military Assistance Command, Vietnam, implemented a pacification strategy in April 1969. Abram's plan elevated the security of the Vietnamese people to top priority, reversing the policies set earlier by General

William Westmoreland (in which providing security was third priority after bringing the enemy's main force elements to battle and training South Vietnamese forces). From April 1969, the Australians increased their efforts to secure the villages of Phuoc Tuy against enemy penetration. Intensive ambushing around village perimeters was implemented and the training of ARVN and village militia forces was begun in earnest. While gaps might remain through which enemy patrols might enter villages, from mid-1969 the enemy was increasingly faced with having to fight their way into and out of the villages.

Considerable Australian effort was also put into training the local government forces of the province. With the exception of the Revolutionary Development Cadre, Province Reconnaissance Units, and some units of the Regional Force, in 1968 provincial militia forces were poorly trained, badly led and indifferently armed. These largely amateur soldiers were mostly based in the villages and hamlets of the province, and were expected to defend their villages against VC/PAVN penetrations. In 1968 and early 1969 most Phuoc Tuy villages lacked the barbed-wire fences, bunkers and compounds that might have enabled their militias to repel attempted enemy penetrations. They were incapable of putting much pressure on the battle-hardened enemy, even when they initiated contacts. They lacked the training to take advantage of a surprised enemy, and could quite often suffer more casualties than their adversaries in these exchanges. Not surprisingly, a 'live and let live' attitude developed in which village militias did not fire on the VC/PAVN if the VC/PAVN did not fire on them.

Throughout 1969, however, the Australians built bunkers and fences and trained these militias, particularly in those villages giving the strongest support to the insurgents. As well as defensive measures, training also emphasised offensive patrolling and ambushing. Gradually, this improved the confidence, combat performance and aggression of the militias. The net result was that the provincial militias stopped waiting in their bunkers for the enemy to initiate contacts and increasingly went out looking for the enemy around their villages, particularly at night. In 1969, slightly more than half of all contacts between the village militias and the VC/PAVN were initiated by the militias. By 1970 this had risen to 65 per cent, and in 1971 to 70 per cent. A gradual improvement in the combat performance of the militias was also evident in their loss ratios: in 1969, when the provincial militias initiated the contact, they achieved a casualty ratio of one villager for every 1.9 enemy casualties; by 1970 this had risen to one provincial soldier casualty for every 2.7 enemy casualties. By this stage the provincial militias were out-fighting the VC around their villages.[19] While there were some notable tactical failures in these militia contacts, it is clear that they were making an increasingly aggressive and effective contribution to the security of the villages.

By these various means, the steady denial of the VC/PAVN night-time village penetrations produced a food crisis for the enemy that began in 1969 and extended until the end of 1971, when Australians troops withdrew from Vietnam. During this period, VC/PAVN night-time movement into villages was regularly interdicted by provincial militias and Australian patrols, while enemy movement between jungle bases was ambushed day or night. The loss of the freedom of entry to the villages forced the VC/PAVN into putting more and more effort into searching for food at the expense of conducting military operations. Enemy-initiated contacts throughout Phuoc Tuy steadily fell over the period from 1969 to the withdrawal of 1ATF in late 1971: in 1969 the enemy initiated 380 contacts in Phuoc Tuy; in 1970 these had declined to 223; and in 1971 had sunk to 135.[20] The enemy was losing control of the night. This is not the picture presented in Hollywood accounts of the war, and it is not the

Vietnam of popular mythology – but it is the war fought by the Australian in Phuoc Tuy Province.

The last of the myths related to the Australian experience in Vietnam concerns the iconic small arms of that war: the AK47 and the M16. The enemy's AK47 has over time taken on the lustre of a 'super weapon', one that is widely thought to have been far superior to its allied equivalent, the M16. A typical example is this glowing testimonial from a US Army officer, Colonel David Hackworth. Hackworth relates that, after jumping into a hole where a bulldozer had just unearthed an AK47 that had been buried for 'a year or so', he shouted to his soldiers 'Watch this guys, and I'll show you how a real infantry weapon works'. He then cocked the weapon and immediately fired 30 rounds. 'That was the kind of weapon our soldiers needed', he later wrote, 'not the confidence-sapping M-16'.[21]

There is no doubt that the AK47 was a robust and highly efficient weapon, capable of operating effectively even when exposed to the mud, dust and water of tropical Vietnam. But did it really so far surpass the M16 as Hackworth implies? It is true that when first introduced into service in the US Army, the M16 was prone to stoppages. High rates of breakdown in any weapon can be extremely confidence-sapping to those soldiers whose lives may depend on their reliability and performance. In this case, however, the explanation was relatively simple. Cleaning kits had not been issued, and training on the care and maintenance of the weapon had been neglected. These and other problems were quickly solved.

It was also true that the M16 was not as robust as the AK47. It was specifically designed to fit under a weight limit and as a consequence was not so tough or rugged. The Australian and American forces, however, had a much more efficient resupply system than did the VC/PAVN. Failed or broken M16s could be replaced with relative ease. But for the VC/PAVN, replacement of a failed AK47 required that a new weapon be shipped down the Ho Chi Minh trail, a long and difficult route even under the best conditions, and one that was also under frequent air attack. The replacement weapon might take months to get into the hands of a soldier in Phuoc Tuy Province. For the VC/PAVN a weapon of robust design, one that above all could survive the rigours of extended combat use in the jungle, was very important.

However, a number of other design features of the AK47 rendered it less salubrious than many allied soldiers thought it to be. On firing a burst, the muzzle tended to climb, causing some of the bullets to pass harmlessly over the target. Later models (such as the AK74) were fitted with a muzzle compensator to counter this tendency. The M16, however, having a 'straight line butt' – in which the axis of the barrel passed in a straight line through the firer's shoulder – and also having less recoil, was far less affected by this tendency. The result was that it was much easier to keep an M16 pointed at the target than it was with the AK47. Although it was heavier, the muzzle velocity of a bullet from an AK47 was also substantially lower than that of the M16, so that while the AK47 bullet could penetrate light foliage and scrub without deflection, the weapon's effective range was shorter than that of the M16. In the give and take of these technical differences, the weapons came out about even.

The most significant disadvantage of the AK47 over the M16, however, was its greater weight. The AK47, fitted with a 30-round magazine, weighed in at 5.22 kilograms; the M16 weighed about 3.30 kilograms when similarly loaded. (For comparison, the Self Loading Rifle or SLR also carried by Australian infantrymen tipped the scale at 4.54 kilograms.) The result was that a man armed with an M16 could carry nearly 2 kilograms more ammunition (or over 120 cartridges) than a man carrying the same weight but equipped with an AK47. Multiply this by the number of men in an Australian platoon equipped with M16s – between 7 and 11 – and the result begins to add up to a substantial advantage in firepower. The typical combat of Vietnam, where contacts were very brief but intense and targets were rarely seen, commonly generated high volumes of fire. Giving away all that extra ammunition was a distinct disadvantage to the AK47, but one that few authors have ever noted.

Of course, not every Australian soldier carried an M16, but neither did every one of their enemies carry an AK47. Insofar as the weapons captured in combat by Australians in Phuoc Tuy represent an accurate sample of the weapons used by the enemy in contact, then AK47s were carried by a little more than 50 per cent of enemy soldiers.[22] However, the proportion of AK47s to other weapons changed over the course of the war, with AK47s being captured in greater proportions in the final years of Australian operations. Thus, although the AK47 was a highly effective weapon, it did not have an overwhelming influence on the battlefield.

The other small arms in enemy use were the SKS carbine, and a range of World War II vintage weapons, rocket-propelled grenades, and modern machine guns. With the exception of the rocket-propelled grenade launcher, especially the RPG7, all of these weapons were somewhat inferior to similar small arms used by the Australians.[23] Some enemy soldiers were also equipped with captured M16s, which suggests that they did not regard that weapon as overly inferior.

A proof of the effectiveness of a small arm is how long it remains in combat service. The AK47 – or its variants – is still to be found on battlefields around the world today, signifying that its design was, and remains, excellent. But the M16 and its variants are also still found on contemporary soldiers. Since both were

'Landmark' battles and the myths of Vietnam

originally fielded forty-odd years ago, the numerous armies that equip their soldiers with these weapons or their more modern variants have been unable to find better weapons. This is a sure sign that both weapons were well designed for their intended purpose.

In any case, many Australian infantrymen preferred the SLR. It was heavier than the M16, longer, only capable of semi-automatic fire – one shot each time the trigger was pulled – and fired a heavy bullet with high muzzle velocity which produced a substantial 'kick'. On the face of it, it seemed a poor weapon by comparison to the AK47 or the M16. But it was robust and reliable. In the jungle engagements typical of combat in Vietnam, the SLR had very high penetrative power. Its bullet might pass through several small trees without deflection, before finding its target. It was popular with Australian soldiers because of its high 'stopping power' – the ability to render an enemy incapable of further resistance with a single shot.[24]

If the AK47 and the M16 could be said to be about equal in their battlefield impact, it is difficult to say this about other notable infantry weapons of the Vietnam War. For example, the enemy's main light machine gun was the Russian-designed RPD. It had a simple and robust design that rarely malfunctioned, and it could stand a considerable amount of operational abuse. In contrast, the Australians used the US-designed M60 machine gun. This was designated a 'general purpose machine gun' and was intended to fill the roles of a sustained fire weapon and that of a light machine gun. The sustained fire role required a belt-fed, heavy-barrelled machine gun capable of being mounted on a tripod for use in fixed positions, such as the defence of the Nui Dat base. The light machine gun role, however, required a light, bipod-mounted weapon for use by soldiers on foot patrols. The two intended uses were fundamentally at odds. The result of trying to reconcile them led to a weapon that was notoriously prone to jamming and malfunctioning. The M60's belt-feed system, for example, tended to draw extraneous matter such as mud and vegetation into the weapon, leading to stoppages. The M60 also suffered stoppages for a range of other reasons and with no gas regulator, its working parts could become slowed by accumulated dirt, oil and dust, with the result that the gun would stop functioning.[25] Finally, the M60 was far from being a 'soldier-proof' design and could be re-assembled incorrectly resulting in a malfunction.

The Australians in Phuoc Tuy addressed the problems of the M60 by training to manage its unreliability. Detailed routine orders were published to guide soldiers safely through many of these issues.[26] Rifle companies introduced rigorous cleaning regimes in an effort to ensure their M60s would function properly when they were needed, and usually the weapon and its ammunition were cleaned twice daily. When on patrol, machine gunners and their 'number two' would often give their weapons an external clean every time the platoon or section stopped for a rest. The Australians were thus largely successful in containing the stoppages of the M60, reducing the rate of failure to 2.7 per cent of contacts in which the M60 was fired.[27] But this machine gun was the mainstay of a rifle section's fire output, and a stoppage – even in a small number of contacts – endangered the survival of the section.

Another enemy weapon clearly superior to any Australian or allied equivalent was the rocket-propelled grenade, the RPG7. It fired a fin-and-spin-stabilised shaped-charge warhead with high accuracy to a range of 500 metres against stationary targets and 350 metres against moving targets. The fuse on its warhead allowed it to penetrate light brush without exploding. By comparison, the nearest equivalent carried by the Australians, the M72 light anti-armour weapon, had an effective range of just

200 metres and its warhead had a very sensitive fuse which often detonated ineffectually when it hit twigs or leaves before reaching its target. Some Australians openly wished they had a weapon which could match the RPG7.[28]

For brutal efficiency in killing and wounding, however, it is difficult to go past the M16 land mine. Although an American weapon issued to its allies, the VC secured a large supply of these mines when the Australians built a barrier minefield between the village of Dat Do and the sea. The minefield was intended to secure the population of Dat Do and other villages against enemy incursions, but it was inadequately defended and the VC lifted many mines and redeployed them against Australian patrols. These M16 mines, together with other landmines of Soviet or Chinese origin and locally manufactured versions, were the enemy's most successful weapons in Phuoc Tuy. With them they caused large numbers of Australian casualties at very low cost to their own forces. Australian soldiers feared them while their senior commanders fretted over the political repercussions of the casualties they caused.[29] The enemy successfully used mostly stolen mines to protect their own base area, the Minh Dam Secret Zone, in the Long Hai hills, from Australian pressure, a feat they were unable to achieve with any other weapon. From this base area the enemy was able to continue the political domination of the people in the villages of Dat Do and Long Dien.[30]

Another measure of the effectiveness of weapons is the level of fear they engender in their targets. The soldiers of the 8th Battalion, Royal Australian Regiment (8RAR) were probably broadly representative of Australian infantry in Vietnam in their reactions to enemy weapons. Most 8RAR soldiers rated 'mines, including M16 mines' as the most feared enemy weapon. Rocket-propelled grenades closely followed, then booby traps and command-detonated mines, each of which were nominated as 'most feared' by more 8RAR soldiers than nominated the AK47. The AK47 was in fact rated 'most feared' by only a very small number of soldiers, on a par with spiked-pit booby traps. Of the eighteen men of 8RAR who were killed in action in Vietnam, only two were killed by AK47 fire while 11 fell to landmines.[31] Although the AK47 was a robust and effective weapon it was not the 'war winner' as some see it. Other weapons in the enemy inventory, including one which the enemy took from the Australian minefield, had a far greater impact on the war.

Contrary to dominant popular public conceptions of Vietnam, influenced to their core by Hollywood imagery and imported American representations, Australia's war in Phouc Tuy Province was never about large-scale landmark battles such as Long Tan. These were aberrations and of minor relevance when compared to the much more common and significant 'contacts' which characterised the face of battle for the men of 1ATF. In addition, prevailing ideas of how completely such battles were 'won' by Australian troops need to be rethought in their fuller political context. Nor do prevailing and enduring ideas of VC/PAVN soldiers 'owning' the jungle or the night have any real resonance or relevance for the Australians in Vietnam – quite the converse. It was the Australians that dominated their enemies in the 'bush' and in the hours of darkness. Last, the powerful idea that Australian and allied soldiers were let down by their personal weapons lacks true substance. The enemy's AK47 was not the war-winner it is often described. Moreover, if any singular enemy weapon can be said to have had the most impact on the Australians in Phuoc Tuy, then it must be their own landmines, stolen and used against them. Australia's Vietnam combat experience was not that of the ARVN or the Americans. Nor in many ways was it the war of the silver screen or dominant public memory. It is time to accept it on its own terms.

Further reading

B. Buick, with G. McKay, *All Guts and No Glory: The Story of a Long Tan Warrior*, Allen & Unwin, Sydney, 2000.

B. Grandin, *The Battle of Long Tan as Told by the Commanders to Bob Grandin*, Allen & Unwin, Sydney, 2004.

R. Hall, *Combat Battalion: The Eighth Battalion in Vietnam*, Allen & Unwin, Sydney, 2000.

P. Ham, *Vietnam: The Australian War*, HarperCollins, Sydney, 2007.

I. Kuring, *Redcoats to Cams: A History of Australian Infantry 1788 to 2001*, Army History Unit, Department of Defence, Canberra, 2004.

G. Lockhart, *The Minefield: An Australian Tragedy in Vietnam*, Allen & Unwin, Sydney, 2007.

I. McNeill, *To Long Tan: The Australian Army and the Vietnam War 1950–1966*, Allen & Unwin/Australian War Memorial, Sydney/Canberra, 1993.

I. McNeill & A. Ekins, *On the Offensive: The Australian Army in the Vietnam War, January 1967–June 1968*, Allen & Unwin, Sydney, 2003.

M. O'Brien, *Conscripts and Regulars: With the Seventh Battalion in Vietnam*, Allen & Unwin/Seventh Battalion, Royal Australian Regiment Association Incorporated, Sydney, 1995.

[10]

THE MYTH THAT AUSTRALIA 'PUNCHES ABOVE ITS WEIGHT'

Albert Palazzo[1]

In recent years, those who belong to the Australian Defence Force (ADF) or who follow or study its activities have witnessed the emergence of a new myth, one that asserts the exceptional prowess of the nation's military on the international stage. Australia is a 'middle power' with a small defence force, yet despite its size it has become common for observers to credit Australian military forces with having a disproportionate effect on the battlefield and by implication, the success of operations. The general idea is that, as a result of its superior training, competency, technology and professionalism, the ADF operates better than equivalent or even larger defence forces. The myth is that the ADF 'punches above its weight'.

There is nothing new in the expression of this type of myth. Indeed, since H.V. 'Doc' Evatt's part in the establishment of the United Nations, the Australian government has used the notion to describe the role played by Australia in foreign affairs and the influence that the country supposedly enjoyed in regional and international forums. Subsequently, the idea became linked to Gareth Evans's time as Minister for Foreign Affairs during the Hawke and Keating governments.[2] However, in recent years the expression has also gained increasing currency within the ADF. The Australian military now describes its fighting worth as 'punching above its weight' and senior officers have regularly employed the phrase to highlight the ADF's performance overseas and the reputation for excellence its members have earned. General Peter Cosgrove (as Chief of the Defence Force), for example, drew attention to the force's achievements in 2004 and to his expectation that the ADF would continue to excel in 2005. Air Marshal Angus Houston (as Chief of Air Force), Lieutenant General Peter Leahy (as Chief of Army), Lieutenant General David Hurley (as Vice Chief of the Defence Force), and Brigadier Craig Orme (as Commander 1st Brigade) among others, have all worked the expression into their addresses.[3]

Its notion has now filtered down through all levels of the ADF. No task is too insignificant to merit the praise of 'punching above one's weight' and the force's junior leaders have used it to extol the superior capabilities and achievements of the men and women they command. For example, the 1st Battalion, Royal Australian Regiment's band, the Royal Australian Navy (RAN)'s minor war vessels, the Army Personnel Agency in Hobart, the Joint Logistic Unit South, the Joint Strike Fighter Industry Team, and the entire Australian Army Pay Corps have all either 'punched above their weight' or have been urged to do so.[4] The skipper of HMAS *Dechaineux* went so far as to describe a better than expected result in a sportsday tug-of-war competition as an instance of the vessel 'punch[ing] above her weight'.[5]

In a wider context there is nothing novel in the use of this expression. Across Australian society and overseas its usage is commonplace, and even the most casual of searches will reveal numerous references to Australian individuals and organisations claiming to 'punch above their weight'. Most are benign, some even comical and one should not take too seriously revelations of inexplicable male success with members of the opposite sex, patriotic rants after the nation's disproportionate receipt of awards at the Cannes Film Festival, the remarkable performance of Rockhampton's youth softball talent, or even a government report which asserts that the Australian cement industry punches above its weight.[6]

It would be easy to react to the ADF's use of this expression with the same incredulity that is used for other areas of Australian society and to dismiss it as comic effect. After all, just how serious was the *Dechaineux*'s captain? However, myths involving a nation's military capability are different. They are serious because war matters, not just for the fate of the men and women who are called upon to fight, but also for the future of the nation upon whose military prowess the outcome of a war hangs. Just as Charles Bean inspired the Anzac legend and the cult of the 'digger' has exaggerated and distorted the narrative of the Australian soldier, the 'punches above its weight' myth misrepresents the ADF's role and accomplishments in its most recent operations.[7] The ADF's belief that it 'punches above its weight' cannot be taken too lightly or be too easily dismissed because in war the stakes are too high. Moreover, the consequences of being seduced by this myth are serious. Unthinking acceptance undermines the ADF's ability to scrutinise its operations, assess its true strengths and weaknesses, and correctly evaluate the organisation's current and future worth, and do so with brutal candour. The ADF's servicemen and women deserve no less, nor does the citizenry which they protect.

There has already been a serious attempt to assess the validity of Australia's claim that it 'punches above its weight'. In 2005, the Australian Strategic Policy Institute published a *Strategic Insights* paper which questioned whether or not Australia was living up to its position as a middle power.[8] Its author, Mark Thomson, compared Australia with other countries across a number of categories including percentage of GDP dedicated to defence, and percentage of population serving in a nation's full-time armed forces. Australia tended to lie in the bottom half of middle powers according to such categories, but given its relatively secure geopolitical situation at the time this result was unsurprising. More significantly, Thomson drew on data from the US Department of Defense's *Report on Allied Contributions to the Common Defence*. This publication provides a comparative analysis of the contribution by NATO and other allied nations to US-supported operations. In categories that covered the allocation of ground troops, naval combat ships, naval supply ships, combat aircraft, transport aircraft and tanker aircraft, this report rated the ADF as offering forces that were generally in balance with the nation's ability to contribute. Australia was most generous in the provision of naval combat vessels, and least generous in the provision of ground combat forces. Thomson's conclusion was that the intensity of Australia's contribution to a range of operations was pretty much what one would expect from a middle power with its population and wealth. While Australia was not shirking its responsibilities, nor was it punching above its weight.

This chapter will look more specifically at some of Australia's most recent operations in order to extend Thomson's analysis and discount this myth once and for all. It will examine the performance of the ADF on three of the force's most recent and important operations: the stabilisation mission to East Timor, and the wars in Iraq and Afghanistan. It is important to note a distinction between the performance of the individual 'digger' and that of the organisation. There is little doubt that today's ADF personnel are highly trained, and the organisation has long rejected the idea of the natural warrior that underpinned much of the cult of the 'digger'. For example, after his return from East Timor in as address to the Sydney Institute, Cosgrove rightly extolled the virtues of the men and women who had served with him.[9] But while individual acts are important, the success of a military operation is measured as a whole. The claim to 'punch above its weight' must apply to the ADF as an entity not to the ordinary digger.

The Australian intervention in East Timor in 1999 was the nation's largest military deployment since the end of the Vietnam War. It was also the first time that Australia acted as the lead nation in assembling and commanding an international coalition. After the outbreak of widespread violence across East Timor following its vote for independence from Indonesia, Australia accepted a United Nations request that it lead a peace-stabilisation mission to restore order in the territory. This mission became known as International Force East Timor, or INTERFET.[10] On 19 September the mission's commander, Major General Peter Cosgrove, visited Dili to hold discussions with his Indonesian counterpart. The next day, Australian ground forces began to arrive at Dili while an international fleet of warships approached the coast.

Over the next weeks, Australian, New Zealand and British servicepeople, along with the personnel of other contributing nations, spread out across East Timor bringing security to the territory. As this took place, Indonesian military forces withdrew while renegade militias were evacuated, disarmed or forced across the border into West Timor. On 23 February 2000, INTERFET came to an end and the operation changed to the United Nations Transitional Administration in East Timor (UNTAET). The Australian-led mission had succeeded in its goals of restoring security to East Timor and laying the foundation for the emergence of a new nation.

INTERFET is usually described as a great success, a point

that is hard to dispute since Timor-Leste (East Timor) took its place among sovereign states in 2002. It was also a relatively cost-free operation, as casualties sustained by the coalition's members were very low. Australia had just two fatalities, both non-battle related. Most importantly, Cosgrove avoided an open breach with the Indonesian military, although it must be admitted that relations between the two countries did worsen considerably, culminating in Jakarta's cancelation of its security agreement with Canberra.

Numerous commentators ascribed Australia's success in East Timor to Cosgrove's skill as a coalition commander as well as to the professionalism of the men and women who served under him.[11] The 2000 Defence 'White Paper' recognised INTERFET as the 'most demanding military operation by the ADF in a generation', and credited its success to the personnel who served and to their 'training, equipment and preparation'.[12] There is much truth in these assertions. Had an Australian soldier panicked during a confrontation with Indonesian forces — and confrontations did occur — and had an exchange of fire resulted, there could have been a dangerous escalation of violence.

While such praise of the 'diggers' is justifiable, it discounts another factor that was also critical to INTERFET's success. The vital contributions by the United States military and the quiet diplomatic pressure that Washington applied to Jakarta are often overlooked or minimised in Australian assessments of the East Timor intervention. This is unfortunate, as it was American military and diplomatic power, or rather the threat of it, that secured Indonesian agreement to INTERFET's deployment, Jakarta's acceptance of the loss of the province, and the Indonesian military's compliance with INTERFET during the handover. Thus the United States shaped the environment in a way that made INTERFET's success possible.

The diplomatic pressure that the United States applied on Indonesia was intense. US President Bill Clinton made it clear to Indonesian President B.J. Habibie that continued economic assistance from the international community was contingent upon the violence stopping in East Timor and the United Nations being allowed to resume its work in the territory. When, at the behest of the US government the International Monetary Fund suspended talks with Jakarta, the spectre of national economic collapse loomed, especially as Indonesia was dependent on external assistance as it struggled to recover from the Asian financial meltdown of 1997. The United States exerted additional pressure through its military-to-military links. The Commander-in-Chief of the US Pacific Command, Admiral Dennis Blair, met with the Commander of the Indonesian National Armed Forces (TNI), General Wiranto, and told him that the United States had decided to sever its military relations with Indonesia. The Chairman of the US Joint Chiefs of Staff, General Henry Shelton, also spoke to Wiranto on several occasions. The thrust of these conversations was that the United States would cut Indonesia off from all US military and financial assistance unless the TNI supported the transition of East Timor to independence. It was after one of these calls that Wiranto recommended to Habibie that Indonesia allow an international peacekeeping force into the province.[13] In its actions, the US government left no doubt that if Indonesia did not adopt 'a constructive approach toward ending the humanitarian disaster in East Timor', the aid money needed to prop up the country would end and the military assistance that the TNI received would cease.[14]

The result of this pressure was that when Australian troops arrived in Dili, they found a delicate situation, but not a warlike one. Indonesia, including its military, had already made the decision that it was in its best interests to withdraw from East Timor and by doing so avoid any escalation with INTERFET. Thus the Australian-led coalition faced a disgruntled Indonesian military, but not an overtly hostile force. Failure was still possible, but success had already been made much more likely thanks to the influence of the United States.

The military support the United States provided to INTERFET sent an equally powerful message to Indonesia's political and military leaders. Significantly, the United States offset a number of ADF capability gaps. As Australians arrived in Dili, they were protected by the US Navy's *Mobile Bay*, a guided-missile cruiser that could defeat any warship or aircraft in the Indonesian arsenal with ease. It remained in place until the TNI had completed its withdrawal. The United States also provided a series of amphibious and logistic vessels. These included the USN *Belleau Wood* and the USN *Peleliu*, while the US Marines that each ship carried offered a further latent threat, although these troops did not go ashore. As the ADF also lacked a deployable theatre-level communications capability, the United States supplied one. Requiring twelve C-5 cargo and one C-17 transport aircraft, the US Army dispatched elements of its 11th Signals Brigade from Arizona to Darwin. The American signallers then transferred to East Timor where they remained until replaced by contractors in mid-December 1999. The United States also provided the operation with intelligence support by placing a team in Darwin with access to the American satellite system. Also to arrive were a small team of CIMIC (civil-military operations) personnel who established an operations centre in Dili and several US Air Force C-130 transport aircraft that joined the Darwin–Dili airbridge, supplementing the limited RAAF capacity. Other nations provided additional aircraft.

A particularly critical capability provided by the United States were the helicopters from the *Belleau Wood* and *Peleliu*. Ground transport was difficult outside of Dili due to the poor quality of the territory's roads, and INTERFET made heavy use of US Marine CH-46 Sea Knight and CH-53E Super Stallion helicopters. In one case a relief organisation wanted to move six tons of supplies from Dili to Suai on the island's devastated south coast. As the organisation had only one truck it estimated that the movement across the island's rugged spine on dirt tracks would take about two months, assuming the wet season did not wash away the roads. Two Super Stallions made the move in an afternoon.[15]

The American contribution to INTERFET's success cannot be ignored if a true assessment of the operation is to be reached. As Alan Ryan has noted, while the American presence 'was not obvious in terms of troops on the ground, it was critical to the success of the mission'. Ryan has no doubt that it was American political leverage, as well as the presence of its warships and Marines offshore, that enabled INTERFET to 'box above its weight'.[16] The Australian Senate recognised this reality by admitting that it was leverage from the United States that persuaded Indonesia to support the intervention, which in turn allowed INTERFET to meet its mandate.[17] One American observer has been a little more generous about the Australian contribution, however. John R. Ballard ascribed the mission's success to a combination of Australian leadership and the unique support capabilities provided by the United States. It was American logistical might, he believes, that made it possible for Australia to serve as an effective lead nation.[18]

All this is not to deny that the ADF did a good job in East Timor. But any assessment of its effectiveness must take into account the American contribution if it is to have any validity and, more importantly, utility to the ADF. In the operation's aftermath a considered analysis of the Australian Army's performance revealed a force that was, despite its level of training and professionalism, fundamentally hollow, lacking in capability, and suffering from major deficiencies in logistics and sustainment capability.[19] There is no doubt that Australia's ability to conduct the operation at all only resulted from the external assistance it received.[20]

It must also be remembered that the East Timor intervention did not provide a full test for the ADF, as it was not a 'war fighting' mission after all. The only real threat that the ADF faced came from the militia bands made up of ill-armed and poorly trained thugs. These had to be treated with care, but they did not pose a credible threat to a professional military organisation. Yet although not a 'real' war, pacifying East Timor still stretched the ADF to an uncomfortable degree and if fighting had broken out, it is questionable whether the organisation had the depth of manpower, equipment and stores to meet and sustain the challenge. Surely this is not what is meant by 'punching above its weight'.[21]

Moving on from East Timor, Australia's participation in the US-led Coalition against Iraq can be divided into two periods: the invasion phase of 2003 (Operation Falconer) and the subsequent search for weapons of mass destruction and rebuilding of Iraq (Operation Catalyst). Both campaigns also brought forth great praise for the performance of the ADF. But, once again, the fact that tasks were done well is insufficient to sustain the myth, for the sum of the Australian effort was less than it at first appears.

The government allocated to Operation Falconer approximately 2500 personnel, divided among sea, land and air task groups. For reasons of space this analysis will focus on the ADF's ground commitment, the smallest of the three ADF environment contingents and one which consisted largely of Special Forces troops. The mission of the Special Forces Task Group was to secure a large section of central al-Anbar province in western Iraq in order to prevent Iraqi forces from firing missiles armed with weapons of mass destruction against Israel. This was a critical mission because if Israel retaliated against Iraq it might lead to the collapse of Arab support for the US-led Coalition. While no Arab state participated in the invasion of Iraq, some did allow the Coalition to operate from their territory, and if they withdrew this permission it would severely compromise the Coalition's ability to prosecute the campaign, if not prevent it entirely.

Upon the war's commencement, the Australians quickly took control of their area of operations, while American and British Special Forces fulfilled similar tasks in their adjacent zones. These Special Forces achieved their mission with great efficiency and Iraq made no attempt to attack Israel. The Australians had numerous armed 'contacts' with Iraqi forces but emerged from all of them victorious and unscathed. Afterwards the Australian commander commented that his men were 'very experienced, very aggressive and very good at what they did', and what they did do to the enemy was 'crush their spirit and will' and force them to 'run or surrender'.[22]

While Australian Special Forces in Iraq deserve the praise they have received, it is still important to factor the nature of their opponent into any assessment of the reasons for their success. After all, war is not a one-sided affair: the strengths and weaknesses of the enemy also matter. Once the capability of the Iraqi military is take into consideration, the degree of the Australian accomplishment becomes less notable, albeit more accurate. The most important factor in the speed with which the Special Forces gained control of their area of operations was not their very high level of skill but the contrasting incompetence of their enemy. Throughout this brief conflict, Coalition forces completely outmatched their opponents, who time and time again displayed poor planning and fighting skills at all levels.[23] The gap between the competency of the Australians and the ineptitude of the enemy was more extreme in the Australian area of operations than elsewhere in Iraq, because circumstances matched elite Special Forces troops against the rear echelon combat service and combat support elements of a demoralised army. The Australians were better trained, armed and equipped and enjoyed total air dominance. When the enemy did not flee, the Australians could and did call on Coalition air support, which ended the matter with brutal efficiency.

It should also be noted that while the Australian Special Forces prevented a missile launch against Israel, the Iraqis did not actually attempt to do so. The Iraqi Army did not have any missile launchers positioned in the Australian area of operations, nor did they attempt to move any there once the war began. It can be debated that it was the skill of the Australians that deterred the enemy from moving rocket launchers into position, but this is a debate that cannot be resolved with any degree of certainty. In addition, as subsequently revealed, Iraq no longer possessed any weapons of mass destruction as it had ended, or suspended, its chemical and biological programs some time prior to the war's commencement.

An event that requires particular comment here is the Australian seizure of the al-Asad air base, a major Iraqi air force facility. This was one of the few events for which the ADF provided a detailed brief to the public and it has been used to highlight the effectiveness of Australia forces. It was also notable as it brought together for the first time Special Air Service (SAS), Commando and Incident Response Regiment soldiers, while flying above in support were RAAF fighters. What is misleading is the government's description of the base's seizure in tones that suggest an epic military feat. In reality the base was abandoned, undefended and littered with scores of inoperable Iraqi aircraft. At most, the

Special Forces had to contend with some armed looters who scattered after a few well-placed shots shooed them on their way.[24]

It is also possible to examine the Australian government's resolve in Iraq from the perspective of per capita commitment. When compared to the contribution of personnel by its allies, the suggestion that Australia 'punches above its weight' does not stand. The table below outlines the commitment by the three major participants in the invasion.

Commitment of Coalition military personnel to the Iraq War (Invasion Phase)[25]

Country	Population (thousands)	Number of military personnel committed	Commitment as percentage of population
United States	290 850	284 450	0.0977
United Kingdom	59 557	46 150	0.0774
Australia	19 903	2 054	0.0103

As would be expected, the United States provided the largest contingent to the Coalition in terms of raw numbers, and by some margin. But what is of more interest is the contribution viewed as a percentage of population. From this perspective the significance of the Australian effort becomes clear. The United States and the United Kingdom contributed personnel in roughly ten and seven times the proportion of Australia.

The commitment figure of 2054 personnel represents the ADF's entire theatre presence in the first phase of operations in Iraq and therefore includes the personnel who served with the air (C-130 transport planes, F/A-18 fighters, and PC-3 Maritime Patrol Aircraft) and maritime task groups (HMAS *Kanimbla*, *Anzac* and *Darwin* and Clearance Diving Team 3). While the above focused on Australia's ground contribution, some reflection on the nature of the larger ADF effort is warranted. While the

RAN's ships and the RAAF's planes did contribute – for example the *Anzac* provided naval gunfire support to the Royal Marines – it is hard to imagine that they were actually needed, given the sheer vastness of the sea and air armada deployed by the senior Coalition partners. It was probably only the RAAF's C130s that made a real difference to Coalition tasking, due to the perennial shortage of air transport that all modern operations seem to face. This is not to say that the personnel serving on Australia's ships and planes did not do their job, it is just that they were not essential and Australia only committed them to the operation to make up numbers, at very little additional risk, and no real benefit to the campaign's outcome as a whole.

After the fall of Baghdad to US forces on 9 April 2003, as represented by the pulling down of the statue of Saddam Hussein in Firdos Square, the war entered its post-conflict phase. Ironically, this phase would prove the most dangerous and challenging for the Coalition as it had to contend with a deadly insurgency while striving to establish a viable successor state to Saddam's regime. Australia never had any intention of participating in the occupation of Iraq, but it soon gave way to requests from the United States for assistance. The ADF gave this mission the name Operation Catalyst.[26]

Again this analysis will focus on the ADF's ground-based contribution to Operation Catalyst. This is not to distract from the RAAF's C130 and P3C aircraft task groups or the RAN ship that continued to serve in the Middle East area of operations. Rather, it is because it was the land-based contribution that served in harm's way, on the ground, inside Iraq. Initially, Australia's assistance was quite small and took the form of a limited number of specialist personnel who deployed for a particular task and for a set period. Such tasks included, for example, assistance in the search for weapons of mass destruction, as air traffic controllers who helped run Baghdad International Airport, and as embedded personnel in US and UK headquarters. In addition, the ADF deployed to Baghdad a security detachment to protect the Australian ambassador and staff. Australia's Middle East headquarters also moved forward to Baghdad in order to be located near the US headquarters.

Despite the initial intent to keep its presence inside Iraq as small as possible, the Australian government gave way to Coalition pressure and eventually deployed a more significant ground force. In April 2005, the ADF provided the al-Muthanna Task Group (AMTG). Its purpose was to protect a Japanese engineering group that was working in the province of the same name. The ADF also deployed the Australian Army Training Team – Iraq (AATT-I), whose task was to help the United States to train the Iraqi Army. Combined, both organisations numbered approximately 500 personnel.[27] In July 2006, AMTG relocated to neighbouring Dhi Qar Province and was renamed Overwatch Battle Group – West (OBG-W). Its new task was to provide operational overwatch to the Iraqi forces based in Dhi Qar and al-Muthanna Provinces, in case the local troops needed assistance. Australia withdrew both groups in June 2008.[28]

Although an insurgency still raged across Iraq, its prosecution was not the mission of the Australians serving with AMTG/OBG-W and AATT-I. Instead, their tasks were to train Iraqi soldiers and officers, and provide operational overwatch in both provinces, the latter a requirement they were never called upon to perform. Countering the insurgents was the job of the other Coalition forces that operated in these provinces, principally the American troops who guarded Main Supply Route Tampa, a key logistical corridor which traversed Dhi Qar. Instead of an aggressive pursuit of insurgents, the Australians adopted a defensive posture, a policy which allowed them to mitigate risk and thereby avoid casualties. The Australians could and did defend themselves if fired upon, but seeking trouble was someone else's business.[29]

Moreover, Dhi Qar and al-Muthanna proved to be among the quietest of Iraq's provinces, and the first to convert to local control. During the course of the war, Coalition forces suffered 99 and eight fatalities in these two provinces respectively. During the period in which the Australians were present, there were only five deaths as a result of hostile fire in Dhi Qar and none at all in al-Muthanna. In fact, both provinces were backwaters. The areas where the insurgency was most active were Basra to the south, al-Anbar to the west, or in Baghdad and its environs. Only the Kurdish regions of the far north were less dangerous. That said, it must still be recognised that threats did exist. Improvised explosive devices were used in Dhi Qar and al-Muthanna, and indeed a number of Australians were wounded in attacks. In addition, rockets did strike the Australian camp at Tallil, which resulted in the deaths of one Romanian and four US soldiers.[30] But such events were comparatively rare, and an Australian risk assessment that needed to include criminal activity, unexploded ordnance left over from the 1991 and 2003 wars, and road traffic accidents did not suggest an area of operations of exceptionally high danger. The characterisation of the Australian area as a 'non permissive battlespace' only served to undercut any claim that Australia punched above its weight in Iraq.[31]

While casualty figures are an imprecise measure of how committed a country is to a military operation, they are indicative. As the United States bore the worst of the combat in the invasion of Iraq and the subsequent insurgency, it is not surprising that it also suffered the greatest number of fatalities: 4462 as of mid-2011. The United Kingdom's loss of 179 personnel was smaller, but still considerable. By contrast, the ADF lost just two soldiers during its entire involvement in the Iraq War, and both deaths were non-battle related.³² That Australia in a military commitment that lasted more than six years and involved over 20 000 personnel can suffer just two fatalities is a great outcome for the organisation and those who serve in it. It is, however, so extraordinary an achievement that it is hard to avoid the suggestion that Australia's commitment to the war was not as robust as that of its allies, and that while the ADF maintained a presence in the Coalition, the inescapable conclusion is that the policy of its deployed forces was to avoid taking any risks.³³

At the time of writing, Australia has lost 27 soldiers in the ongoing war in Afghanistan. These personal tragedies do suggest that Australia is attempting to contribute more in a combat sense to the US-led Coalition there than it did in Iraq. Australia was also one of the first countries to join the United States in attacking al-Qaeda and their Taliban protectors, and its Special Forces troops served with distinction in the war's opening phase in 2001 and 2002. The soldiers of the Australian SAS received particularly high praise for their performance during Operation Anaconda in March 2002, when they saved a party of US soldiers from two downed Chinook helicopters who were in danger of being overrun.³⁴ US personnel who got to know the Australian Special Forces described them in glowing terms, calling them 'pros' and the 'hardest looking men in Bagram'.³⁵ After working with the Australian SAS, the then Brigadier General James Mattis remarked, 'we Marines would happily storm Hell itself with your troops'.³⁶

Australia withdrew the SAS from Afghanistan in 2002 in order to have them available for the war with Iraq, and the nation did not return a field force to Afghanistan until September 2005. By 2011 this deployment had grown to approximately 1550 personnel supported by a further 800 serving elsewhere in the Middle East. The operational name given to the Australian contribution to the war in Afghanistan is Operation Slipper.

Since re-engagement in 2005, the Australian area of operations has been Uruzgan Province in Afghanistan's south-east. The ADF contingent's mission is to train and mentor the Afghan National Army's 4th Brigade, build the capacity of the Afghan National Police in the province, and improve the capacity of the provincial government to deliver essential services to the population. In addition, the Australian Special Operations Task Group's mission is to disrupt insurgent operations and supply routes in the region. Based outside of Afghanistan but providing support to Operation Slipper are RAAF transport and surveillance elements, a detachment of gunners serving with the British Army in Helmand Province, embedded personnel serving on NATO and US staffs, as well as a RAN major fleet unit operating in the Persian Gulf and Arabian Sea.[37]

In assessing the role of the ADF in the war in Afghanistan it is not yet possible to examine it from the perspective of outcomes achieved. Even the comparison of Australian accomplishments with those of other Coalition partners is problematic due to the limited information available. Moreover, there is considerable doubt among defence thinkers that Australia and its partners are even pursuing an achievable strategic goal. For example, the Provincial Reconstruction Team has completed an impressive list of reconstruction projects, yet the jury is still out on the effectiveness of such aid programs in winning the 'hearts and minds' of a people. Operational outcomes, therefore, are still too undecided to serve as useful guides for determining the mission's overall success or failure.

It is necessary, therefore, to look at the Australian role in the war in Afghanistan not in isolation but rather in comparison with that of a defence force of another country. In its commitment to this conflict, Canada offers useful points of comparison with Australia. Canada and Australia share a common language, cultural values and history, and both rely on mineral extraction for much of their national wealth. Each country also has a close military relationship with the United States. While Canada is approximately 50 per cent larger than Australia in population, its defence expenditure and size of its armed forces are roughly the same. In 2009, Canadian and Australian defence expenditure were also almost identical at US$19 575 and US$19 515 million respectively, while the number of full-time personnel fielded by the Canadian forces was 66 000 versus 57 000 for the ADF.[38]

A superficial review of these figures suggests that Australia is attempting to do more with less, since its military share of GDP is higher on a per capita basis – US$892 versus US$580. Yet, when operational commitments are taken into account, the difference in the two nations' degree of willingness to use military force dramatically changes the equation. A one-to-one comparison leads to the conclusion that it is Canada, not Australia, that is punching above its weight in Afghanistan.

Both countries are currently participating in numerous operations around the world, representing a mix of peace-keeping, peace stabilisation and war fighting missions in places such as Sudan, Sierra Leone, the Balkans, the Middle East, Afghanistan and Timor-Leste. There are approximately 2900 ADF personnel serving on ten international deployments, while Canada has about 3900 personnel serving on 14 international deployments.[39] For both Australia and Canada, the most significant mission is Afghanistan, although Canada has also recently become involved in the effort to impose a 'no fly zone' on Libya, a task to which it has assigned another approximately 650 personnel.[40]

In its commitment to Afghanistan, Canada has taken responsibility for Kandahar province and deployed a combined arms battalion-size battle group based upon the 1st Battalion Royal

22e Regiment. In support, Canada has deployed its own artillery, engineer, armoured reconnaissance and tank elements. Also in Kandahar Canada has fielded an Operational Mentor and Liaison Team, a Civil-Military Co-Operation Team, an engineering team and additional support services. Canada has also deployed an air wing that includes three C-130 transports, six CH-47D medium-lift helicopters (more than the entire ADF inventory, it should be noted), and eight CH-146 Griffon utility helicopters, and has chartered additional medium-lift helicopters from a commercial provider. The Canadian contingent totals over 3000 personnel. In addition, serving under Canadian command in Kandahar is a battalion of US infantry from the 82nd Airborne Division with supporting cavalry elements from the 10th Mountain Division.[41]

Not only is the size of the Canadian contingent twice that of Australia, but its composition is a balanced combined arms team that is aligned for combat rather than the ADF's preference for mentoring, reconstruction and social empowerment. In Uruzgan, only Special Forces troops have the specific task to hunt down and kill the enemy, while the rest of the ADF deployment's focus is on less risky undertakings. In addition, the Australian contingent has not taken complete responsibility for the province, but shares this with the United States and remains dependent on US resources for much of its support. The contrast in posture means that Canadian troops are exposed to more danger, and the casualty figures mirror this. To date Canada has lost 156 soldiers in Afghanistan, compared to 27 Australians.[42]

Canada is in the heart of the conflict and it is one of the countries which have not shirked from the threat of losses. When it first deployed to Afghanistan, Canada had decided against sending tanks. Its leaders soon changed their minds and sent out the force's elderly Leopard I vehicles. Canada then quickly upgraded its armour force by acquiring the newer and more capable Leopard II tank. Canada has also deployed a fleet of helicopters, whereas Australia maintains only two Chinooks in the theatre, and then for only an eight-month interval. The Australian Army's sizeable fleet of Blackhawk helicopters remains at home and the Australians in Afghanistan instead rely on Coalition partners for the extra lift they need. Canada finds utility in employing the symbol of land power projection – the tank – whereas Australia's state-of-the-art M1 Abrams tanks remain in Darwin, without any prospect for operational experience.

There have been suggestions that Australia should do more, to make a larger and more powerful contribution to the war in Afghanistan. Retired Major General Jim Molan has frequently called for the deployment of a brigade group to Afghanistan,[43] yet successive Australian governments have decided that Australia is already doing enough.[44] The result is that, while reports of the high regard in which the US-led Coalition holds Australia continue to be released, there are signs of a changing attitude. US General David Petraeus did single out Australia for praise, but he did so while fishing for a larger commitment – an opportunity the Australian government declined.[45] Assessments in recent books place Australia above the league of many 'do-nothing' partners, but still well below the efforts of other countries.[46] As one Australian commentator has observed, 'instead of impressing its allies, Australia's heavily circumscribed commitment dismays them with its timidity'.[47] Australia's forces in Afghanistan serve with national caveats designed to limit what they are allowed to do, and are similar to the ones that were in place for the war in Iraq. There is little doubt that these restrictions annoy the leaders of Australia's partners, but they also understand the game and accept that domestic concerns trump the preferences of coalition partners, particularly in wars of choice.[48] Elsewhere, the nature of

Australia's commitment has been described as 'a politically safe deployment, designed to demonstrate Australia's commitment to the war on terror without incurring electorally unpalatable casualties'.[49] These are hardly ringing endorsements.

If the ADF does not punch above its weight, then what is its true nature? Through design, the ADF is a provider of niche capabilities to international coalitions. This has been a deliberate and long-standing policy and practice of the government: in fact it dates to the nation's founding. Even the Australian Imperial Forces of the two World Wars were not independent armies, but worked within a coalition upon which they relied for much of their support and sustainment. For example, the tank was a critical factor in the Australian successes at the Battles of Hamel and Amiens in World War I, yet Australia did not raise any tank units. So strong has been the preference to field niche forces that it is no longer clear that Australia would want, or even could, initiate a military operation unilaterally. Moreover, this trend has been reinforced by the ADF seeking greater inter-operability with the military forces of the United States.[50]

Being a niche provider is not necessarily a bad thing: indeed it represents a sound strand of strategic thinking by the nation's political and military leaders. By being willing to provide a coalition partner with effective niche forces, Australia has been able to provide for its broader security needs at a relatively affordable cost. This has also allowed Australia to achieve desirable international goals that might not otherwise have been available, including the ANZUS Alliance and a free trade deal with the United States. With relatively small contributions, Australia has fulfilled international obligations and enjoys a high standing with its coalition partners.[51]

Furthermore, being a niche provider is not incompatible with the claim to punch above its weight, because some parts of ADF's forces do just that. Rather it is the myth's universal application that needs to be checked. For example, the Australian Army's Special Forces are justifiably held in high regard by the nation's allies and, perhaps alone amongst the rest of the ADF, they do punch above their weight.[52] US officials sincerely describe the Australian SAS as 'shit hot' and acknowledge that their own military personnel 'love to work with them'.[53] However, such comments are not indicative of the organisation as a whole, and too many examples exist where the applicability of 'punching above its weight' is patently false. Can an army that is unable to wage combined arms warfare, or a navy that fails to have any submarines or major amphibious vessels fit for sea, or an air force that nurses its aging jets on the promise of the joint strike fighter, realistically claim to be an above-average organisation?[54]

This myth is an especially pernicious one because it prevents the ADF from realistically assessing its own worth. Instead, it encourages the mistaken notion that Australian military personnel can do anything, anywhere, and do it better than anyone else. In war, this is a dangerous belief to hold, particularly when the ADF does so little to back it up. Our coalition partners are realists, and they accept that there are domestic political limitations on what Australia can provide. They are content to accept a largely symbolic presence, as was the case in post-invasion Iraq and for much of the war in Afghanistan. Officials in Washington are also aware that it is the political fact of Australia's contribution that really matters, not its composition. However, our coalition partners are also composed of people, some of whom have written letters to the families of soldiers who have died under their command, soldiers who fought with quiet dignity and without vocal claims to greatness. There are signs of the beginning of a change of attitude in the United States from those who have sacrificed so much towards those who contributed so little.

Whether this affects Australia's strategic relationship is yet to be determined.[55]

This myth is dangerous for another reason, for it encourages wishful rather than clear, realistic thinking. It prevents the ADF itself from perceiving what it really is: a niche provider of discrete military elements to coalition warfare. In assessing Australia's military worth, it is best to start from a point of reality rather then one of bravado. If being a niche contributor is openly acknowledged, than it can be assessed; if found undesirable it can be changed. If the ADF requires more 'weight', a case can be made for it receiving a larger share of the nation's wealth. In understanding the true nature of the force the government and the ADF can make plans and policies backed by what the force can and cannot do. National security is just too important to allow the 'punching above its weigh' myth to survive any longer.

Further reading

Australian Department of Defence, *The War in Iraq: ADF Operations in the Middle East in 2003*, DoD, Canberra.

J.R. Ballard, *Triumph of Self-Determination: Operation Stabilise and United Nations Peacemaking in East Timor*, Praeger, Westport, 2008.

B. Breen, *Mission Accomplished, East Timor: The Australian Defence Force Participation in the International Forces East Timor (INTERFET)*, Allen & Unwin, Sydney, 2001.

B. Breen & G. McCauley, *The World Looking Over Their Shoulders: Australian Strategic Corporals in Somalia and East Timor*, Land Warfare Studies Centre, Canberra, 2008.

C.A. Collier, 'A new way to wage peace: US support to Operation Stabilise', *Military Review*, January–February 2001, pp. 2–9.

P. Cosgrove, *My Story*, HarperCollins, Sydney, 2007.

D. Horner, 'Deploying and sustaining INTERFET in East Timor in 1999', in P. Dennis and J. Grey (eds.), *Raise Train and Sustain: Delivering Land Combat Power*, Army History Unit, Canberra, 2010, pp. 204–29.

A.J. Molan, *Running the War in Iraq: An Australian General, 300 000 Troops, the Bloodiest Conflict of our Time*, HarperCollins, Sydney, 2008.

P. Pigott, *Canada in Afghanistan: The War so Far*, Dundurn Press, Toronto, 2007.

M. Thomson, 'Punching above our weight: Australia as a middle power', *Strategic Insights*, 18, Australian Strategic Policy Institute, 2005.

H. White, 'The road to INTERFET: Reflections on Australian strategic decisions concerning East Timor, December 1998–September 1999', *Security Challenges*, 4(1) Autumn 2008, pp. 69–87.

L. Windsor, D. Charters & B. Wilson, *Kandahar Tour: The Turning Point in Canada's Afghan Mission*, Wiley, Mississauga, 2010.

[11]

CRITICAL REFLECTIONS ON THE AUSTRALIA–US ALLIANCE

Michael McKinley

Australia's military relationship with the United States of America, formalised by the ANZUS Treaty of 1951, is officially acknowledged as the Australian Defence Force's 'most important defence relationship'. The 2009 Defence White Paper, an important planning document that forms the foundation of future Defence capabilities, asserts that:

> In day-to-day terms, the alliance gives us significant
> access to materiel, intelligence, research and development,
> communications systems, and skills and expertise that
> substantially strengthen the ADF ... Without access to US
> capabilities, technology, and training, the ADF simply could
> not be the advanced force that it is today, and must be in the
> future, without the expenditure of considerably more money.[1]

This White Paper is part of a long and continuing tradition of frequent, regular and meaningful professions of faith in the alliance. Such faith, such unquestioning and uncritical certainty in the absolutely indispensible nature of the Australian–US alliance, lumbers along in the background of defence debate in this country, no matter what contrary evidence the historical record might contain. Although there are often debates in the media and think-tanks about whether Australia should contribute to a particular US-led military operation, most of these discussions are largely conducted over tactical issues such as what kinds of forces should be deployed: the number of infantry, the number of ships and aircraft, or the degree of logistic support. These debates occur, however, within a shared framework of agreement: that the alliance with the United States is vital to our 'national interest' and must be protected by regular acts that affirm its ongoing importance. A more fundamental question is rarely asked, and almost never answered in any depth: is the Australia–US the alliance worth it? This basic question is the subject of this chapter. In all likelihood an attempt to answer it will attract various charges of impiety for proposing that ANZUS, an article of faith, be subject to an impudent test of facts, but then that is the very nature of the myth under investigation here.

Although the world in which the 1951 ANZUS Treaty was signed has changed dramatically, official proclamations about its continuing relevance are as confident as ever. Thus it was that in 1991, Australian Foreign Minister Gareth Evans responded to the ending of the Cold War by stating that:

> Our alliance is as relevant as it ever was, as the world changes around us. It is ever more multi-dimensional in character; it is frank and robust when it needs to be; and it totally mutually supportive when it needs to be. In this sense, ours is not only an alliance of democracies, but also a thoroughly democratic alliance …
>
> Ultimately, it is because Australians and Americans believe in the same things – democracy, freedom and human rights – that our alliance relationship will endure, will adapt and

will go on contributing to the building of a safer and fairer world.[2]

For Evans, the passing of the Cold War in no way required a reconsideration of the Australia–US alliance, or indeed any thought that the historic justification for the United States' dominant role in the West's defence against the Soviet Union might also have passed. Indeed, Evans and his ilk asserted the exact opposite, as did Prime Minister Julia Gillard, on 10 March 2011, with her near-to-tears address to a joint session of the US Congress and her insistence that the United States be at the centre of a new world order.

For reasons of space, this chapter will discuss briefly only four of a range of propositions that, despite decades of political and public rhetoric, call the contemporary alliance into question. The first is that, historically, alliances do not produce the public good – peace – that their proponents claim. Second, the available evidence does not show that Australia receives the particular benefits that the alliance's proponents claim. Third, the United States is a bad alliance partner: it is overly disposed to the use of force and coercive diplomacy, is war-prone, and its wars generally demonstrate neither a fidelity to international law nor even the US Constitution. Last, the intellectual architecture of US foreign and security policy prevents the development of politics that advance the cause of peace.

In theory, alliances such as ANZUS are supposed to deliver physical security in an anarchic world of nation states which, even in the twenty-first century resembles, at heart, something of 'state of nature' described 360 years ago by Thomas Hobbes in *Leviathan*. Under this assumption Australia, traditionally defined as a predominantly Anglo-Celtic colony in a region from which it is alienated, must seek its security through an alliance with a dominant power of similar values, history and politics. In considering this view, it is important to begin with an elementary point about the burden of proof: those who advance a proposition are required to provide the evidence for it. Thus, those who assert that alliances deliver a peaceful strategic environment are required, under standard rules of logic and argument, to show the evidence for their assertion. It will not do to simply assert that alliances produce these benefits and then require sceptics to provide contrary evidence. Yet this evidentiary burden is never met adequately by supporters of alliances.

For sceptics, however, there is ample analytical support in the form of John Vasquez' *The Power of Power Politics*, which examined the international relations 'power politics' literature from the late 1950s to the 1980s to evaluate its explanatory power in regard to international phenomena. After surveying the field of relevant accounts, Vasquez' conclusion was a demolition of the *realpolitik* argument for alliances:

> It is now clear that alliances do not produce peace but lead to war. Alliance making is an indicator that there is a danger of war in the near future ... This means that the attempt to balance power is itself part of the very behaviour that leads to war. This conclusion supports the earlier claim that power politics is an image of the world that encourages behaviour that helps bring about war.[3]

Vasquez then asks a valuable political question: 'Since it is now known that alliances, no matter what their form, do not bring about peace ... what causes actors to seek alliances?'[4] For Australia specifically, the record indicates that since 1945 its alliances have been efficient and effective instruments for involving the country in war. Interestingly, although the popular public view is that Australia has been basically at peace since 1945, the historical record proves otherwise: for over 40 'operational' or war-fighting years within this 66-year period, Australian Defence Force personnel have served in no less than seven conflicts (the Malayan Emergency, Korean War, Vietnam, Indonesian Confrontation, the 1990–1991 Gulf War, Afghanistan, and the Iraq War) all as a direct or indirect consequence of alliance membership.

As to the security guarantees that an alliance with a dominant power might offer, it cannot be emphasised strongly enough that the historical record again offers little comfort. Consider the Australia–Great Britain relationship of the late 1930s and early 1940s. In return for Australia's commitment to Britain's defence in 1939, the latter promised to defend Australia from any Japanese attack with little real thought or concern for the possibility of it ever being implemented. When, however, such a guarantee was required to be implemented, Churchill not only tried to prevent substantial American forces being sent to the Pacific, but even attempted to delay the repatriation of Australian troops to a country that was basically defenceless before the advancing Japanese forces. To the Australian government of the time, the British decisions of 1942 which determined the fall of Singapore, and thus the peril which Australia faced, were an 'inexcusable betrayal'. Even US General Douglas MacArthur, Supreme Commander of Allied Forces in the Southwest Pacific Area from April 1942, thought the abandonment of British promises to the Dominions reeked of treachery.[5]

Such perfidy, nevertheless, would seem to have been a matter of policy for Great Britain. According to papers captured from the British steamer *Automedon* by the Germans, after they had sunk it off the Nicobar Islands in November 1940, the British War Cabinet had by that date already abandoned any hope of saving Singapore and Malaya in the event of a Japanese attack, and were communicating this to their Commander-in-Chief, Far

East, Air Chief Marshall Sir Robert Brooke-Popham. Churchill was thus not only aware that this secret would soon be passed to Japan but decided that the loss of the documents was so sensitive that it, too, was a secret, and so allowed Australia to continue pouring reinforcements into Singapore.[6] Little succour remains for those who hope against hope that the world is any less cynical and amoral today than it was in the past.

Nevertheless, defenders of the Australia–United States alliance go on to claim that Australia obtains certain 'practical benefits' from its defence relationship. For example, the 2009 White Paper on Defence claims that:

> Australia's defence relationships also strengthen the ADF by providing access to equipment, intelligence and training opportunities. Ultimately, our defence relationships are designed to underpin the possible use of military force ... What the alliance means for our direct security is that the associated capability, intelligence and technological partnership, at the core of the alliance, is available to support our strategic capability advantage in our immediate neighbourhood and beyond. This is indispensable to our security.[7]

To evaluate this assertion, it is necessary to appraise the first four of the following claimed benefits because they are considered to be the most important, and they tend to shape the level, nature, and even the need for the last three:

1. access to, and political influence with, US policy-makers and decision-makers
2. the exchange of a significant amount of strategic intelligence data in general, and receiving relevant US intelligence in particular

3   security through formal and informal guarantees of assistance between the United States and Australia, in particular the ANZUS Treaty
4   access to state-of-the-art US-manufactured defence equipment and logistics and other forms of support in both peace and war
5   inclusion in US–allied military exercises
6   the exchange of defence-scientific material and personnel; and
7   exchanges in the field of defence education and training.

Moreover, these 'practical benefits' are said to flow to Australia within the context of commonalities – history, values, political character and interests – which apparently exist between Australia and the United States.

As far as political influence is concerned, it should first be noted that those who claim that the alliance gives Australia political access to, and influence over US decision-makers at the highest levels seldom write for publication. When they do, their work is often unverifiable, anecdotal and selective. Additionally, claims of political influence are exaggerated due to organisational interest, bureaucratic rivalry, necessary and unnecessary secrecy, and different levels of knowledge and ignorance. Thus they cannot meet the burden of proof of providing the evidence for a proposition themselves, rather than merely requiring doubters to provide contradictory evidence.

For doubters, however, once again we see from the numerous autobiographical, biographical and scholarly accounts of Australia–United States relations since 1945 (around a hundred volumes), that there is no justification for accepting the claim that alliance membership delivers Canberra any real political influence over Washington. Certainly, there are occasional references in various memoirs, but the scholarly accounts are generally silent on the issue. Furthermore, a US Audit Office report to Senator John Glenn, which was subsequently released under the Freedom of Information Act, showed not only the United States' consistent lack of interest in even 'consultation' with the Australian government, but also the latter's dissatisfaction with this ongoing state of affairs.

Australia's lack of influence over the United States was, in fact, well publicised during a series of conferences held in the late 1980s after New Zealand barred nuclear-armed or nuclear-powered ships from using its ports or entering its territorial waters. In these and other meetings, US officials made it clear that Australian (and New Zealand) views simply did not count in the final analysis. As James Rosenau concluded, 'it could hardly be more clear cut: the ANZUS countries are as far removed perceptually from the United States as they are geographically'.[8]

One of the most important defence activities of the state is the gathering of information, and the subsequent analysis of it, to the point at which it becomes intelligence product suitable for informing domestic and foreign policy. For that reason intelligence must subjected to a systematic, disciplined and deep questioning, and must be especially concerned with fundamental concepts, principles, theories, issues and problems. When analysing the intelligence that the United States shares with its allies, friends and partners of convenience, however, it must be understood that this material is never given altruistically, but always with the intention of influencing the policy and strategy of the recipient countries. The need to question this alleged 'jewel in the crown' of the alliance benefits is crucial given that the United States has a record of frequent intelligence failure on many of the most significant events and developments in the post-1945 world. To take only some examples of – publicly acknowledged

– failures, the intelligence agencies of the United States did not foresee: the first Soviet atomic bomb; North Korea's invasion of South Korea in 1950; China's intervention into the Korean War the same year; the Hungarian uprising of 1956; the launching of Sputnik in 1957; Fidel Castro's victory in 1959 and the subsequent placement of Soviet missiles in Cuba in 1962 (and, of far greater significance, that some of these weapons were armed and operational); the Soviet Union's invasion of Czechoslovakia in 1968; the massive Soviet effort in the mid-1960s to match the United States in strategic missile numbers and capabilities; the 1973 Middle East war; India's acquisition of a nuclear capability in 1974; the overthrow of the Shah of Iran in 1979; the Soviet invasion of Afghanistan in the same year; the rise of Japan as a major economic power, the emergence of inflation as a chronic problem of all industrial nations, and the decline in productivity of all Western powers in the 1970s; and, almost inexplicably, the striking loss of leadership on the world stage by the United States in the period following its defeat in Vietnam. This was followed by the strategic surprise generated by the disintegration of the principal focus of US intelligence, the Soviet Union, in 1992.

After the Cold War, of course, the pattern went unchanged, with a lack of warning in respect of the Asian Financial Crisis of 1997 and the Indian nuclear tests of May 1998, to take just two well-known examples. Unsurprisingly, the shock and after-effects of US strategic-level intelligence failures in the twentieth century continued into the twenty-first: on 11 September 2001 four civilian airliners were hijacked and three of them flown into government and public buildings in the United States as part of a terrorist strategy. In all between 3000 and 4000 innocent people were killed in a period of less than one hour. The US intelligence community – funded at the time to the tune of at least US$30 billion annually, consisting of at least 39 organisations, and having access to at least 75 000 personnel – failed to foresee or prevent these attacks. Aside from acts of violence against its citizens, the United States (and the rest of the world) have since 2008 lived with the failure to predict, let alone comprehensively understand, the economic meltdown still under way and known popularly as the Global Financial Crisis.

There have also been regular and catastrophic US intelligence failures in which political, social and economic signals have been ignored, not recognised, or discounted. For Australia, moreover, we know from the public record that the United States refused to provide intelligence about events in an area of 'prime political and strategic concern to Australia'. During the Chinese invasion of Vietnam in early 1979, for example, the American cut-off of intelligence 'meant that the first warning Australian intelligence officials had of the actual invasion ... came from the public announcement by the Chinese'. For two days prior to and one day after the invasion, US signals intelligence were not made available to Australia, with the first official (Australian) explanation being that, for much of this time, the United States had decided to stop collecting such material.[9] What actually took place in this case was an abandonment of formal agreements and informal understandings that had been given for nearly forty years of intelligence co-operation, in a matter of critical importance to Australia, in an area of operations where Australia had, less than five years earlier, fought a war alongside the United States as one of its allies, and at a time when the conservative government in Canberra was staunchly pro-American and pro-alliance. It was, therefore, a remarkable event in its own right since it suggests the United States distrusted an enthusiastic ally. Of course, since it remains a solitary case in terms of the public record, its capacity to instruct and to inform is limited.

Great scepticism must nonetheless be exercised about claims

of alliance benefits in the area of intelligence sharing by the United States, with its structural weaknesses, technological inducements to intelligence failure, penetration and compromise, and actual intelligence disappointments and strategic surprises wrought on it over many years. For Australia, too, the benefit is even more dubious because it creates a syndrome of dependency. And related to this are issues of breaches of sovereignty, the provision of intelligence always being in the interests of the provider, the quantity and quality of intelligence received, the diplomatic costs of membership in an intelligence-sharing network, and the subversion of Australian foreign policy by the intelligence network of a foreign country. Over and above these costs can be added other costs to Australia: dishonesty and deceit, international and national legal transgressions, and breaches of declared national codes of ethics. The price then is as extensive as it is profound, and in Australia's case they seem to have been incurred for no appreciable advantage to Australian foreign and security policies. Moreover, according to Australian ministerial statements, the arrangements which give rise to them do not appear to be actually necessary for such foreign and security policies.[10]

A third assertion often made by those who defend the alliance with the United States is the so-called 'populist' case: that Australia is supposedly vulnerable, or even militarily indefensible. Yet this view is not regarded as credible by the more intellectual members of the foreign and defence policy community. In fact, as Paul Dibb demonstrated in the late 1980s in an argument that is still relevant today, Australia is defensible at many levels of threat. Furthermore, earlier works by, among others, Desmond Ball and Robert O'Neill, show that even with the best will in the world, there are scenarios or conditions which might prevent the United States from committing itself to the defence of Australia in times of peril.[11] According to this latter analysis, although US assistance might be essential to overcome challenges above the spectrum of relatively low-level conventional conflict, this country would 'understand' that the resources of the United States were finite and, ultimately, would be applied in areas of its own more immediate interest.

Were the United States to provide military support to Australia in a high-level conventional conflict, however, we can reach only a rather pessimistic conclusion about its capabilities. If we examine the period since 1950 – that is, the period punctuated by the Korean War, Vietnam, 'Operation Enduring Freedom' in Afghanistan and 'Operation Iraqi Freedom' in Iraq – we find that US military efforts have been and remain in serious trouble. The year 1950 is significant here since it was, according to one archetypical study towards the end of the Cold War by two leading US strategic analysts, 'the last major victory for American arms'.[12] This reference was not to the Korean War as such, but to the landings on the mainly undefended Inchon Peninsula which led eventually to the retaking of Seoul. In the next four decades to the end of the Cold War, we find that US military efforts are no model of competence or success. From the record – which includes the debacle in Indo China, and over 120 specifically designated rescue and other missions in that conflict, through still more rescue missions such as those in support of the *Mayaguez* and the hostages in Teheran, and interventions-cum-invasions such as those in Beirut, Grenada and Panama – the armed forces of the United States have performed in a manner which encourages neither confidence in themselves nor on the part of allies operating with them, or in receipt of a US security guarantee.[13]

This record since 1950 is clear, broadly agreed upon, supported by specialists from across the political spectrum, and based on criteria established by the US military itself. For reasons of space, let us take Richard Gabriel's conclusion to his 1985 study as a representative sample:

> The American military is in serious trouble. Its recent historical record, to say nothing of its disastrous performance in Vietnam, has been marked far more often by failure than success. Its military plans have been unrealistic and unsuccessful. The officer corps by any historical standard is lacking in the spirit and expertise that have characterised the more successful officer corps in history. Worse, it is infected by habits and values which are characteristic of many of the worst officer corps in history. The record is clear that the officer corps has failed the single test of a successful army, the ability to perform well in the field of battle.[14]

Despite its apparent success, 'Operation Desert Storm' in Iraq in 1991 provided nothing of substance to improve this assessment. The overwhelming majority of the Iraqi forces in the conflict realised that retreat had proved impossible, resistance futile, and capitulation and surrender wise. So they adopted a military version of what in legal terms is known as the plea of 'No Contest'. Accordingly, they offered no defence in 1991: a fact that should have been remembered during the long aftermath of the 'Mission Accomplished' banner being hung from the superstructure of the USS *Abraham Lincoln* on 1 May 2003 as a backdrop for President George W. Bush's victory speech. While some commentators began to regard the American generals as, in the words of *Newsweek* magazine, 'genius generals', it should be remembered that they did no more than defeat the qualitatively inferior conventional forces of a Third World country by bringing to bear the largest military alliance of advanced, industrialised (and other) states since World War II.[15]

Nor, more recently, have either Operation Enduring Freedom

or Operation Iraqi Freedom provided evidence which would challenge such conclusions. Consider again a summary of the evidence: in Afghanistan, a US-led and US-dominated NATO force, acting without United Nations authority, invaded the country with the objectives of not only dismantling the Al-Qaeda terrorist organisation and ending its use of Afghanistan as a base, but also removing the Taliban regime from power and creating a viable democratic state. The operation, in these terms, has largely been a military-strategic failure. In the course of this failure, the United States has deployed over 100 000 troops of its own, but after a decade of fighting has little to show for the overall costs. While it is undoubtedly the case that Al-Qaeda has been seriously and probably permanently disrupted, its legacy and imitators are now well and truly distributed and entrenched throughout Pakistan and North Africa. The Taliban itself, despite the presence of the US, NATO and other international forces, not to mention the considerable presence of private military contractors, appears to be able to indefinitely sustain a strength of 10 000 to 12 000 personnel. Fighting between the Taliban and the occupation forces claims from 1000 to 4000 civilian lives every year, with the Taliban being responsible for only 30–40 per cent of these civilian deaths. In the name of military necessity, the war has extended spatially into Pakistan and acts as another destabilising influence on a country already characterised by civil unrest. As for the benefits of replacing the Taliban, religious minorities are still persecuted; women are still raped, otherwise abused and denied education, including basic literacy; and the country continues to produce 95 per cent of the world's supply of opium, most of which is processed into heroin to supply a US$65 billion industry for a global population of 15 million addicts, of whom 100 000 die every year. This is a dubious report card.

Alternatively, in 2003 the United States and its coalition of eager allies invaded Iraq illegally and on thin pretexts that must be considered incredible, if any respect at all is paid to the expert testimony on matters of weapons of mass destruction and international terrorism. The country's basic infrastructure was destroyed, and under US military oversight was ethnically and religiously cleansed to a greater degree than under the old regime. In addition, the battlefields of this and the earlier US-led invasions were liberally contaminated by the aerosol powder produced during impact and combustion of depleted uranium weapons – essentially a mist of deadly, carcinogenic and mutagenic radioactive particles with a half-life (depending on the isotope) of between 700 million and 4.5 billion years, and which attack the kidney, brain, liver and heart among other organs. By definition, these consequences determine that its use constitutes a war crime, not only against the people of Iraq, but also against those who will be affected into the future as the winds scatter where they may the particles of the close to 2000 tons of depleted uranium particles.

For those with a strategic memory which includes the Vietnam War, the US's policy of 'Iraq-ization' was all too familiar: as US political patience faded, the costs climbed, and the mission seemed not quite 'accomplished', US policy-makers announced that the Iraqi forces were now sufficiently competent to take over, and that US forces could withdraw – either from the country entirely, or away from the cities and into the less threatening countryside. And this was not the conscript US Army of the 1960s and 1970s, but an 'all-volunteer' force supposedly built on the lessons of that period. But in its lack of success it remained comparable. Unlike Vietnam, however, the United States resists complete withdrawal in Iraq, meaning that its forces of around 40 000 hardly increase Iraqi security but rather act as a lightening rod to those forces which would weaken it further. After more than 1.4 million violent deaths in the period since 2003, and ongoing and bloody civil strife into late 2011, claims of even a purely military victory are impossible to entertain, as are notions of Iraq as an emerging politically democratic (or even democratically tending), geographically unified, religiously and ethnically tolerant, constitutional nation state. Should a reader doubt this, consider why it is that nowhere is there any serious mention of 'victory' in the contemporary official discourse on Iraq, or in the foreseeable prospects for Afghanistan in the US, NATO and ISAF projections.

Another major assertion made by those who champion the Australia–United States alliance is that Australia gains access to US-manufactured state-of-the-art defence equipment and weapons systems. At the outset, let it be conceded that defence projects in general are notorious for running over time, over budget and, even then, producing weapons and technologies that fail to meet the performance criteria expected. The questions that arise, then, are why this problem for US industry continues; and why, moreover, is it effectively indulged by Australia in its alliance relationship? The former is more easily approached because there is an extensive historical public record. For sceptics of this assertion, the point is not that access as such is denied (although in some cases it is); rather, that the access is compromised by the incompetency, inefficiencies, excesses and questionable (even criminal) practices of the American military procurement processes.[16]

Between 1960 and 1987, a range of investigating authorities undertook twelve major, independent studies of the US defence acquisition process. These studies are backed up by many inquiries conducted by the General Accounting Office and, since 2004, the Government Accountability Office (both conveniently GAO), an independent non-partisan agency which investigates how the US government spends taxpayer dollars. Of these twelve major, independent studies, this chapter touches on one conducted by

Ronald Fox and James Field of the Harvard Business School. In 1974 Fox, as sole investigator and author, had written *Arming America: How the US Buys Weapons*, but in 1984 he began a second study which led to his joint work. The initial Fox–Field finding was that most of the problems reported in Fox's earlier work not only still existed, but in some cases had worsened. Moreover, the relationship between government and industry had deteriorated, and weapons costs had increased at a rate far greater than costs in the rest of the economy. Despite the large number of studies and the similarity of their findings, virtually all attempts to implement improvements had failed. The magnitude of just the criminal aspect of this malaise can be gauged by extracts from some 32 reports cited by Fox and Field:

> Procurement fraud is derived from essentially three corrupt practices – product substitution, cost mischarging and defective pricing.
>
> At any given time, according to the sworn testimony before Congress given by Joseph Sherick, Inspector General for the Department of Defense, in 1985, about 1000 cases were under way.
>
> Sherick also testified that he had 45 of the Department of Defense's top 100 contractors under investigation for possible criminal activities, and that these 45 included 9 out of the top 10 of DoD's contractors. The particular forms of wrongdoing included overcharging, kickbacks, bribery, bid-rigging and false claims.[17]

Perhaps all of this might even be acceptable if the weapons systems produced were of a high quality, but that too is dubious. Indeed such practices are notorious for producing some of the worst and/or over-priced weapons of the post-World War II age:

the F-15E fighter, the B1 and B2 bombers, the Ballistic Missile Defense program, the Maverick anti-tank missile, the Aegis tracking system, the C-17 transport aircraft, the Advanced Medium-Range Air-to-Air Missile, the Black Hawk helicopter, the C-130J Transport aircraft, the C-5A and C-5B transport aircraft, the C-17 Airlifter, the Comanche Helicopter, the Crusader Howitzer, the FA-22 fighter aircraft, the Joint Strike Fighter (JSF), the Marine Expeditionary Force Fighting Vehicle, the Patriot missile system, the Stryker Armoured Vehicle, the V-22 Osprey aircraft, the Global Hawk drone aircraft (Block 30), coffee machines and pilots' arm-rests that were charged out by Lockheed at US$7600 and US$670 respectively, and so on. Even Australia's own F/A-18 aircraft was not without reproach, being both deprived of important components by their US manufacturer, and having experienced a 58 per cent cost increase over the period 1981 to 1986. More recent Australian weapons procurement experience – the Joint Strike Fighter and the Wedgetail airborne early warning and control aircraft – has been little different.

Nor has the situation changed for the better in the past quarter century. In 2008, the GAO reviewed the Pentagon's major procurement programs and concluded that '95 major systems had exceeded their original budgets by a total of US$295 billion ... were delivered almost two years late on average [and] none had met all of the standards for best management practices during their development stages'.[18] Moreover, auditors stated that the Defense Department showed few signs of improvement since the GAO began. In 2011, the GAO audit found that one-third of US Defense Department weapons programs since 1997 had cost overruns by as much as 50 per cent over their original projections.[19] Yet, because of what is known as the 'termination liability cost' for cancelling a contract, vested interests argue that it should be maintained because the actual payout to the company in question would be so high that it makes economic sense to continue.[20]

In Australia, there is a partial, concealed and an accommodating understanding of these phenomena. Andrew Davies and Peter Layton provide what is probably the typical response from mainstream defence and strategic studies analysts:

> Defence projects the world over have a history of running over budget, behind schedule, or both. And the more research and development required, the longer the schedule delays and the greater the cost overruns. Accurately estimating the capability, cost and delivery timetable of a new piece of equipment is as much art as science, especially if novel technologies or manufacturing techniques are involved.[21]

The problem here is compounded by various further factors: confidential settlements which hide dangerous corporate behaviour; bureaucratic infighting; the pretense, as opposed to the reality, of oversight; the 'revolving door' syndrome whereby some former government officials and retired military officers move into highly paid consultancies for the Pentagon even while they are also working for companies seeking Defense Department contracts; the pervasive and corrosive influence of money in the decision-making process and the consequent division between careerists and ethical professionals in the senior military and civilian ranks; the US government's refusal to make a legislatively mandated database of the personnel involved in the revolving door arrangements; the drastic reduction in the oversight of contracts by the Defense Contract Audit Agency; and the resort to 'budget games, lies, half-truths and misrepresentations' in testimony to Congress during hearings on the Defense Authorization and Appropriation Bills. Added to these must be the same patterns of corporate behaviour seen in the Project for Government Oversight's 2009 Federal Contractor Misconduct Database: the top five corporations with the highest misconduct rate – Lockheed Martin, Boeing, Northrop Grumman, General Dynamics and Raytheon – were all leading defence contractors.[22]

It is fundamentally important to note that none of this finds a place in the alliance debate in Australia, or even in the specialist analyses of the government-funded, policy-oriented think-tanks. Moreover, given the Lockheed bribery scandals of the 1970s, the Savings and Loan scandals of the 1980s and 1990s, and the endemic criminal behaviour which led to the current Global Financial Crisis, it is surely reasonable to wonder whether the defence industries of the United States share the excesses of Wall Street.

Alarmingly, using only examples since 2006, there is a body of evidence which suggests that the United States is acting as a role model for Australia in this regard. In that year, the extremely important $400 million electronic warfare self-protection system for the RAAF's F/A 18 fleet, being built by BAE Systems at the Royal Australian Air Force Base, Edinburgh, was scrapped after being shown to be an expensive failure. Significantly, the decision to proceed with it in the first place in a politically sensitive state for the government of the day had been taken against expert advice.[23] Three years later, the Australian National Audit Office tabled its report on the Super Seasprite helicopters for the RAN, which established not only that defence planners had wasted at least $1.4 billion on the project to buy eleven of the aircraft, but had 'failed to properly inform their minister about concerns the project should be scrapped'.[24] Then, in 2010 it came to light that private firms which had been allocated thousands of dollars by the Defence Department for 'hotel accommodation, horseback trail rides, and use of an executive jet' reported they had no knowledge of such contracts. This was followed by a report that a crucial Defence Department information system upgrade for keeping track of billions of dollars worth of assets was not only late and $30 million over budget, but that a company that the government had excluded from it on the grounds of conflict of interest in 2005 – KPMG – was now involved to the extent of at least 41 contracts.[25] Three months later it was revealed that Australian government aviation contracts had been awarded to 'companies that secured their bids with inside information about tenders provided by senior public servants'.[26] It would be easy, of course, to continue citing more examples to the extent that they would almost become an end in themselves. While there is little to be gained from this there is little doubt, however, that there is a proliferation of such cases in the United States, and a growing incidence of them in Australia.

To state the case most baldly, and to borrow from the title of Geoffrey Perret's work, the United States is 'a country made by war'.[27] Notwithstanding the American Revolution, the War of 1812 and the US Civil War on its own soil, the United States had by 1942 already shown its war-proneness by its role in the Spanish-American War, the Mexican War, and World War I. By 1980, the United States had managed to participate in eight international wars at a cost of nearly 700 000 dead. On average, each of these wars lasted longer (33 months versus 22 months) and cost more lives (83 000 versus 68 000) than those of Imperial Britain.[28] It also must be remembered that, once committed to a war, states tend to forget the past and need to learn anew the costs to be borne. Wars tend to be long and expensive in human terms, and wars fought by major powers are particularly long and particularly expensive. And minor powers aligned with major powers share the risks and eventually the significant costs of such conflicts. US military interventions, whereby a US force was deployed on foreign soil, are therefore relevant to the central argument of this chapter. Since 1900, 71 such initiatives have taken place, 15 in the period from 1945 to 1991. And this count leaves to one side the 215 occasions in the period from 1946 to 1975 when the United States used its armed forces as a political instrument without actually committing any violence.[29]

War-proneness and a habit for coercion and intervention do not of themselves disqualify the United States as an appropriate ally if the country were acting out of necessity, or perhaps, even legally. But the evidence is not favourable here either. As Melvin Small has argued, of the six major wars which the United States has fought (including both World Wars and Korea), 'necessity' as a justification was found wanting in virtually every case.[30] Nor were those conflicts in the post-1945 period either (domestically) constitutional or, more recently at least, in accordance with international law. As regards the former, two leading US constitutional lawyers, Michael J. Glennon and Louis Henkin (acknowledged by Theodore Draper as 'the doyen of constitutional scholars'), have in separate accounts concluded that wars since 1945 have not been constitutionally sanctioned but presidentially arranged without congressional authorisation.[31] The Reagan administration had difficulty even in maintaining international legal norms in the exercise of US foreign policy. In Stuart Malawer's study of 32 major US foreign policy decisions taken by that administration, he identified only five as broadly complying with the standards of international law. The remaining 27 represented deviations from these norms which varied from moderate to significant, but in any case suggested a careless and certainly patterned disregard for them.[32]

Nearly a quarter of a century later, the record is unchanged: the invasions of and subsequent wars in Panama, Afghanistan and Iraq were all either illegal in their initiation, in how they were fought, or in the manner in which prisoners and non-combatants were treated – or all three. Indeed, the record includes 'the violation of international agreements, the use of prohibited weapons, crimes of aggression, military attacks on civilian populations, support for war crimes by proxy [and] support for death squads and torture'.[33] Of greater significance is the fact that, even where the perpetrators are known to the US government and the crimes in question are *prima facie* covered by US law, the decision has been taken not to press charges and prosecute, even when there is an admission of responsibility for the crime. Instead, successive administrations have declared that the president may order the extrajudicial assassinations of American citizens living overseas.[34]

For the student of US politics and society, one of its most striking features is its openness. This is not to say that there is no deceit, secrecy, or hidden government – on the contrary, these most assuredly abound – but the openness of the United States at least allows political analysts to examine them in approximate terms. Indeed, US writers are exhibitionists in terms of the pathologies embedded in their national ideology. There is a consensus that the ideology of the United States emphasises patriarchy, individualism and the country's Anglo-Saxon heritage to the point of racism. Inseparable from this are both the consequences of the historical origins of the European settlement of America and its abundance of natural resources, and of the dominant political economy – the need for territory and markets, and a belief in what is known as 'American exceptionalism'. Together they have induced a sense not just of nationalism, but of national mission, a tendency to universalise the American experience and either export it, impose it, or both. This tendency makes the United States impatient with those states slow to grasp the 'truth' and even hostile to other forms of social and political revolution and development.

Since the contradiction between being 'exceptional' and asserting the universal relevance of the US ideas and ideologies is never (nor can it be) resolved, the United States continually collides with a world of adversaries and enemies, almost all of them of its own making. Believing it is 'exceptional', it believes it is also invincible. Believing it is 'exceptional' and the instrument of a universal mission, it tends neither to compromise nor to trust diplomacy. It tends, therefore, to decide in solitude, and to act unilaterally.[35] The Global War on Terror – with its declaration of a war against an abstract noun and an unknown enemy, effectively a declaration of perpetual war – only confirms this tendency. All of this has real and significant consequences for the United States' allies like Australia, for this is an intrinsic part of the nature of the power we chose to attach ourselves to.

It remains then to ask two questions: why is the Australia–US alliance so privileged and unchallenged in Australian security and strategic discourse? Now as much as ever, as Australia agrees to host US troops in Darwin from 2012. And what do we make of the claims made on the alliance's behalf? The first admits no easy answer because, ultimately, defenders of the alliance possess a temperament of conviction in things that can only be believed with their eyes and ears closed. Faith, in other words, is the currency here, not rationality. The second is definitely easier: the claims are at best the repetition of myth, at worst they are fiction. They have become, in the poetic turn of Dylan Thomas, 'the hissing of the spent lie'. Both reign nevertheless, standing reminders of a myth that is killed again and again, and again and again comes back to life.

Further reading

Commonwealth of Australia, *Defending Australia in the Asia-Pacific Century: Force 2030*, Defence White Paper 2009, Australian Government, Canberra, 2009.

R. Drinnon, *Facing West: The Metaphysics of Indian Hating and Empire Building*, Schocken Books, New York, 1990.

M. McKinley, 'Discovering the "idiot centre" of ourselves: Footnotes to the academic and intellectual culture of the Australian security policy discourse', *AntePodium: An Antipodean Journal of World Affairs*, 4, 1996.

——, 'The co-option of the university and the privileging of annihilation', *International Relations*, 18(2), 2004.

——, *Economic Globalisation as Religious War: Tragic Convergence*, Routledge, London, 2008.

M. McKinley (ed.), *The Gulf War: Critical Perspectives*, Allen & Unwin, Sydney, 1995.

B. Toohey & M. Wilkinson, *The Book of Leaks: Exposes in Defence of the Public's Right to Know*, Angus & Robertson, Sydney, 1987.

J. Vasquez, *The Power of Power Politics*, Rutgers University Press, New Jersey, 1983.

[12]

MONUMENTAL MISTAKE: IS WAR THE MOST IMPORTANT THING IN AUSTRALIAN HISTORY?

Peter Stanley

Although much of the thrust of writing about Australia in the twentieth century would lead you to think otherwise, war is not the only or the worst affliction that Australians suffered in this period. One small and personal case in point is the family of George Henderson Smith, killed on Gallipoli on 26 April 1915 with the 11th Battalion. The Australian War Memorial preserves the letters of condolence that his family received and the obituaries they collected. They make heart-breaking reading, and suggest the depth of the family's loss. But George's death seems not to have been the greatest trial that the Henderson Smiths suffered. George was the son of Perth businessman Robert Henderson Smith, who kept a detailed diary-cum-commonplace book. This diary, only available in the State Library of Western Australia in Perth, reveals that George's death was only one of the tribulations that his family and especially Robert faced during the war years. Robert's wife Eleanor had been mentally ill with 'delusions and nervous twitchings' from before the war. Their daughter Nell refused to accept her mother's condition, and indeed, Robert felt, was 'quite incapable of understanding'. Managing what seemed to be Nell's growing mental illness added to Robert's woes. Then early in 1917 another daughter, Barbara, suddenly sickened and died. Suffering himself from severe headaches and insomnia, Robert wrote in January 1918 that 'my life appears to be one long anxiety'. Later that year he wrote to the Claremont Hospital acknowledging that his wife's condition – what the doctor called 'deep-seated delusions' – had been 'a matter of great grief'. The strain made his surviving son Max 'nervy and irritable'. Nor did the Armistice bring peace. Nell's mental illness, Robert conceded in 1919, was also hopeless.[1] What was worse for the Henderson Smiths: the loss of George or the intractable, incurable mental illnesses of Eleanor and Nell? Whose loss hurt more: George's or Barbara's? Of course, there is no way to measure the suffering that Robert and his family bore. All we can say is that war was only a part of it.

So, finally, we come to the most persistent myth of all: that war is central to Australia's history, the biggest thing in it. This idea stems from the familiar idea that the landing on Gallipoli represented 'the birth of a nation'.[2] This proposition implies that history is a mystical rather than a human process, and no one ever actually explains what 'the birth of a nation' actually means. It is certainly a persistent idea. In July 2011, Air Chief Marshal Angus Houston accepted the appointment to chair the Anzac Centenary Advisory Board. In his first public pronouncement, Houston said that 'it was on the shore of Gallipoli and the battlefields of western Europe where our nation was defined, where our nation was born'. Air Chief Marshal Houston is not alone. Standing at Anzac Cove on Anzac Day 2010, young Melbourne builder Chris Barr declared 'This is where the history of our country begins'. At least Air Marshal Houston went on to say 'I relish the challenge in getting it right'.[3] Is he getting it right to make such a claim?

This idea that war is central to Australia's history and identity is, I confess, one I spent years fostering and justifying. When I worked at the Australian War Memorial (1980–2007), I would occasionally draft a speech or talk for someone more senior, and later for myself. In explaining the significance of military history to Australia – which it was part of my job to encourage – I often found myself adding a line to the effect that 'war has been one of the most significant influences on Australia's history and on the lives of its people'. Superficially, this statement seems justifiable, even self-evident. Consider the numbers involved in the world wars overseas, the colossal casualties, the magnitude of suffering or – and this was the clincher – the way that, in the wake of the Second World War, non-British migration changed Australia's demographic composition forever. No longer required to advocate the claims of military history for my daily bread, I am now, however, less sanguine about such rhetoric: indeed, some may see me as an apostate – one who recants a former item of faith. Has war really been so significant to Australia's experience of history as a nation? Should Australians today think that war as an historical force deserves a pre-eminent position? If not, what other aspects of the historical experience should we regard as equally or even more significant?

This chapter examines these questions in three ways. First, it looks at recent arguments critical of the centrality of Anzac Day in unduly skewing Australian history towards war. Second, it considers other aspects of Australian historical experience that could be used to complement the attention accorded to war in justifiable and proportional ways. Third, it considers the continuing case of the world war memorials proposed for the shore of Canberra's Lake Burley Griffin, as a way of evaluating whether or not war justifies its supposed centrality in Australia's history.

We do, however, need to keep this re-evaluation and these

questions in perspective, and strenuously avoid any suggestion that we might be decrying or denigrating those who experienced war and its effects, especially on individuals and families. No one would doubt the importance of wartime experience either for individuals or families, or as a significant factor in shaping crucial aspects of the national experience. In discussing the place of war in the national historical experience, we would do well to recall the 102 000 Australians who did not return from war, or the even more numerous Australians who returned wounded in mind or body. But the significance of war's effects on Australia can be magnified unduly, and this is increasingly the case. Anzac Day especially has been harnessed to serve the purposes of the state – since 11 September 2001 a state in a condition of 'war'. We might therefore begin by enquiring whether Anzac Day explains the primacy of war as the principal contemporary vehicle of Australia's national history.

In 2010 Marilyn Lake and Henry Reynolds published their provocative collection of essays *What's Wrong with Anzac?* With collaborators Mark McKenna and Joy Damousi, they argued that 'Australian history has been thoroughly militarised'. They argued that Anzac has become, as Mark McKenna put it, Australia's 'most powerful myth of nationhood'.[4] Military history has colonised the school curriculum, and dominated any other single aspect of Australia's history in popular publishing (with the possible exception of 'true crime'). Lake documented the extraordinary and unparalleled expansion in budgets devoted to promoting the study of war in Australian schools, an effort principally funded by the Department of Veterans' Affairs (DVA). 'Why', she asked, 'is one federal government department funded to produce history materials when other federal government departments are not?'[5] It is a telling question. The idea of Anzac enjoys a privileged place in education, and indeed in Australian life. Why is this?

In the rhetoric of Anzac Day today, 25 April 1915 marks the point when Australia 'became a nation' or 'gained nationhood'; at which, as Charles Bean put it, 'the consciousness of Australian nationhood was born'. As Mark McKenna asked in his chapter of *What's Wrong with Anzac?*, what did this do to the long history of the struggles for representative government in the Australian colonies; the creation of an Australian identity; the attainment of Federation in 1901; and the decade of nation-building that followed?

Contrary to post-Vietnam expectations of thirty years ago, Anzac Day has not died. In fact, it has gained in support, in numbers attending Anzac Day ceremonies at home and abroad, in the attention military history is accorded by publishers and the media, and in its place in school curricula. All of this essentially endorses a positive view of Australia's involvement in war, regardless of the historical circumstances of the conflict.

Barbecue chat analysis of the resurgence of Anzac Day generally gives John Howard (prime minister from 1996 to 2007) responsibility for encouraging, sanctioning, fostering or even funding the greater attention that Anzac Day received. As McKenna shows, however, in terms of the rhetoric of Anzac as the 'real Australian national day', the process began under Bob Hawke (prime minister 1983–1992). Certainly his successor Paul Keating (prime minister 1992–1996), whose government funded the 'Australia Remembers' year of 1995, must also bear a major share of the responsibility for what has effectively become a bipartisan support for elevating the standing of Anzac Day over the past twenty years. The result is that in the first decade of the twenty-first century, far from eroding, Anzac Day is entrenched as the *de facto* national day, eclipsing an Australia Day hampered by multiple disadvantages. Australia Day occurs during the summer holidays, enjoys lukewarm support outside New South Wales, and is seemingly fatally tainted by the connotation that it celebrates what is widely seen as the European invasion of the continent. These disabilities leave Anzac Day triumphantly in possession of the field, bolstered by the greater support it enjoys among the public, the media, governments and publishers all eager to establish it as the anniversary of Australia's supposed birth as a nation.

The tone is indeed 'triumphant'. Anzac Day has changed from being an occasion for public mourning for those sacrificed in an imperial cause to a celebration of those who died 'to keep Australia free'. The word that most often recurs on Anzac Day is not 'remembrance', 'sadness' or 'grief', and still less any expression of regret that Australia committed itself as a nation to so many conflicts in such a short national history. Rather, it is 'pride'. Many Australians are 'proud' of their nation's military history. They express pride in its volunteer tradition, in the way it 'punched above its weight' in war, of the skill, courage, ingenuity and general martial proficiency that Australian troops are said to have exhibited – all themselves myths already demolished in this book. Often Australians talk as if Australians alive today took part in the events that they commemorate: they talk about 'us' and 'we' even though no one alive today actually lived through or remembers the Great War . Now 'we' talk about 'us' on Gallipoli and 'Our Anzac pride', as the *Herald Sun* put it on 25 April 2010.

The sheer numbers of war dead – what I might formerly have called 'the magnitude of sacrifice' – might seem to explain why war has attracted such attention. War – and especially the Great War – saw such concentrated slaughter that it has tended to overwhelm or dull critical responses. Charles Bean's heartfelt observation that Pozières ridge is 'more densely sown with Australian sacrifice than any other place on earth' is always before us, and it takes an effort of will to look beyond it.[6] For example, it is true that one in five of those members of the Australian Imperial

Force (AIF) who served overseas died; but that does not equate to a fifth of Australian men or their families. Only about four in ten 'eligible' men volunteered to serve overseas, so perhaps something like one family in ten actually lost a son, husband or brother. Of course the question is complicated by what constitutes a 'family', and is bedevilled by double- or even triple-counting: many men would be both brothers and sons; some would be fathers too; tragically, some families lost more than one member. It is at least a long way from Philip Knightley's claim of one family in two. Not that anyone really knows. No one has done the detailed demographic and genealogical research required for a definitive answer. I am just suggesting we be careful. Arithmetic like this might seem either heartless or ghoulish. But it is necessary, because it requires a stern discipline to keep in perspective the lives that war has cost Australia over the course of the twentieth century, or at least in the first half of it.

One of the themes of this chapter is that Australians have been content to allow wars and war remembrance to become the preserve of uniformed members of the defence services. So note that while the figure of '60 000 dead in the Great War' is one of the most well-known Australian historical statistics, hardly anyone but specialist medical or social historians can tell you that 12 000 people, the great majority civilians, died in the influenza epidemic that followed in that war's immediate wake. Were these people not also victims of war? According to the Australian War Memorial, if they died in uniform they were, but as civilians they were not. Yet surely the flu victims were at least indirect victims of war, as much as soldiers who died accidentally before embarking for overseas service (who nonetheless qualify for the 'Roll of Honour'). Here the actual effects of a war are skewed because the idea of a Roll of Honour ascribes some civic virtue to the deaths recorded. This is a nonsense, of course: we surely ought to list

Australian deaths due to the Great War as 72 000, just as we routinely include civilian deaths in the death tolls of other wars: the Soviet Union in 1941–1945, say, or Korea in 1950–1953.

We can settle the question of war's effects for the second half of the century quite simply. It can be safely asserted that the experience of war left Australia largely untouched for the decades after 1950. The nation was technically fighting wars for about half of that half-century: in Korea for three years; Malaya for a decade; Vietnam for a further decade (the latter over-lapping with the 'Confrontation' with Indonesia); and the brief Gulf War occupying a few months in 1990–1991. These wars were largely fought by regular services, although conscripts provided about 40 per cent of the army's strength in Vietnam. Despite dramatic opposition to the Vietnam War in its final years (evoking comparisons with the turmoil of the conscription debates of 1916 and 1917), such anti-war feeling was both short-lived and had few enduring ramifications for society. The brief opposition to Australian involvement in the Gulf War had even less social or political aftermath. In short, in the second half of the twentieth century, war rarely intruded on Australian domestic concerns. (Again, this is not to deny the long-lasting effects on the 50 000-odd Australians who fought in Vietnam, or the small number of regular service personnel or families on whom the burden of the past decade of conflict has fallen.)

If we make a claim, however, for war's pre-eminence based on how many Australians have lost their lives fighting, perhaps we ought also to consider the argument that at least as many, or even more, have died from other causes worthy of regard. Data from the Australian Bureau of Statistics and other sources of longitudinal historical figures (such as *Australians a Historical Library* and, to be honest, *Wikipedia*) suggest that alternative causes of death warrant examination as historically significant.

The largest single cause of death in twentieth-century Australia (besides 'natural causes') has been motor vehicle accidents. The Australian Bureau of Statistics history of road fatalities refers to the historical 'war on the roads': from 1925 to the end of the century, over 160 000 Australians died in motor vehicle accidents.[7] Deaths due to road accidents increased as car ownership and reliance on road transport rose until some 3798 people died in 1970 alone. Since then the rate of accidents has fallen, due to innovations such as seat belts, drink-driving laws, safer cars and better driver behaviour. Still, in the decade of the 1990s just short of 20 000 Australians died in motor vehicle accidents; in the first five years of the twenty-first century 8283 died in road accidents and 143 000 were injured – almost as many as were wounded in the four years in the Great War. Considering these figures against Australia's losses in war we find that, in the course of just three years, as many Australians died on the roads as died, for instance, as prisoners of the Japanese. As many people died on Australia's roads as died at Tobruk over precisely the same time period. The effect is arguably greater among the living. Each year, three times as many Australians are injured in road accidents (about 30 000) as were wounded fighting Germany in the Second World War (about 9480).[8] Arguably, more Australians have been touched by the trauma of car accidents killing loved ones, friends or neighbours than have been affected by deaths in war, yet we do not see calls to erect a National Motor Vehicle Accident Memorial. The idea might seem almost offensive, but why should we not remember motor vehicle accident victims as comparable those who 'gave' their lives in war?

One of the most striking tables in the *Historical Statistics* volume of *Australians: A Historical Library* is devoted to infant mortality. It shows that, over the years of the two world wars respectively, no fewer than 33 000 and 30 000 infants died in

Australia. Certainly that is fewer than died as young men in battle, but in the five years following each war a further 42 000 and 25 000 died respectively, and they went on dying, year after year, regardless of whether the nation was at war.[9] Naturally the numbers and the proportion that died declined as hygiene and medical science improved (from annual figures of 10 000 in 1901 to just 2500 in 1979) but the total of deaths – about 600 000 in the course of the century – surely dwarfs the sum of misery inflicted by war. This everyday suffering is of course part of the human condition: but what makes it less worthy of notice? What memorial should it justify?

Similar cases could be made for remembering deaths from, say, tuberculosis, from various cancers, or from the quaintly named statistical category 'mental and nervous diseases'. Among such causes we might count suicide. Although nowhere as deadly in absolute numbers, suicide continues to take a shocking toll, especially among teenagers, and accounting for about a quarter of the deaths of all men in their early 20s. Just as deaths from suicide are distributed unevenly by age, so are they also disproportionately found geographically. In 1998, there were 1589 suicides in capital cities, 511 in other urban areas and 557 in rural areas. Given how urbanised is contemporary Australia, this 557 represents a much greater impact among young men in the country. The Bureau of Statistics explains these grossly disproportionate deaths by pointing to such factors as greater access to firearms, rapid technological changes and living in a climate of economic uncertainty.[10] In such figures are written the history of modern Australian rural life, its pressures and challenges – and its tragedies. It seems peculiar at best and grotesque at worst that a country should valorise on memorials in country towns the sacrifice of its young countrymen at places like the Nek and Beersheba, but ignore the experience of their counterparts a couple of generations away. To what degree are the Nek and suicide among rural young men two sides of a coin?

Suicide might be compared to the loss of life through drug use. Bureau of Statistics figures suggest that some 13 304 Australians died of 'drug-induced deaths' between 1991 and 2001. Calculating 'years of potential life lost' in 2001 alone gave a staggering total of 37 386 for, like soldiers, most of those dying were teenagers or young adults.[11] Again, these deaths are widely distributed and regarded as a private tragedy rather than a cause for public commemoration; and yet the loss to both families and the community must surely be as severe.

Then there are other causes of death that might seem worthy of remembrance. Taking the statistics for disasters or accidents resulting in more than ten deaths, we get the following indicative figures from 1788 to the present:

- Shipwrecks – at least 3000 deaths
- Heat waves – at least 2500 deaths
- Cyclones and storms – at least 1800 deaths
- Bushfires – over 800 deaths
- Industrial (mostly mine) accidents – 450 deaths
- Air accidents – at least 340 deaths
- Floods – at least 285 death
- Rail accidents – at least 230 deaths.[12]

These figures suggest the price that the continent exacts from those who live here: over 5000 people have died from cyclones, storms, bushfire and extreme temperatures. Several thousand people have died in ships bringing them to this country – including, recently, 50 asylum-seekers who are not included in the figure. As the response to the 2009 Black Saturday fires in Victoria demonstrated, Australians care deeply about those affected by such natural disasters. Speaking of the work of fire services,

Monumental mistake

Prime Minister Kevin Rudd described fire-fighters as Anzacs: but perhaps it would be more fitting to devote greater attention to those affected by such events in their own terms. Why does Australia as a nation accord greater privilege to a person in a khaki uniform than to someone in a yellow or orange overalls? Why should deaths in shipwrecks not be remembered as heroic and tragic? Why should the victims of mine disasters be forgotten when the victims of what might be called obscure and pointless imperial adventures of wars of diplomacy in south-east Asian jungles are valorised in perpetuity?

Such questions might seem impertinent; the answers may seem obvious. I think they are worth pondering. Realistically, however shocking these figures might be, it is unlikely that those who died from these non-warlike causes will be commemorated, for several reasons. Car accident deaths are horrific but rarely heroic. They are diffuse, spread across the nation. In the last decade about 20 000 Australians died on the roads, representing a death toll equal to that in the Vietnam War every three months. But because they occur in small numbers throughout the decade, and attract only local media attention unless the crashes are large or especially lethal, the effect is diminished. However tragic, deaths on the roads differ from death in war because deaths in war come in the service of the nation, and it is the nation that decides that they will be made a fuss of, whether that means a state funeral on return from Afghanistan, a huge and impressive national memorial or official commemoration. We tend to regard such commemoration as natural or organic or justifiable because Australia has always done it. But as a nation we can decide what we commemorate and how. We could as a nation choose to commemorate these losses as well as (not instead of) those who have died in war.

The point about deaths due to drug use, suicide or motor vehicle trauma is that they do not occur only when uniformed forces enter combat in battles overseas: they happen every day, in communities and homes and on roads in every part of Australia. They must surely have affected every single family in the country, in one form or another. Again, this is not to decry or diminish the deaths of those who have served and died in war. But it is important to consider them in perspective. We might ask: why would we as a nation especially remember those who die in one situation – in uniform often in battle – while so persistently ignoring other forms of death that also bring suffering and grief to families and loved ones? Are deaths in war different to deaths in peace-time? Of course they are. First, Australians who have died in war have usually (with two significant exceptions) placed themselves in danger of death voluntarily.[13] Second, and more significantly, those who have died in war have generally served formally as members of uniformed services. It is significant that the few exceptions – merchant seamen and civilians killed in bombing – are largely denied formal commemoration. At the Australian War Memorial, merchant seamen do not appear on the Roll of Honour but are consigned to panels on a memorial outside the building, while the civilian dead of Darwin, although buried in a Commonwealth War Graves Commission cemetery at Adelaide River, are not actually recorded in the Roll of Honour at all. This reminds us forcibly that commemoration in war in Australia is very firmly reserved for uniformed members of the armed services. In Australia, death in uniform (not in battle, mind, but in uniform) is accorded a privileged status.

So, many argue, should it be. They will remind us that Australia's war dead 'gave their lives'. They will remind us that many of those deaths came in horrific ways: cut to pieces by shrapnel on the Somme; succumbing to gas gangrene at Ypres; starving and ill on the Burma–Thailand railway; in lonely jungle clearings anywhere from Ambon to Bougainville. They will remind us that many died heroically: facing death in seemingly futile attacks on Gallipoli or at Fromelles; standing to their guns as ships sank; withstanding attacks by superior numbers at Isurava; and in actions from Pink Hill in South Africa in 1900 to nameless fire-fights in Afghan villages this very year. They will remind us that about a third of these deaths have left no trace, in that thousands were posted 'missing'. They will remind us that every one of those deaths left grieving families. All this is true. The 102 000 Australians who have died in war have often died in horrible ways, sometimes heroically but too often to no clear purpose, very often without trace and all leaving behind grieving loved ones. Yet it still does not adequately explain why war should be accorded such a privileged place in Australian history.

If Anzac Day is, as its proponents aver, a day devoted to remembrance (and not to the celebration of a bombastic national identity), then surely it could readily accommodate the remembrance of those Australians who have died other than in wartime? It could, but realistically it probably never will. Deaths in war are sanctioned, indeed, sanctified, by the nation. Remembrance is orchestrated by organised bodies such as ex-service organisations. No such large organisations speak for the victims of car accidents, suicide or drug use. The overall effect of this, however, is to skew our understanding of the experience of Australian history.

Surely many deaths – in a bush fire, by suicide, from an overdose – can be regarded as just as horrible as deaths in war? Surely deaths due to suicide or drugs, or to a speeding teenage driver, can be seen as equally futile? Surely every death leaves a family distraught, asking unanswerable questions about why a young man or woman has died? They do: but deaths other than war are not remembered publicly because war occupies a privileged place in the way we as a nation think of our history. In this Marilyn Lake is right. No other aspect of Australian history has anything remotely as powerful as its own agents whose task is to lobby to ensure that that aspect is accorded such prominence. Indeed, so much do we take for granted this privileging of military history that to point it out is at first sight either ludicrous or sacrilegious, like asking why we wear trousers and skirts or, say, why we accord everyone the vote. It is so intimately a part of the texture of our society that to question it is to contest a fundamental assumption. Of all comparable Western democracies, however, only Australia accords war service and sacrifice a ministry of government (in the Department of Veterans' Affairs) that enjoys such influence. This is not to mention its own national museum in the Australian War Memorial – indeed, the most handsomely funded and largest museum in the country. What other aspect of Australian history is accorded its own national day? Why should that be?

The answer is only partly that war, and specifically the world wars, were events of such profound effect on Australian society that they justified a response in keeping with the magnitude of the effects. After all, other countries, ones even more profoundly affected by one or both of the wars, did not do all or most of these things. But the Australia of 1914–1918 and 1939–1945 recognised the magnitude of sacrifice by creating enduring ways of remembering. Among other things they created a vast administrative edifice of 'repatriation' to care for those affected by war, erected memorials in every state capital, town and suburb, built national memorials in Canberra, at Villers Bretonneux and Gallipoli, supported the creation of war cemeteries and commissioned series of official histories and the archival collections that sustained them. (And note that except for the construction of state and local memorials, this huge effort was almost all undertaken by agencies of the national government.) All this was understandable (even if it was actually rather more than comparable countries did). It was arguably a fitting response by those actually affected by war.

Nowadays, however, with the increasing commoditisation of the Anzac 'brand', war is being promoted as central to the Australian historical experience. This process has been occurring for over a decade, regardless of political party in power and more as a response to bureaucratic enterprise and the centralising imperatives of media and 'event management' than by conscious manipulation. In 2003 the then prime minister, John Howard, proclaimed – at the opening of the Australian War Memorial in London – that 'Anzac Day remains more evocative of the Australian spirit than any other day in our calendar'.[14]

The effect of this argument and perception is to diminish other manifestations of 'the Australian spirit'. There are, perhaps, many contenders for ways of evoking the Australian spirit – whatever that may be. A cursory list could encompass qualities such as the stamina of convicts; the mateship of bushmen; the endurance of colonial pioneers; the boldness of settlers; the enterprise of gold-seekers; the initiative of migrants (of any period); the attachment to fairness by those who strove for justice; the egalitarianism of members of the labour movement; the resilience of Indigenous people; and so on. Each of us could find historical models representing 'Australian values'. Each of these archetypes, and the qualities they could represent, has been celebrated in songs, stories, literature, art, history and fiction. None, however, has gained anything like the popular attention and regard as has the archetype of the 'digger', partly at least because government has sedulously cultivated no other aspect of Australian history. Clearly, the labour movement has a sectional appeal, as do Indigenous heroes: the digger, however, can be represented as apolitical, and able to encompass all military endeavour, adapting from the classic citizen soldier of the world wars to the regular ethos of the Australian Defence Force as it has developed over the decades after 1945.

As we have seen, the periodic trauma of the two world wars was – thankfully – not repeated in the succeeding half century or later. Korea and Vietnam brought suffering to families, but had no major impact on the nation as a whole. Yet involvement in further wars was incorporated into the rhetoric of Anzac, sometimes seamlessly, sometimes with some stretching, but all bolstered, especially in the past decade, by a concerted effort by government to maintain the privileged position that war exerts over the national historical understanding. The result is that it has been possible to assert that military history's archetypal digger remains 'more evocative of the Australian spirit' than any other figure.

One of the principal ways this occurs is that Anzac Day has become a commodity, able to be managed and indeed manipulated. Anzac Day brings an annual flood of emotion, some of it heartfelt and raw, some ersatz and some frankly manufactured. Still, in 2012 there are several Australian families this Anzac Day who will be remembering Australian soldiers who were alive last Anzac Day. This has been going on now for the past decade, and shows no sign of ending. That alone makes the day different now, and we need to respect that emotion. But Anzac Day overwhelmingly relates to a war that happened almost a century ago. As the centenary of the Great War approaches, we see no diminution of interest in that conflict; rather the opposite. This growing interest can be exaggerated. Much is made, for instance, of the back-packer phenomenon on Gallipoli, although many fewer young people visit Gallipoli than go to Surfers Paradise or Bali for 'schoolies week'. Still, we can agree that interest in the Great War generally is not diminishing. The recent release of the recommendations of the bipartisan Centenary of Anzac Commission suggests that even if Australians do not actually know much about the war (or the century of conflict that followed it) they somehow know that it is important and think that the government ought to be doing something about it.

This relationship with the Great War is often seen sentimentally. Popular treatment of it often proceeds from quite misleading assumptions. For example, there is a presumption that it is a part of every Australian family's history, that we all have a personal connection to Gallipoli or the Somme (or Kokoda or Changi or wherever). In the Australian War Memorial's excellent on-line gallery, which provides terminals for visitors to search databases and digitised sources, a sign invites visitors to look up 'relatives' who served in war. The assumption is clear. The arithmetic as ever eludes me, but with only 40 per cent of Australian men actually serving in the war of 1914–1918, and at least 40 per cent (and probably more than half) of today's population hailing from elsewhere, the chances that any given Australian visitor to the War Memorial has an Anzac in the family is probably quite remote. For most visitors, the Anzac is most likely related to someone else. War memory, therefore, arguably belongs most directly to old Anglo-Celtic families who know of and value their direct connections with those who served in or lived through the Great War. Logically, even if we count connections made by marriage, they must be a relatively small minority. So even though the loss of 60 000 dead in that war traumatised a society of 5 million, looking at that loss through a demographic telescope in 2011 reveals a relatively small impact on or connection with most people in a nation now of over 22 million. Still, the myth persists. A web-based amateur essayist asserts that 'Anzac has become a central part of family life and an element in the transmission of family memories'.[15] Plainly, though, it is not for everyone, or even most. One of the challenges that the Anzac Centenary Commission faces is to find ways to enable non-Anglo-Celtic Australians to understand Anzac Day.

For this essentially minority interest to remain of such central concern, several main carriers work to perpetuate and transmit the idea of Anzac: government; veterans' groups and the media. Each has a legitimate interest in and agenda for continuing to commemorate Anzac Day, and each contributes to the way the day is marked. Although they constitute a minority, no one would deny that large numbers of the descendants of 'old Australians' regard the day as a significant part of their identification with family, community and nation. No one would deny the sincere and just attachment they hold towards the day and all it represents. There are, however, limits to that attachment, as the case of the proposed new world war memorials in Canberra suggests.

One of the tests of whether war occupies a prime position in Australia's conception of its history might be seen in the erection of – or the failure to erect – two memorials to the world wars on the shore of Lake Burley Griffin in Canberra. The debate over the need for and nature of these edifices exposes the arguments relevant to this myth. Here is the story, so far.

In 2005 the private company Memorial(s) Development Committee (MDC) proposed to the National Capital Authority (NCA, the agency responsible for the federal areas of Canberra) that it approve two new memorials dedicated to Australia's involvement in the two world wars. The NCA swiftly and seemingly enthusiastically endorsed this proposal, and steered the plan through the National Capital Memorials Committee (a committee nominally chaired by the prime minister). The company comprised a group of ex-servicemen, ex-officers of no outstanding public profile; most, except its spokesman, former army officer Mike Buick, remain effectively anonymous. But they soon acquired influential friends and supporters. The NCA entered into a favourable memorandum of understanding with the MDC, and the National Capital Memorials Committee both endorsed the idea and (on the NCA's recommendation) allocated the proposed memorials a lake-side site on what is known as the Rond Terraces. Successive governors general – Michael Jeffrey and then Quentin Bryce (and Mr Michael Bryce) – accepted invitations to become MDC's patrons. The MDC claim to have obtained the support of two prime ministers – John Howard and then Kevin Rudd – and between the two prime ministerial endorsements the Department of Veterans' Affairs donated $250 000 to conduct a design competition.

By late 2008 the MDC had seemingly secured a prime site, bipartisan political backing, an architect and a design, and only awaited NCA approvals (and donations of $21–25 million) before work to erect the memorials could commence. The proposed design, by Brisbane firm Richard Kirk, comprised two 20-metre monoliths incorporating various design elements, including a 'field' of illuminated poppies and ideas such as panels listing Australia's 100 000 world war dead by the communities from which they hailed.[16] After five years of representations at the highest levels of government, the MDC's members, faceless or not, could have had reason to believe that once they had secured enough of the (somewhat sizeable) donations they required, their task was within sight of accomplishment.

The MDC's plans, however, had not gone unnoticed by several interested parties. Members of the Walter Burley Griffin Society expressed concern that the proposed memorials compromised one of the principal elements in Walter and Marion Mahoney Burley Griffins' vision for the design of Canberra. A quite different group, the Medical Association for the Prevention of War, noticed that the memorial represented a massive and prominent endorsement of a militarist conception of Australian history, and that it would probably only be possible by donations from arms manufacturers and companies that made their profits through defence contracts. Individuals who valued or used the lake shore and felt that the memorials would unjustifiably curtail broader, community-based uses of the Rond Terraces also began to feel or express unease. Each time the proposal was mentioned in the *Canberra Times*, it attracted a flurry of letters expressing concern or outright opposition.

The MDC issued a brochure explaining its proposal, a document that suggested both that it was ignorant of the setting and indeed of the history to which it professed to be devoted. It depicted the 'two massive granite memorials' on what it seemed to think was called 'Anzac Avenue'. (Not only is the boulevard called 'Anzac Parade', but the Rond Terraces are not on it.) The MDC also seemed unaware that a major national memorial service occurred at the Australian War Memorial at dawn each Anzac Day. How else could they propose that their memorial be illuminated by the rising sun at dawn on 25 April? Further, the MDC seemed uncertain whether the memorials would commemorate all those who served, or only those who died. In endorsing the project, its 'inception patron', Tim Fischer (a serial supporter of wacky military historical ideas, such as pardoning the convicted multiple murderer 'Breaker' Morant) explained that it would allow 'Nurse Vivian Bullwinkel of Sandakan' (a place Sister Bullwinkel never saw) and Roden Cutler 'of the Syrian campaign' (a country Roden Cutler never saw) to gain 'collective recognition'.[17] Presumably by some perverse reasoning, arguably the two best known veterans of the Second World War needed to be remembered in some additional way. The brochure revealed that MDC's proposal, although supported at high levels, was at best half-baked.

In October 2010, the various groups which had individually expressed opposition came together as the Lake War Memorials Forum, a loose coalition of concerned citizens. Some represented groups such as the Walter Burley Griffin Society or the Medical Association for the Prevention of War, others (such as several architects or historians) acting as individuals. The forum was formed without a formal constitution or office-bearers, but out of groups acting in broad concert. Its campaigning coalesced after a report on the Canberra ABC television program *Stateline*. Opponents from these various groups expressed their views – that the memorials embodied an unwelcome militarism, conflicted with Griffin's vision, and unnecessarily sought to duplicate (and detract from) the functions of the Australian War Memorial. Crucial to the forum's case was the covert nature of the process that the MDC and the NCA had followed thus far. The MDC's members had not, however, sought or welcomed public comment on the proposal. Indeed, they had assumed that the Australian community would accept as self-evident that commemoration of war was unquestioned. The following six months were to disabuse them of that comfortable assumption. It is this response that makes the case of the lake war memorials so relevant to discussion of the myth in question.

The MDC's case for the erection of the memorials was disarmingly simple: indeed, it comprised only one (highly arguable) proposition. It argued that, as several other conflicts in which Australia had participated were represented in memorials on Anzac Parade, why should not the two world wars. The MDC discounted the Australian War Memorial, a massive edifice a few hundred metres distant at the head of Anzac Parade. It argued disingenuously that, because it commemorated the Australian dead of *all* wars, it did not constitute a memorial to the world wars (conveniently ignoring that 100 000 of the 102 000 names on its Roll of Honour related to those wars). Although this argument seemed to convince no one who was not an office-bearer of the NCA, it had sufficed to gain the MDC a prime spot of commemorative real estate, and soon afterwards government funding for a design competition.

Despite consistent opposition in the local press, between its inception in 2005 and late 2010 the MDC had never actively tested its proposal against public opinion. On 21 October 2010, however, it held a small 'consultation' at the Ainslie Football Club. The event involved about a dozen invited guests and mostly comprised presentations by MDC's architects or consultants, explaining and justifying the choice of site and design. When some of those present questioned the need for the memorials they were firmly told that such questions were beyond the scope of the gathering.[18] The MDC disdained debate. Its vice chairman replied to a three-page letter discussing counter-arguments merely with 'your unsurprising opinions are noted and do not dissuade either I or my fellow committee members from our purpose'.[19]

By contrast, the Lake War Memorials Forum adopted an essentially open approach, creating a website and inviting contributions and comments, posting copies of all letters to the editor, articles and op-ed pieces that appeared, regardless of whether they were for or against the memorials. In fact, virtually all the comment that appeared, on the forum's website or in the media generally was opposed to the memorials, and overwhelmingly so. The forum website invited visitors to 'vote' and leave a comment, using software that prevented multiple votes. As of 18 July 2011, 356 people had voted – all but eight against the proposed memorials. Many also left comments. Most were Canberrans, but there were dozens of people from interstate. Several common trends became apparent, as in these representative contributions:

> I am an ex-servicewoman and mother of a serving soldier.
> What more can be said about World Wars that is not already conveyed by the AWM?
> O'Connor, ACT

> Apart from looking pretty ugly, I express concern on behalf of my father, now deceased ... he would be horrified at this glorification of war.
> Birchgrove, NSW
>
> I believe that those courageous and honourable souls who gave so much ... would not seek this 'extra' glorification.
> Evatt, ACT
>
> While I pay my respects to the fallen – after all, my grandparents lost 9 relatives, cousins and closer, in the two world wars ... I believe a line has to be drawn before we get to warrior worship.
> Ryde, NSW[20]

More than one letter to the *Canberra Times* began 'my immediate family lost two members in each of the world wars ...'. Others, such as historian Professor John Mulvaney – who decried the memorials as 'vulgar and costly blots on the landscape' – were veterans but did not say so.[21] The newspaper's correspondence columns, which had become a principal site of debate, showed the proportion of letters against the proposal far outweighed those agreeing with it: over eighty letters appeared, with fewer than six arguing in its favour. On radio a similar proportion prevailed. While Canberra's federal representatives (of both parties) proved to be wary of doing anything as risky as expressing an opinion, Mike Buick was and has remained virtually the only MDC representative speaking publicly for the memorials.

In contrast to the MDC, the Lake War Memorials Forum welcomed public comment, holding a public meeting in the Albert Hall. A dozen notable figures spoke against the proposal. They included novelists and poets such as Marion Halligan and

Geoff Page, journalists and historians such as Geoff Pryor and Michael McKernan, heritage experts such as Dianne Firth, and included both a former director of the Australian War Memorial, Brendon Kelson, and a former chief of the Air Force, Air Marshal David Evans. The striking feature of the meeting, which voted unanimously against the memorials, was that almost all of the participants were over 50, and that opposition to the memorials came from precisely the generation that might have been expected to be most favourably disposed toward them. A great many of those objecting to the memorials were in fact children of Second World War veterans. Indeed, soon afterwards, the two largest RSL sub-branches in the ACT voted unanimously to 'not support' the memorials. Even the director of the Australian War Memorial, Major General Steve Gower, published his view that the proposal was 'unconvincing' and he later spoke against it to a Joint Standing Committee on the subject.[22]

It would seem that if various commentators from a retired air marshal, the children of world war veterans and the director of the Australian War Memorial have spoken in concert, the MDC has misjudged Australians' willingness to accept the endless commemoration of the two world wars. While the great majority of those who attended the meeting and who responded to the forum's website support the existence and the work of existing commemorative institutions, notably the Australian War Memorial, there is a definite and vocal move against the creation of further monuments to war. Soon after, the Report of the Anzac Centenary Commission reached a similar conclusion. It had commissioned social research which found that 'there was no particular need seen for a new permanent memorial to be established to mark the 100th anniversary of Anzac Day'.[23]

The fate of the world war memorials is not yet decided. Thanks to some energetic work in alerting ordinary citizens to their nature and likely impact, and some effective counter-lobbying by some of the members of the forum, the memorials' fate is a great deal less certain than it was. This also, therefore, suggests that concerns over the paramountcy of war in Australian history as a whole might be less acute than Marilyn Lake and Henry Reynolds feared. Perhaps the ultimate failure of the lake war memorials proposition – as I believe it will fail – will come to be seen as the turning point in Australia's love-affair with war.

What do we make of all this? We have a fairly clear disjunction between the way many Australians view their military history (essentially uncritically) and the way many historians regard it (dismayed by the way official agencies have fostered an unbalanced view of Australia's history). We see that one aspect of the Australian historical experience – war – increasingly tends to crowd out or overwhelm all other aspects, even though many other parts of Australia's history are worthy of attention and empathy. We find that when a small group in Canberra propose to erect monolithic new memorials to the world wars, large numbers of the children and grandchildren of those who served in those wars go to some trouble to oppose the idea. We find that despite official support for the memorials, large numbers of ordinary Australians (that is, *not* historians) turn out to public meetings, submit comments to websites and write to newspapers complaining that there is more to Australia than war and that a memorial duplicating the existing Australian War Memorial is not needed or wanted.

So, is war the most important single thing to have happened in Australia's history? Three years away from the events that will happen at Anzac Cove on 25 April 2015, the prospect of treating Australian military history in proportion seems to hang in the balance. On the one hand, assuming that the push from government, the media, populist publishers and authors to celebrate Anzac will not abate, we can probably expect to see the myth entrenched. On the other hand, if more historians and their readers and viewers take a more critical approach to military history, try to keep it in perspective and show that other aspects of the Australian historical experience are compelling, significant and important, then perhaps 2015 will see Australian history in better shape.

Journalist Paul Kelly wrote on Anzac Day 2011 that 25 April is said to have become 'entrenched as the authentic national day', describing the annual AFL match at the Melbourne Cricket Ground as 'an open-air shrine'. But he also looked forward to 2015, to an Anzac Day that is 'a muscular event, strong enough to tolerate different views, on guard against too much emotionalism and intellectually honest about the history'.[24] We can certainly hope so.

Further reading

K. Inglis, *Sacred Places: War Memorials in the Australian Landscape*, Melbourne University Press, Melbourne, 2008.

Lake War Memorial Forum, website, <www.lakewarmemorialsforum.org>, (accessed 26 September 2011).

M. Lake & H. Reynolds (eds), *What's Wrong with Anzac? The Militarisation of Australian History*, UNSW Press, Sydney, 2010.

Parliament of Australia, Joint Standing Committee on the National Capital and External Territories, *Inquiry into the Administration of the National Memorials Ordinance 1928*, 2011, <www.aph.gov.au/house/committee/ncet/memorials/subs.htm>, (accessed 26 September 2011).

EPILOGUE

Every page of this book challenges some of the more grievous misconceptions of this nation's military past. Yet the list is not exhaustive. There remain fables left untouched, and conflicts left uncovered. As long as modern-day Australian nationalism, our sense of self, and collective identity are sourced from the imagery of past military conflicts, we will continue to draw what we need from the past without worrying too much about actually occurred.

If our contemporary social and psychological need to venerate the concept of 'Anzac' continues – as both a national day of celebration and a wider anchor of what it might mean to be an Australian – then the Allied invasion of Turkey in 1915 will persist as the birthplace of the Australian military tradition. Similarly, as long as the name and connotations of 'Anzac' are evoked so regularly, and used so widely to re-affirm the ties between Australians and New Zealanders, then the origins of the relationship will be glossed over in favour of modern warm and satisfying feelings of military kinship reflected backwards. Whenever we feel anxious about the moral legitimacy or practical utility of the conflicts in which we have found (and still find) ourselves, then we will fall back into the comforting solace of having been tricked, coerced or blindly stumbled into other people's wars. There is no guilt, no recrimination and no need for reflection under this mistaken interpretation. In much the same way, the social, ideological or intellectual need to include Australian women within the Anzac fable, and a general refusal to accept Australian military experiences within a global context, will continue the distorted historical representation of female involvement in the nation's wars. The same sort of thing might be said of the impact of Hollywood imagery, or more agenda-driven interpretations of specific conflicts like Vietnam, which continue to resist or retard detailed and realistic analyses of the experience of Australian troops abroad. As long as Anzac imagery remains heavily focused on 'diggers', mud, trenches and bayonets, then the experiences and contributions of those who fought at sea – and in the air for that matter – will remain under-represented.

The contemporary Anzac legend has become an idealised representation of the values most of us aspire to, or even imagine we possess simply as part of the label 'Australian'. It continues to prompt popular interpretations of real historical events that may only have a tenuous connection to fact. The archetypical Anzac is physically imposing, mentally stoic, yet mercurial in spirit. He is rough around the edges, but has an unflappable sense of fair play, natural justice, and deep democratic urges. He fights hard but plays by the rules. He is distinct insofar as he is an eager volunteer with no desire to kill, but rather resigned to do his terrible duty by his nation and his mates. He is not a conscript, for compulsion is too close to reluctance. He is, unfortunately, far too often let down by the incompetence of his military and political leaders. His mistakes, such as they are, are not really his. He may be uneducated and unruly, but he is nonetheless clever. Perhaps he had to be, coming from the bush? He is always white. Essentially masculine, 'he' cannot comfortably be a 'she' – despite the degree the legend is often twisted in an attempt to make such an accommodation. Those who fail to fit this mould, or fail to celebrate it, run the risk, perhaps, of seeming un-Australian.

So long as such stereotypes exist, so long as such nonsense

drowns out the more complex and less idealised reality, then deeper understandings of Australians in war, their actions as human beings in extraordinary circumstances, and the purposes, conditions and reasons for their sacrifices, will remain difficult to grasp. The power of such ill-informed imagery has real, identifiable and ongoing effects. The indomitable, glorified Anzac image pushes politicians, policy-makers and the public alike to sprout the flawed preconceptions that Australian troops invariably 'punch above their weight'. Such chimeras are dangerous foundations for historical interpretation, not to mention contemporary decision-making at all levels.

At a deep and fundamental level, the power of Anzac and the dominance of military history within the national 'story' tends to subordinate, subsume and suffocate the non-military aspects of Australia's past. And there are many: we were one of the first nations in the world where all men and women had the vote, for example, and we have always enjoyed, in general terms, remarkably high levels of education, health, political and social freedoms, and high standards of living for such a young country. There are countless inspiring and heroic slices of the Australian historical saga that do not require war-oriented myth-making – or its associated exaggeration, sanitation or fabrication. Some readers will find it ironic that the authors of this volume, mainly people who earn a living as military historians or professional historians with at least a passing interest in military affairs, are the first to concede this point. Australia and Australians are far more than the sum of their military past.

There is no doubt that the myths and misunderstandings addressed in this book fulfil important social needs. That they are untrue may seem largely beside the point. But they *are* not true – and we should not forget it. Such ideas are historical fiction, not history. As far as the authors of this book are concerned, accuracy, impartiality, attempts at rational objectivity – what might be called the search for 'truth' – matter. They are important. They mean something worthwhile. They fill a social need as well, perhaps even a higher one.

The 'Anzac legend' is probably the most frequent phrase in *Anzac's Dirty Dozen*. This is unavoidable. The whole issue of myth-making in regard to the military heritage of this country is complicated by what has become our national 'founding' story – the idea of Anzac. Like most national myths, Anzac is based on inspiring narratives, concepts and images about a country's past. It can represent what we want to unite us and affirms a set of self-perceived national values. It contains symbolic meaning and often serves social and political purposes. In some respects Anzac fulfils what might be called a secular religious function. Importantly, it is based on, but does not necessarily reflect, historical fact. The Anzac myth involves fictionalised exaggerations of actual incidents. It commonly disregards inconvenient historical details, and subverts or reinvents the past to fit the legend. Prior to 1914, Australians saw themselves as part of the mighty British Empire and were proud of that fact. Concepts of Australian nationhood were complicated by shared imperial heritage as a Dominion and strong continuing connections with 'the mother country'. To many early twentieth-century Australians, their country lacked one key experience, which to that generation mattered above all others: Australia had not yet, as a nation, faced a trial by arms.

From the first news of Australian participation in the British amphibious assault on the Dardanelles in 1915, Australians were told that their country had at last 'come of age'. Deeds at Gallipoli, and later in Flanders and Palestine, filled a vacuum for the newborn nation. During the inter-war period, the idea of 'Anzac' came to represent a distinct collection of values, both real and imagined. It embodied the perceived comradeship of frontline soldiers, the rejection of conventional discipline, physical strength, egalitarianism, loyalty, self-sacrifice, courage and early twentieth-century Australian conceptions of masculinity. It was centred on success, not defeat. Even at its genesis, a marked strategic failure like Gallipoli was redefined as a triumph of endurance and a celebration of 'Australian' virtues.

As part of the developing Australian national consciousness, the interwar period saw the glorification of the martial achievements of newly returned servicemen. The legend grew into an inescapable social force increasingly tied to the core of national identity. Its powerful symbolism permeated all aspects of life. It was reproduced in schools, championed by veterans' associations claiming to represent the body of men at the heart of the legend, and reaffirmed on 25 April each year at various memorial 'shrines', large and small, in every Australian city and town worthy of the name. Even the word 'Anzac' became sacred and legally protected under various Acts in 1920.

In times of crisis, turmoil or soul-searching, societies usually fall back on national traditions. For Australians, even now, it is Anzac. And the legend is getting stronger. The number of politicians invoking rousing Anzac rhetoric, the size of Anzac Day marches (despite the dwindling number of 'traditional' veterans), the number of Australians on annual 'pilgrimages' to Anzac Cove, flag in hand or draped over their shoulders – is evidence enough of this.

The authors of this book recognised from the beginning that the subjects we were taking on, and our conclusions, might set us on a collision course with the Anzac legend. At one level, we embrace this: legend should not substitute for history. It is a myth, and however powerful and pervasive, it has in fundamental ways obscured more about the past than it has revealed.

But at another level there is no collision. We are historians. In no way do we seek to undermine the foundations of Anzac just for the sake of appearing subversive. Nor do we reject the idea that some social good can flow from the Anzac legend – despite the exclusive nature of its white, Anglo-Saxon, male and 'macho' orientation. All we ask is that legend not be mistaken for history.

Let us conclude with the words of an official historian, someone who was there. Our book has examined key and thematic issues in Australian military history. It has applied an analytical torch to subjects more used to veneration and commemoration than to rigorous analysis. Yet in military history, critiquing a misinterpretation is not the same as criticising the participants. We do not minimise, undermine or forget the sacrifices made by Australian servicemen and women of years past. On the contrary, we honour them, but we do so with an objective recognition of their deeds. We honour them as rational, reflective people, ordinary human beings, not fabricated myths. Surely they are worthy of as much. As Charles Bean wrote of the real Anzacs, let us once again reaffirm that 'nothing can alter now' what such individuals accomplished:

> The good and the bad, the greatness and the smallness of their story will stand. Whatever the glory it contains nothing can now lessen. It rises, and will always rise, above the mists of ages, a monument to great-hearted man; and, for their nation, a possession forever.[1]

NOTES

1 Australian military history doesn't begin on Gallipoli
Craig Wilcox

1 Pooley to Maj. Sherbon, 12 November 1912, Mitchell Library, ML MSS 1261/3.
2 K. Windschuttle, 'The myths of frontier massacres', parts 1–3, *Quadrant*, October–December 2000; and *The Fabrication of Aboriginal History*, vol. 1, Macleay, Sydney, 2002.
3 K.S. Inglis 'Anzac: The substitute religion' (first published 1960), in his *Observing Australia*, Melbourne University Press, Melbourne, 1999, ch. 3; and *Sacred Places: War Memorials in the Australian Landscape*, Miegunyah Press, Melbourne, 1998.
4 D. Horner, *Australia's Military History for Dummies*, Wiley, Brisbane, 2010, p. 71.
5 *Adelaide Register*, 14 February 1921, p. 5.
6 P. Kelly, 'The next Anzac century', *Weekend Australian*, 23–24 April 2011, Inquirer, p. 2.
7 *The Australian*, 25 April 2011, p. 7.
8 K. O'Brien & M. Peacock, 'War Memorial battle over frontier recognition', *7.30 Report*, Australian Broadcasting Corporation, 26 February 2009; *Canberra Times*, 23 December 2010, p. 5.
9 J. Laffin, *Anzacs at War*, Horwitz, Sydney, 1982 (first published 1965), ch. 2; N. Bleszynski, *Shoot Straight, You Bastards!*, Random House, Sydney, 2003 (first published 2002), pp. 159–63.
10 B. Beresford (director), *Breaker Morant*, South Australian Film Corporation, 1979; Bleszynski, *Shoot Straight, You Bastards!*
11 For example E. Willmot, *Pemulwuy, the Rainbow Warrior*, Weldon, Sydney, 1987; P.W. Newbery (ed.), *Aboriginal Heroes of the Resistance*, Action for World Development, Sydney, 1999 (first published 1988), part 1.
12 Notably I. Clendinnen, *Dancing With Strangers*, Text, Melbourne, 2003.
13 J.H. Elliott, 'The very violent road to America', *New York Review of Books*, 9 June 2011, pp. 64–67.
14 Two notable contributions have been H. Reynolds, *The Other Side of the Frontier*, James Cook University, Townsville, 1981, and P. Stanley, 'Soldiers and fellow countrymen in colonial Australia', in M. McKernan & M. Browne

(eds.), *Australia: Two Centuries of War and Peace*, Australian War Memorial, Canberra, 1988.
15 I. Keen, *Aboriginal Economy and Society*, Oxford University Press, Melbourne, 2003, p. 264.
16 A.W. Howitt, *The Native Tribes of Southeast Australia*, Aboriginal Studies Press, Canberra, 1996 (first published 1904), pp. 351–52.
17 H. Allen (ed.), *Australia: William Blandowski's Illustrated Encyclopaedia of Aboriginal Australia*, Aboriginal Studies Press, Canberra, 2010 (plate first published 1862), p. 129.
18 J. Connor, 'The frontier war that never was', in C. Stockings (ed.), *Zombie Myths of Australian Military History*, UNSW Press, Sydney, 2010, ch. 1; *The Australian Frontier Wars*, UNSW Press, Sydney, 2002.
19 T.F. Bride (ed.), *Letters from Victorian Pioneers*, Government Printer, Melbourne, 1898, pp. 43, 151–53, 187.
20 J. Grey, *A Military History of Australia*, Cambridge University Press, Melbourne, 2008 (first published 1990), p. 39; Horner, *Australia's Military History for Dummies*, p. 49.
21 *The Australian*, 26 June 2008, p. 3; Battle for Australia Commemoration National Council, 'Battle for Australia' website, <www.battleforaustralia.org.au>.
22 *Sydney Herald*, 16 July 1832, p. 2.
23 See for example *Sydney Morning Herald*, 22 March 1858, p. 2; *Argus* (Melbourne), 19 July 1860, p. 5.
24 *Advertiser* (Adelaide), 27 July 1860, p. 2.
25 A. Jose, 'Sydney and district in 1824 as described by a French visitor', *Royal Australian Historical Society Journal and Proceedings*, 10(4), 1924, p. 222.
26 *Record of the Imperial Representative Corps Trip Australia and New Zealand 1900–1901*, Army & Navy Cooperative Society, London, 1901, p. 44.
27 D. Horner (ed.), *The Battles that Shaped Australia*, Allen & Unwin, Sydney, 1994.
28 E.W. O'Sullivan, *The Power of Mounted Riflemen*, Age, Queanbeyan, 1894, conclusion.
29 Report by Maj. Gen. James Bevan Edwards on local forces and scheme for organising Australia's military forces, Qld *Journals of the Legislative Council*, 1889, 39(1), p. 779.
30 Evidence by Col. Stokes to Royal Commission into the NSW military service, NSW *Votes and Proceedings of the Legislative Assembly*, 1892, 7(52), p. 162.
31 C.N. Connolly, 'Manufacturing spontaneity: The Australian offers of troops to the Boer War', *Historical Studies*, 18(70), April 1978, pp. 106–117; L.M. Field, *The Forgotten War*, Melbourne University Press, Melbourne, 1979, ch. 1.
32 Gov. Gormanston to secretary of state for colonies, 6 March 1900, UK National Archives, CO 280/403, f. 57 (microfilmed by the Australian Joint Copying Project).
33 Nearly 5000 men joined Boer War contingents from late December to mid-1900 (C. Wilcox, *Australia's Boer War*, Oxford University Press, Melbourne, 2002, pp. 391–407); a net 6568 became citizen soldiers in 1900 (N. Meaney, *The Search for Security in the Pacific*, Sydney University Press, Sydney, 1976, p. 271); and more than 19 000 joined rifle clubs during the same year (*Year-Book of Australia for 1900*, pp. 626–33; *Year-Book of Australia for 1901*, pp. 601–609).

34 Wilcox, *Australia's Boer War*, pp. 102–108, 346.
35 Gen. Carew to Maj. Poore, 19 June 1900, [UK] National Archives, WO 105/19, T/36/2.
36 *Sydney Morning Herald*, 9 May 1900, p. 7.
37 R. Kipling, *Traffics and Discoveries*, Macmillan, London, 1904, p. 87.
38 C.J. Dennis, *The Moods of Ginger Mick*, Sydney University Press, Sydney, 2009 (first published 1916); C.E.W. Bean, 'The Australian', *Sydney Morning Herald*, 22 June 1907, p. 6; and *The Story of Anzac*, Angus & Robertson, Sydney, 1941, vol. 1, pp. 46–47.
39 *Christian Science Monitor*, 18 February 1911, p. 30.
40 J. Barrett, *Falling In*, Hale & Iremonger, Sydney, 1979, chs 4-5.
41 Lt Gen. L.B. Concannon, 'The psychology of a citizen company', *Commonwealth Military Journal*, January 1913, p. 40.
42 Report by Gen. Sir Ian Hamilton on an inspection of military forces of the Commonwealth of Australia, Cwth *Parliamentary Papers*, 1914, 2(14), p. 45.
43 *Sydney Morning Herald*, 6 October 1913, p. 8.
44 *Argus* (Melbourne), 11 April 1896, p. 11.
45 Capt. J.H. Watson, 'The Royal Navy's contribution to Australian history', *Royal Australian Historical Society Journal and Proceedings*, 3(7), 1916, pp. 326–51.
46 Old Chum (J.M. Forde), 'Old Sydney', *Truth* (Sydney), Sunday editions, 21 February–7 November 1909.
47 'What is the story of Elands River?', *Life* (Melbourne), September 1907, pp. 214–216, and October 1907, pp. 337–41.
48 *Age*, 25 May 1915, p. 9
49 Assuming an Aboriginal population of around 300 000, with 60 000 sometimes engaged in formal fighting.
50 There were 29 000 members of military forces in Australia (Meaney, *Search for Security in the Pacific*, p. 270–71), with some among the 12 000 serving with Australian contingents in South Africa (State Records of WA series 1496 item 1769/010); plus at least 26 000 rifle club members (*Year-Book of Australia for 1901*, pp. 601–609); and a possible 5000 Australians with non-Australian contingents in South Africa.
51 Based on 46 000 members of military forces, plus 48 000 rifle club members (*Official Year Book of the Commonwealth of Australia 1901–1914*, pp. 939, 943).

2 The 'superior', all-volunteer AIF
John Connor

1 J. Monash, *The Australian Victories in France in 1918*, Hutchinson & Co, London, 1920, pp. 2, 287, 291.
2 P. Adam-Smith, *The Anzacs*, Thomas Nelson, Melbourne, p. 298; K.S. Inglis, 'Anzac and the Australian military tradition', *Current Affairs Bulletin*, 64(11), April 1988, p. 6; J. King, *The Western Front Diaries: The Anzac's own Story, Battle by Battle*, Simon & Schuster, Sydney, 2008, p. 367; <www.sandsofgallipoli.com.au/collections/sog05.php> and <www.learningonline.com.au/topics/10/books/54/chapters/1246>, (both accessed 1 July 2011).
3 C.E.W. Bean, *The Australian Imperial Force in France During the Allied*

Offensive 1918, Official History of Australia in the War of 1914–1918, vol. 6, Angus & Robertson, Sydney, 1942, pp. 5, 485–86 & 402; J. Grey, *A Military History of Australia*, Cambridge University Press, Melbourne, 3rd edn, 2008, p. 111; and *The Australian Army*, Oxford University Press, Melbourne, 2001, p. 41; P. Dennis et al., *The Oxford Companion to Australian Military History*, Oxford University Press, Melbourne, 2nd edn, 2008, p. 156; <www.awm.gov.au/encyclopedia/conscription/ww1.asp>, (accessed 1 July 2011).

4   I.F.W. Beckett, *Ypres: The First Battle 1914*, Pearson Education, Harlow, 2004; and *The First World War: The Essential Guide to Sources in the UK National Archives*, Public Record Office, London, 2002, p. 121; M. Middlebrook, *The First Day on the Somme*, (orig. 1971) Penguin, Harmondsworth, 1984; R. Prior & T. Wilson, *The Somme*, Yale University Press, New Haven, 2005; W. Philpott, *Bloody Victory: The Sacrifice on the Somme and the Making of the Twentieth Century*, Little Brown, London, 2009.

5   Beckett, *First World War*, pp. 122–23.

6   For 1917 see R. Prior & T. Wilson, *Passchendaele: The Unknown Story*, Yale University Press, New Haven, 1996; March 1918, see M. Middlebrook, *The Kaiser's Battle, 21 March 1918: The First Day of the German Spring Offensive*, (orig. 1978) Penguin, Harmondsworth, 1983; and for November 1918, see G. Sheffield, *Forgotten Victory: The First World War ~ Myths and Realities*, Headline, London, 2001; and P. Hart, *1918: A Very British Victory*, Wiedenfeld & Nicolson, London, 2008.

7   For the introduction of conscription in New Zealand, Canada and Newfoundland, see P. Baker, *King and Country Call: New Zealanders, Conscription and the Great War*, Auckland University Press, Auckland, 1988; J.L. Granatstein & J.M. Hitsman. *Broken Promises: A History of Conscription in Canada*, Oxford University Press, Toronto, 1977; P.T. McGrath & C. Lucas, 'Newfoundland', in Lucas (ed.), *The Empire at War*, vol. 2, Oxford University Press, London, 1923, p. 307.

8   C. Puglsey, 'At the Empire's call: New Zealand Expeditionary Force planning 1901–1918', in J.A. Moses & C. Pugsley (eds), *The German Empire and Britain's Pacific Dominions 1871–1919: Essays on the Role of Australia and New Zealand in World Politics in the Age of Imperialism*, Regina Books, Claremont CA, 2000, pp. 221–38; J. Crawford, '"New Zealand is being bled to death": The formation, operations and disbandment of the Fourth Brigade', in J. Crawford & I. McGibbon (eds), *New Zealand's Great War: New Zealand, the Allies and the First World War*, Exisle Publishing, Auckland, 2007, pp. 250–65; I. McGibbon (ed.), *The Oxford Companion to New Zealand Military History*, Oxford University Press, Auckland, p. 118.

9   J.L. Granatstein & D.F. Oliver (eds), *The Oxford Companion to Canadian Military History*, Oxford University Press, Toronto, 2011, pp. 85, 123 & 190; T. Cook, *Shock Troops: Canadians Fighting the Great War 1917–1918*, Viking Canada, Toronto, 2008, p. 504.

10 D. Fitzpatrick, 'Militarism in Ireland 1900–1922', in T. Bartlett & K. Jeffery (eds), *A Military History of Ireland*, Cambridge University Press, Cambridge, 1996, p 388.

11 P. Orr, '200 000 volunteer soldiers', in J. Horne (ed.), *Our War: Ireland and the Great War*, Royal Irish Academy, Dublin, 2008, pp. 63–77; T.P. Dooley,

Irishmen or English Soldiers? The Times and World of a Southern Catholic Irish Man (1876–1916) Enlisting in the British Army during the First World War, Liverpool University Press, Liverpool, 1995.

12 For example, like Australia, Irish farmers enjoying a wartime boom would have opposed conscription as it would take away their agricultural labourers, and the Irish urban working class would have been 'war weary' due to price increases in food and other necessities: see D. Fitzpatrick, 'Home front and everyday life' and N. Puirseil, 'War, work and labour', both in Horne (ed.), *Our War*, pp. 131–42, 181–94; P. Travers, *Conscription: War, Nationalism and Revolution in Ireland 1914–1918*, Four Courts Press, Dublin, 2000.

13 For example, Bean included a table in his official history that compared enlistment of the Dominions according to 'estimated total white male population': Bean, *Australian Imperial Force in France*, p. 1098.

14 B. Nasson, *Springboks on the Somme: South Africa in the Great War 1914–1918*, Penguin, Johannesburg, 2007, pp. 65, 125, 161–62 & 158–59.

15 S.D. Pradhan, 'Indian Army and the First World War', in D.C. Ellinwood & S.D. Pradhan (eds), *India and World War I*, Manohar, New Delhi, 1978, pp. 51 & 55. For recent contributions on India in the war, see S. Das, 'India and the First World War', in M. Howard et al. (eds), *A Part of History: Aspects of the British Experience of the First World War*, Continuum, London, 2008, pp. 63–73; and 'Indians at home, Mesopotamia and France 1914–1918: Towards an intimate history', in S. Das (ed.), *Race, Empire and First World War Writing*, Oxford University Press, Oxford, 2011, pp. 70–89.

16 R. Smith, *Jamaican Volunteers in the First World War: Race, Masculinity and the Development of National Consciousness*, Manchester University Press, Manchester, 2004, pp. 80 & 90.

17 A. Osuntokun, *Nigeria in the First World War*, Longman, London, 1979, p. 269.

18 T.P. Parsons, *The African Rank-and-File: Social Implications of Colonial Military Service in the King's African Rifles 1902–1964*, Heinemann, Portsmouth NH, 1999, pp. 2 & 18.

19 J.N.I Dawes & L.L. Robson, *Citizen to Soldier: Australia before the Great War ~ Recollections of Members of the First AIF*, Melbourne University Press, Melbourne, 1977, pp. 47 130.

20 Dawes & Robson, *Citizen to Soldier*, pp. 45–46 (apprentice); 49 (bank); & 119–20 (stockmen).

21 Dawes & Robson, *Citizen to Soldier*, p. 112; and A.W. Martin, *Robert Menzies: A Life*, Melbourne University Press, Melbourne, 1993, vol. 1, pp. 29–30.

22 E. Scott, *Australia during the War*, The Official History of Australia in the War of 1914–1918, vol. 11, Angus & Robertson, Sydney, 1936, pp. 310–312.

23 Dawes & Robson, *Citizen to Soldier*, pp. 13–14. It is interesting to note that escaping the control of farmer-fathers was a major motivation for young Irishmen joining the IRA during the Irish War of Independence (1919–1921): see P. Hart, *The IRA and its Enemies: Violence and Community in Cork 1916–1923*, Oxford University Press, Oxford, 1998, chs 7 & 8.

24 J. McQuilton, *Rural Australia and the Great War: From Tarrawingee to Tanganbalanga*, Melbourne University Press, Melbourne, 2001, pp. 175–76.

25 See in general M. Crotty, *Making the Australian Male: Middle-Class Masculinity 1870–1920*, Melbourne University Press, Melbourne, 2001; the engine cleaner

is quoted in Dawes & Robson, *Citizen to Soldier*, p. 117; and for feathers, M. McKernan, *The Australian People and the Great War*, Thomas Nelson, Melbourne, 1980, pp. 29 & 185–86.

26 *West Australian*, 19 April 1915, p. 6; and M. Haig-Muir, 'The economy at war', in J. Beaumont (ed.), *Australia's War 1914–18*, Allen & Unwin, Sydney, 1995, pp. 97–98 & 109.
27 Dawes & Robson, *Citizen to Soldier*, pp. 155–58.
28 E. Greenhalgh, 'Australians broke the Hindenburg Line', in C. Stockings (ed.), *Zombie Myths of Australian Military History*, UNSW Press, 2010, pp. 70–71.
29 R. Stephenson, 'The 1st Australian Division in 1917: A Snapshot', in P. Dennis & J. Grey (eds), *1917: Tactics, Training and Technology*, Proceedings of the 2007 Chief of Army Military History Conference, Australian Military History Publications, Sydney, 2007, p. 42.
30 G.D. Sheffield, 'Military revisionism: The case of the British Army on the Western Front', in M. Howard (ed.), *Part of History*, pp. 1–2.
31 J. Bailey, 'British artillery in the Great War', in P. Griffith (ed.), *British Fighting Methods in the Great War*, Frank Cass, London, 1996, pp. 23–49; P. Chasseaud, 'Field survey in the Salient: Cartography and artillery survey in the Flanders operations in 1917', in P.H. Liddle (ed.), *Passchendaele in Perspective: The Third Battle of Ypres*, Pen & Sword, Barnsley (Yorks), 1997, pp. 117–39; A.P. Palazzo, 'The British Army's Counter-Battery Staff Office and control of the enemy in World War I', *Journal of Military History*, 63(1), January 1999, pp. 55–74.
32 J. Coates, *An Atlas of Australia's Wars*, Oxford University Press, Melbourne, 2nd edn, 2006, pp. 78–79.
33 G.D. Sheffield, 'The indispensible factor: The performance of British troops in 1918', in P. Dennis & J. Grey (eds), *1918: Defining Victory*, Proceedings of the Chief of Army's History Conference held at the National Convention Centre, Canberra 28 September 1999, Army History Unit, Canberra, 1998, pp. 72–95.
34 Greenhalgh, 'Australians broke the Hindenburg Line', p. 86.

3 What about New Zealand? The problematic history of the Anzac connection
Chris Clark

1 C.E.W. Bean, *The Australian Imperial Force in France 1917*, The Official History of Australia in the War of 1914–1918, vol. 4, Angus & Robertson, Sydney, 1933, pp. 732–33; see also A.G. Butler, *The Digger: A Study in Democracy*, Angus & Robertson, Sydney, 1945, p. 18.
2 F. Glen, 'ANZAC today: What does ANZAC mean to contemporary New Zealanders?', *Wartime*, Official Magazine of the Australian War Memorial, 14, Winter 2001, p. 10.
3 F. Waite, *The New Zealanders at Gallipoli*, 2nd edn, Whitcombe and Tombs, Auckland, 1921, p. 300.
4 D.O.W. Hall, *The New Zealanders in South Africa 1899–1902*, Department of Internal Affairs, Wellington, 1949, pp. 9 & 88; see also J.L. Mordike, *An Army for a Nation: A History of Australian Military Developments 1880–1914*, Allen & Unwin, Sydney, 1992, p. 112.

5   Mordike, *An Army for a Nation*, pp. 111–113.
6   C. Coulthard-Clark, *Duntroon: The Royal Military College of Australia 1911–1986*, Allen & Unwin, Sydney, 1986, pp. 24 & 34.
7   C.E.W. Bean, *The Story of Anzac: From the Outbreak of War to the End of the First Phase of the Gallipoli Campaign, May 4, 1915*, The Official History of Australia in the War of 1914–1918, vol. 1, Angus & Robertson, Sydney, 1921, pp. 27–28; see also Mordike, *An Army for a Nation*, p. 244.
8   Bean, *The Story of Anzac*, pp. 28 & 30.
9   Bridges to Sir Ronald Munro-Ferguson (Governor-General of Australia), 31 October 1914, Novar Papers, National Library of Australia, Item MS 696/3557.
10 C. Pugsley, *Gallipoli: The New Zealand Story*, Hodder & Stoughton, Auckland, 1984, p. 69.
11 Pugsley, *Gallipoli*, p. 81.
12 Bean, *The Story of Anzac*, p. 129.
13 K. Fewster, *Gallipoli Correspondent: The Frontline Diary of C.E.W. Bean*, Allen & Unwin, Sydney, 1983, p. 39.
14 Fewster, *Gallipoli Correspondent*, pp. 47–48.
15 Pugsley, *Gallipoli*, p. 94.
16 P.A. Pedersen, *Monash as Military Commander*, Melbourne University Press, Melbourne, 1985, p. 50n.
17 Bean, *The Story of Anzac*, pp. 117–118.
18 A prime example of a New Zealander in the AIF was Captain Alfred Shout, who won the Victoria Cross serving with the 1st Battalion at Lone Pine. Another was Major W.L.H. Burgess, a permanent officer who happened to be on exchange in Australia when war began and found himself commanding the 9th (Tasmania) Battery at Gallipoli. Burgess stayed with the AIF and ended the war as brigadier-general commanding the artillery of the 4th Australian Division. After the war, as a Major General, Sir William Sinclair-Burgess was both General Officer Commanding and Chief of the General Staff, New Zealand Military Forces.
19 J. Jupp (ed.), *The Australian People: An Encyclopedia of the Nation, its People and their Origins*, Cambridge University Press, Melbourne, 2001, p. 603.
20 Bean, *The Story of Anzac*, p. 301.
21 Pugsley, *Gallipoli*, pp. 15, 109, 115 & 353.
22 Pugsley, *Gallipoli*, pp. 16, 153.
23 Bean, *The Story of Anzac*, p. 516.
24 Bean, *The Story of Anzac*, p. 516n.
25 J. Crawford (ed.), *No Better Death: The Great War Diaries and Letters of William G. Malone*, Reed Books, Auckland, 2005, p. 166.
26 Crawford, *No Better Death*, pp. 167 & 179–80.
27 Crawford, *No Better Death*, p. 283.
28 Birdwood, 'Foreword', in Waite, *The New Zealanders at Gallipoli*, p. xviii.
29 The Australian War Memorial in Canberra holds one of the six watercolours that Moore-Jones painted of 'The Man with the Donkey' (see AWM ART92147) along with several copies of the photo on which it was based, taken by Sergeant J.G. Jackson of the NZEF on 12 May 1915 (see AWM negatives A01011 and P03136.001).

30 H.S. Gullett, *The Australian Imperial Force in Sinai and Palestine 1914–1918*, The Official History of Australia in the War of 1914–1918, vol. 7, Angus & Robertson, Sydney, 1944, pp. 58–59.
31 Gullett, *The Australian Imperial Force in Sinai and Palestine*, pp. 210–11.
32 F.M. Cutlack, *The Australian Flying Corps in the Western and Eastern Theatres of War*, The Official History of Australia in the War of 1914–1918, vol. 8, Angus & Robertson, Sydney, 1923, pp. 3 & 10.
33 C.E.W. Bean, *The Australian Imperial Force in France during the Main German Offensive, 1918*, The Official History of Australia in the War of 1914–1918, vol. 5, Angus & Robertson, Sydney, 1937, p. 704.
34 D. Horner, *Blamey: The Commander-in-Chief*, Allen & Unwin, Sydney, 1998, pp. 192–93 & 208.
35 J. McLeod, *Myth & Reality: The New Zealand Soldier in World War II*, Heinmann Reed, Auckland, 1986, p. 32.
36 Horner, *Blamey*, p. 215; see also J. Hetherington, *Blamey: Controversial Soldier*, Australian War Memorial, Canberra, 1973, pp. 165–66.
37 G. Hermon Gill, *Royal Australian Navy 1939–1942*, Australian War Memorial, Canberra, 1957, pp. 519–21 & 646–47.
38 Horner, *Blamey*, p. 437.
39 Hetherington, *Blamey: Controversial Soldier*, p. 319.
40 R. Jackson, *The Berlin Airlift*, Patrick Stephens, Wellingborough, 1988, p. 58.
41 Interview with Squadron Leader C.A. Greenwood, 1980, Imperial War Museum, Item 9961/3/3.
42 J. Cannon (ed.), *Mediterranean Mission: A Pictorial Record of No 78 (F) Wing, RAAF*, David Waddington, Malta, 1955.
43 R. O'Neill, *Australia in the Korean War 1950–1953*, vol. 1: *Strategy and Diplomacy*, Australian War Memorial, Canberra, 1981, pp. 80–81.
44 N. Bartlett (ed.), *With the Australians in Korea*, Australian War Memorial, Canberra, 1954, p. 68.
45 R. O'Neill, *Australia in the Korean War 1950–1953*, vol. 2: *Combat Operations*, Australian War Memorial, Canberra, 1985, pp. 144–45 & 151.
46 Bartlett, *With the Australians in Korea*, pp. 104–105.
47 O'Neill, *Australia in the Korean War*, vol. 2, p. 158.
48 P. Edwards, *Crises and Commitments: The Politics and Diplomacy of Australia's Involvement in Southeast Asian Conflicts 1948–1965*, The Official History of Australia's Involvement in Southeast Asian Conflicts 1948–1975, Allen & Unwin, Sydney, 1992, pp. 359–60.
49 Captain Morrie Stanley was later viewed as 'the Kiwi hero of Long Tan' and, for his part in that battle, was included in an Australian Unit Citation for Gallantry shortly before he died: *Canberra Times*, 18 September 2010.
50 L. McAulay, *The Battle of Long Tan: The Legend of Anzac Upheld*, Arrow Books, Sydney, 1987, pp. 24 & 40.
51 I. McNeill & A. Ekins, *On the Offensive: The Australian Army in the Vietnam War 1967–1968*, The Official History of Australia's Involvement in Southeast Asian Conflicts 1948–1975, Allen & Unwin, Sydney, 2003, pp.162, 164 & 536 n. 92.
52 McNeill and Ekins, *On the Offensive*, p. 162.
53 McNeill and Ekins, *On the Offensive*, pp. 163–64.

54 P. Londey, *Other People's Wars: A History of Australian Peacekeeping*, Allen & Unwin, Sydney, 2004, p. 114.
55 *RAAF News*, March 1986, p. 1; April 1986, p. 3.
56 D. Stevens (ed.), *The Royal Australian Navy*, The Australian Centenary History of Defence, vol. 3, Oxford University Press, Melbourne, p. 245.
57 P. Dennis et al., *The Oxford Companion to Australian Military History*, Oxford University Press, Melbourne, 1995, p. 395.
58 Department of Defence media release MECC 273/11, 2 July 2011, <www.defence.gov.au/media/DepartmentalTpl.cfm?CurrentId=12073>, (accessed 25 July 2011).
59 Prime Minister Helen Clark, 27 April 2008, <www.sydneyarchitecture.com/PYR/PYR11.htm>, (accessed 21 September 2011).
60 K. Hunter, 'States of mind: Remembering the Australian–New Zealand relationship', *Journal of the Australian War Memorial*, 36, May 2002, <www.awm.gov.au/journal/j36/nzmemorial.asp>, (accessed 25 July 2011).

4 Other people's wars
Craig Stockings

1 'Other peoples wars', in *John Pilger's Australia*, Ovation Entertainment, 2010.
2 For a survey of published accounts of this attitude or interpretation see D. McLean, 'Australia and the Cold War: A historiographical review', *International History Review*, 23(2), June 2001, pp. 299–321.
3 P. Keating, *Major Speeches of the First Year*, ALP, Canberra, 1993, p. 59.
4 M. Lake et al., *What's Wrong with Anzac?*, UNSW Press, Sydney, 2010, pp.164–65.
5 The canal certainly did represent a key point of communications for Britain with its colonies before 1913, but after the outbreak of war it carried little trans-oceanic traffic. The passage to it via the Mediterranean route (Gibraltar–Port Said) was actually voluntarily abandoned by British shipping to Australia from as early as April 1940.
6 D. Day, *The Politics of War*, HarperCollins, Sydney, 2003, pp. 17–18.
7 Day, *The Politics of War*.
8 See A. Meaher, *The Road to Singapore: The Myth of British Betrayal*, Australian Scholarly Publishing, Melbourne, 2010.
9 P. Calvocoressi, G. Wint & J. Pritchard, *Total War: The Causes and Course of the Second World War*, vol. 2, Penguin, New York, 1989 (2nd edn), pp. 266–76; and Day, *The Politics of War*, p. 16.
10 S.F. Rowell, *Full Circle*, Melbourne University Press, Melbourne, 1974, pp. 42–43; T.A. Gibson, '"Bayonets about the crown": The record of the Australian Army in the Second World War', *Army Quarterly*, 56(1), April 1948, p. 167; G. Long, *To Benghazi*, Australian War Memorial, Canberra, 1961, pp. 34–35.
11 D.M. Horner, *High Command: Australia and Allied Strategy 1939–1945*, Allen & Unwin, Sydney, 1982, p. 23.
12 An expectation both in line with the principles of imperial defence and referred to with considerable regularity in the deliberations and reports of the Committee of Imperial Defence throughout the 1930s: 'Report by Sir Maurice

Hankey, Secretary to the Committee of Imperial Defence, on Certain Aspects of Australian Defence, November 1934', in J. Robertson & J. McCarthy, *Australian War Strategy 1939–1945*, University of Queensland Press, Brisbane, 1985, p. 25 (document 17).
13 Horner, *High Command*, pp. 24–25; Long, *To Benghazi*, p. 37; Day, *The Politics of War*, pp. 20–21.
14 Military Board Report, 'The raising of a special force for continuous service either in Australia or overseas, 13 September, 1939', in Robertson & McCarthy, *Australian War Strategy 1939–1945*, p. 27 (document 19); Minute, CGS to Adjutant General, 'Designation of the Special Force', 26 September 1939, National Archives of Australian (NAA), series MP508/1, item 96/750/2; Draft Australian Army Order (AAO), 'Second Australian Imperial Force', 24 November 1939, NAA MP508/1, 240/751/11.
15 Memorandum, Secretary of the Army to Secretary Department of Defence Coordination, 'AIF Army Personnel: Complete Records from Inception to Enlistment', 15 November 1941, NAA MP508/1, 304/750/17; Telegram, Army Headquarters to all Military District Headquarters, 8 October 1939, NAA MP508/1, 96/750/2; Minute, Adjutant General to CGS, 'Organisation and Distribution of AIF', 9 November 1939 & Tables of Special Force District Quotas, NAA MP508/1, 96/750/3.
16 J. Popple, 'The first and the finest', *Australian Defence Force Journal*, 39, March–April 1983, pp. 35–36.
17 Robertson, *Australia at War 1939–1945*, p. 40.
18 Cable (no. 191 – Most Secret), Eden to Whiskard, 8 September 1939, in Robertson & McCarthy, *Australian War Strategy 1939–1945*, p. 26 (document 18).
19 AHQ, Notes on formation and future employment of 2nd AIF, 28 November 1939, NAA MP729/7, 51/421/2, Part 1; Robertson, *Australia at War 1939–1945*, pp. 37–39.
20 Day, *The Politics of War*, p. 22.
21 'Agreed conclusions of discussions between officials, held at the War Office on 3rd November, 1939', in Robertson & McCarthy, *Australian War Strategy 1939–1945*, p. 33 (document 22); P. Badman, *North Africa 1940–1942: The Desert War*, John Ferguson, Sydney, NSW, 1987, p. 12; Robertson, *Australia at War*, pp. 37–39.
22 Horner, *High Command*, pp. 28–29; Day, *The Politics of War*, p. 33.
23 Notes of conference, Military Board and Blamey, 13 November 1939, NAA MP729/7, 51/421/2, Part 1; Cables (various), Menzies/Casey, 17–21 November 1939, NAA MP729/7, 51/421/2, Part 1.
24 Horner, *High Command*, p. 29.
25 Robertson, *Australia at War*, pp. 37–39; Minute, Secretary for Defence to Squires, 21 November 1939, NAA MP729/7, 51/421/2, Part 1.
26 Casey to Menzies, 23 November 1939, NAA MP729/7, 51/421/2, Part 1.
27 Cabinet Decision (Full Cabinet) 'Despatch of 6th Division overseas', 28 November 1939, in Robertson & McCarthy, *Australian War Strategy 1939–1945*, p. 38 (Document 25); Horner, *High Command*, p. 30.
28 See B. Farrell & G. Pratten, *Malaya 1942*, Army History Unit, Canberra, 2009; Day, *The Politics of War*, p. 32; Robertson, *Australia at War*, p. 40.

29 Horner, *High Command*, pp. 32 & 37.
30 Report, 'The AIF's first year abroad', Australian War Memorial, series 54, item 524/7/1; Long, *To Benghazi*, pp. 68–69.
31 G. Blainey, 'We weren't that dumb', <www.theaustralian.com.au/news/arts/we-werent-that-dumb/story-e6frg8nf-1225848127735>, (accessed 23 February 2011).
32 See J. Mordike, *An Army for a Nation*, Allen & Unwin, Sydney, 1992.
33 See C. Wilcox, *Australia's Boer War: The War in South Africa 1899–1902*, OUP, Melbourne, 2002.
34 Quoted in R. Thompson, *Australian Imperialism in the Pacific: The Expansionist Era 1820–1920*, Melbourne University Press, Melbourne, 1980, p. 129.
35 Blainey, 'We weren't that dumb'.
36 F. Bongiorno & G. Mansfield, 'Whose war was it anyway? Some Australian historians and the Great War', *History Compass*, 6(1), 2007.
37 Bongiorno & Mansfield, 'Whose war was it anyway?'
38 Blainey, 'We weren't that dumb'.
39 See P. Stanley, 'Dramatic myth and dull truth: Invasion by Japan in 1942', in C. Stockings (ed.), *Zombie Myths of Australian Military History*, UNSW Press, Sydney, 2010.
40 The British Commonwealth Far East Strategic Reserve was a joint British, Australian and New Zealand military force created in the 1950s and based in Malaya. The idea of this force was to act as a point of forward defence and protect collective interests in south-east Asia from both internal and external communist threats. The Reserve was made up of an infantry battalion and a carrier group, supported by squadrons of aircraft.
41 G. Woodard, *Asian Alternatives: Australia's Vietnam Decision and Lessons on Going to War*, Melbourne University Press, Melbourne, 2004.
42 *The Age*, 31 July 2002.
43 Quoted in J. Beaumont et al., *Ministers, Mandarins and Diplomats: Australian Foreign Policy-Making 1941–1969*, MUP, Melbourne, 2003, p. 151.
44 Beaumont et al., *Ministers, Mandarins and Diplomats*, pp. 149–50.
45 See G. Pemberton, *All the Way: Australia's Road to Vietnam*, Allen & Unwin, Sydney, 1987; and the official history of the war, P. Edwards & G. Pemberton, *Crises and Commitments*, Allen & Unwin, Sydney, 1992.
46 See G. Sheridan, *The Partnership: The Inside Story of the US–Australian Alliance under Bush and Howard*, UNSW Press, Sydney, 2006.

5 'They also served': Exaggerating women's role in Australia's wars
Eleanor Hancock

1 J. Damousi, 'Why do we get so emotional about Anzac?', in M. Lake et al., *What's Wrong with Anzac? The Militarisation of Australian History*, UNSW Press, Sydney, 2010, pp. 102, 106. For an earlier analysis of one of the commemorations that promoted this revival, as well as some of the problems it raised, see E. Reed, *Bigger than Gallipoli: War, History and Memory in Australia*, University of Western Australia Press, Perth, 2004, pp. 123–31, 164–65, 170–75.

2   'Women and defence', in J. Beaumont (ed.), *Australian Defence: Sources and Statistics*, The Australian Centenary History of Defence, vol. 6, Oxford University Press, Melbourne, 2001, p. 357. Social changes did mean that some 1000 Australian women lived and worked in Vietnam during the Vietnam War in various capacities, plus about another 1000 military nurses: S. McHugh, *Minefields & Miniskirts: Australian Women and the Vietnam War*, Doubleday, Sydney, 1993, pp. ix, 102.

3   This can be seen in the conflating of critical academic military history and uncritical popular history in M. Lake, 'How do schoolchildren learn about the spirit of Anzac?', in Lake et al., *What's Wrong with ANZAC?*, pp. 136–37. On this topic more widely see J.A. Lynn, '"Rally once again": The embattled future of academic military history', *Journal of Military History*, 61(4), 1997, pp. 777–89.

4   H. Reynolds, 'Are nations really made in war?', in Lake et al., *What's Wrong with ANZAC?*, p. 43. On the wider implications of this, see R. White's stimulating observations, which need to be developed further: 'War and Australian society', in M. McKernan & M. Browne (eds), *Australia: Two Centuries of War & Peace*, Australian War Memorial, Canberra, 1988, pp. 391–95.

5   'Introduction', B. Caine et al. (eds), *Australian Feminism: A Companion*, Oxford University Press, Melbourne, 1998, p. x.

6   Reed, *Bigger than Gallipoli*, pp. 12–13, 71–82, 84, 86–90, 122–24, 143–51.

7   Numbers taken from C. Kenny, *Captives: Australian Army Nurses in Japanese Prison Camps*, University of Queensland Press, Brisbane, 1986, p. xi. Of course those Australian women who had emigrated and lived in other countries at war, including civilian internees of the Japanese, did share such experiences. The ambiguous status of the civilian internees appears to have ensured that they have not gained the same national attention as the POW nurses: C. Twomey, *Australia's Forgotten Prisoners: Civilians Interned by the Japanese in World War Two*, Cambridge University Press, Melbourne, 2007, pp. 3–7, 15–17, 207.

8   P. Adam-Smith, *Australian Women at War*, Thomas Nelson Australia, Melbourne, 1984, p. 14; S. de Vries, *Heroic Australian Women in War: Astonishing Tales of Bravery from Gallipoli to Kokoda*, HarperCollins, Sydney, 2004, p. xxiii.

9   See A.G. Butler on the qualities suiting women to nursing: *The Australian Army Medical Services in the War of 1914–1918*, vol. 3, Australian War Memorial, Canberra, 1943, pp. 585–86; also L.A.G. Turner, 'Captive women: Re-writing women into the Anzac myth', hons thesis, UNSW/ADFA, Canberra, 2000, pp. 5–7.

10 K. Harris, *More than Bombs and Bandages: Australian Army Nurses at Work in World War I*, Big Sky, Sydney, 2011, p. 221.

11 R. Rae, *Scarlet Poppies: The Army Experience of Australian Nurses during World War I*, College of Nursing, Sydney, 2005, p. 231.

12 Harris, *More than Bombs and Bandages*, p. 3.

13 S. Pedersen, 'Britain's second most famous nurse', *London Review of Books*, 33(8), 14 April 2011, p. 19.

14 Department of Veterans' Affairs, *Just Wanted to be There: Australian Service*

Nurses 1899–1999, Commonwealth of Australia, Canberra, 1999, pp. 110–111. Rae implies that the attention given to nurses in the official history is inadequate: Rae, *Scarlet Poppies*, p. 20. The chapter devoted to the Australian nursing service in the Australian official medical history is greater than the six pages for its Canadian counterpart in the Canadian official medical history: A. MacPhail, *The Medical Services: Official History of the Canadian Forces in the Great War 1914–1919*, F.A. Acland, Ottawa, 1925, pp. 224–30.

15   J. Bassett, *Guns and Brooches: Australian Army Nursing from the Boer War to the Gulf War*, Oxford University Press, Melbourne, 1992, p. 1.
16   Harris, *More than Bombs and Bandages*, p. 2. Rae, *Scarlet Poppies*, p. 7; P. Rees, *The Other Anzacs: Nurses at War 1914–1918*, Allen & Unwin, Sydney, 2008.
17   Rae, *Scarlet Poppies*, p. 228.
18   'Women and defence', pp. 366–67, lists six specialist studies of the various nursing services. The studies by Rae, Rees and Harris have appeared since.
19   The figures given for women serving in the Australian Land Army range from 3068 to 7000: Adam-Smith, *Australian Women at War*, p. 377 (3068); Reed, *Bigger than Gallipoli*, p. 79 (7000).
20   Harris, *More than Bombs and Bandages*, pp. 11–12.
21   Rae, *Scarlet Poppies*, p. 53.
22   These very rough computations are based on the population figures in 'POP 26-34 Male Population, colonies and states 1828–1981' and 'POP 35-43 Female Population, Colonies and States 1828–1981', J.C. Caldwell, 'Population', in W. Vamplew (ed.), *Australians: Historical Statistics*, Fairfax, Syme & Weldon, Sydney, 1987, pp. 27–28. The numbers for the 2nd AIF are taken from 'Australian Army', in Beaumont, *Australian Defence: Sources and Statistics*, p. 120. The numbers in the women's services are taken from Adam-Smith, *Australian Women at War*, p. 377. It should be noted that Hasluck's figures for those in the women's services are considerably more conservative: 44 707 in 1943 and 43 600 in August 1945: P. Hasluck, *The Government and the People 1942–1945: Australia in the War of 1939–1945*, series 4 (Civil), vol. 2, Australian War Memorial, Canberra, 1970, pp. 269 and 613 respectively.
23   <www.dva.gov.au/commmems_oawg/commemorations/education/Documents/DVA_Women_in_War_part3.pdf>, (accessed 1 July 2011).
24   Department of Veterans' Affairs, *Just Wanted to be There*, pp. 48–49.
25   Department of Veterans' Affairs, *Just Wanted to be There*, p. 5; see also Rae, *Scarlet Poppies*, pp. 7, 141.
26   Butler, *Australian Army Medical Services in the War of 1914–1918*, vol. 3, p. 584.
27   Department of Veterans' Affairs, *Just Wanted to be There*, pp. 56, 57, 60, 62–63, 71, 94, 104–105; Rae, *Scarlet Poppies*, pp. 23, 231; Harris, *More than Bombs and Bandages*, pp. 24, 130–31; Adam-Smith, *Australian Women at War*, pp. 2, 375. On this process, see also Turner, 'Captive women', passim.
28   Harris, *More than Bombs and Bandages*, pp. 152–55, 192, 196, 199, 211, 216.
29   M. McKernan, *The Australian People and the Great War*, Nelson, Melbourne, 1980, pp. 78–82, 93, 129, 130–31, 144, 223; P. Grimshaw et al., *Creating a Nation*, McPhee Gribble, Melbourne, 1994, pp. 255–56; K. Darian-Smith, 'War and Australian society' in J. Beaumont (ed.), *Australia's War 1939–1945*, Allen & Unwin, Sydney, 1996, p. 62.
30   The WRANS and WAAAF were not allowed to serve overseas at all: 'Women

and defence', Beaumont, *Australian Defence: Sources and Statistics*, pp. 351–52.
31 J. Thomson, *The WAAAF in Wartime Australia*, Melbourne University Press, Melbourne, 1992, pp. 268–72.
32 Quoted in Adam-Smith, *Australian Women at War*, p. 368.
33 Grimshaw et al., *Creating a Nation*, pp. 200–202, 209. Darian-Smith writes of 'thousands of women' recruited into the auxiliary services and the Women's Land Army: *On the Home Front*, p. 54.
34 I. Beckett, *The First World War: The Essential Guide to Sources in the UK National Archives*, Public Record Office, Kew, 2002, p. 204; K. Robert, 'Gender, class, and patriotism: Women's paramilitary units in First World War Britain', *International History Review*, 19(1), 1997, pp. 52–53.
35 Thomson, *The WAAAF in Wartime Australia*, pp. 2–3.
36 Entry for 15 February 1944, Gavin Long diary, Australian War Memorial, series 67, item 1/4. I am grateful to Dr Kent Fedorowich for this reference.
37 J. Damousi & M. Lake, 'Introduction', in *Gender and War: Australians at War in the Twentieth Century*, Press Syndicate of the University of Cambridge, New York, 1995, p. 8.
38 Grimshaw et al., *Creating a Nation*, p. 260 – no source given.
39 Darian-Smith, *On the Home Front*, p. 57.
40 'Conflicts and overseas deployments', in Beaumont, *Australian Defence: Sources and Statistics*, p. 320.
41 Percentages are calculated from the figures given in S.J. Butlin & C.B. Schedvin, *War Economy 1942–1945: Australia in the War of 1939–1945*, series 4 (Civil), vol. 4, Australian War Memorial, Canberra, 1977, p. 51.
42 White, 'War and Australian society', p. 410.
43 These figures are drawn from E. Hancock, 'Employment in wartime: The experience of German women during the Second World War', *War & Society*, 12(2), 1994, pp. 43–68. On women's combat see P. Biddiscombe, 'Into the maelstrom: German women in combat 1944–1945', *War & Society*, 30(1), 2011, pp. 61–89. German women fired anti-aircraft guns, which women in Britain were officially excluded from doing: J. Schwarzkopf, 'Combatant or non-combatant? The ambiguous status of women in British anti-aircraft batteries during the Second World War', *War & Society*, 28(2), 2009, pp. 105–31.
44 See for example the comments that seem to blame professional military historians for not making more of women's experiences in S. Buttworth, 'Antipodean iconography: A search for Australian representations of women and war', *Outskirts: Feminisms along the Edge*, 6, 2000, <www.chloe.uwa.edu.au/outskirts/archive/volume6/buttsworth>, (accessed 26 June 2011).

6 The nonsense of universal Australian 'fair play' in war
Dale Blair

1 J. Monash, *The Australian Victories in France in 1918*, Lothian Books, Melbourne, rev. edn, 1923 [1920], p. 229.
2 T. Hyland, 'Of law and war: Our military justice system distinguishes us from the Taliban – let it run its course', *Sunday Age*, 17 October 2010, p. 19.
3 *Age*, 20 October 2009; *National Times*, 10 December 2010.

4   K. Fewster, *Gallipoli Correspondent: The Frontline Diary of C.E.W. Bean*, Allen & Unwin, Sydney, 1983, p. 83.
5   Fewster, *Gallipoli Correspondent*, p. 83.
6   Fewster, *Gallipoli Correspondent*, pp. 82–83.
7   Fewster, *Gallipoli Correspondent*, p. 83.
8   C.E.W. Bean, *Official History of Australia in the War of 1914–1918: The AIF in France 1916*, vol. 3, Angus & Robertson, Sydney, 1936 [1929], p. 514.
9   Bean, *Official History of Australia in the War of 1914*–1918, pp. 514–515.
10 J. Keegan, *The Face of Battle*, Jonathan Cape, London, 1976, pp. 48–49, 51.
11 Bean, *Official History of Australia in the War of 1914–1918*, p. 772.
12 Bean, *Official History of Australia in the War of 1914–1918*, p. 772, n. 115.
13 W.D. Joynt, *Breaking the Road for the Rest*, Hyland House, Melbourne, 1979, p. 129.
14 Keegan, *The Face of Battle*, p. 51.
15 Bean, *Official History of Australia in the War of 1914–1918*, vol. 3, p. 772, n. 115.
16 *International Law Concerning the Conduct of Hostilities: Collection of Hague Conventions and Some Other Treaties*, International Committee of the Red Cross, Geneva, 1989, pp. 24–25.
17 R.S. Corfield, *Don't Forget Me, Cobber: The Battle of Fromelles 19/20 July 1916: An Enquiry*, Corfield and Company, Rosanna (Vic.), 2000, p. 455. Relevant portions of the manual are reproduced on pp. 453–63.
18 Corfield, *Don't Forget Me, Cobber*, p. 455.
19 J. Bourke, *An Intimate History of Killing: Face-to-Face Killing in Twentieth Century Warfare*, Granta Books, London, 1999, p. 177.
20 For example, the circular 'Prisoners of War', Xth Corps No. I.G. 33/36, dated 20 March 1915, Australian War Memorial (AWM) Series 27, Item 424/5.
21 Circular, 'The Soldiers' Don'ts of International Law', AWM 27, 424/7.
22 E. Gorman, *With the Twenty-Second: A History of the 22nd Battalion, AIF*, H.H. Champion, Australasian Authors' Agency, Melbourne, 1919, pp. 9–10.
23 Letter (unsigned), AWM 27, 424/12.
24 Letter (unsigned) to Australian administrative HQ, London, AWM 27, 424/12.
25 R. McMullin, *Pompey Elliott*, Scribe, Melbourne, 2002, p. 647.
26 Gellibrand to Bean, (undated), AWM 3DRL 6673, 419/8/1.
27 Bean to Gellibrand, 18 March 1918, AWM 3DRL 6673, 419/8/1.
28 Diary of Private T.J. Cleary, 24/1/18, cited in B. Gammage, *The Broken Years: Australian Soldiers in the Great War*, Penguin, Melbourne, 1975, p. 258–59.
29 See for example incidents cited by repatriated Australian POWs: statements by Private K.S. Ross, 28 February 1919, AWM 30, B.5.44; Private A.D. Stone, 23 January 1919, AWM 30, B.16.11; Corporal A. McKee, 17 December 1918, AWM 30, B.14.5.
30 Bean, *Official History of Australia in the War of 1914–1918*, vol. 3, pp. 248–49, and n. 10.
31 E. Wren, *Randwick to Hargicourt: History of the 3rd Battalion*, Ronald G. McDonald, Sydney, 1935, pp. 196–97.
32 Wren, *Randwick to Hargicourt*, p. 199.
33 Diary of Sergeant A.E. Matthews, 3rd Battalion, AWM 2DRL 219, p. 7.

34 Wren, *Randwick to Hargicourt*, p. 200.
35 J. Dower, *War without Mercy: Race and Power in the Pacific War*, Faber & Faber, London, 1986, p. 71.
36 P. Ham, *Kokoda*, HarperCollins, Sydney, 2010, p. 564
37 Dower, *War without Mercy*, pp. 70–71. I have heard of similar incidents related by Vietnam veterans of Viet Cong being thrown from helicopters all off the record and, as such, inadmissible as evidence..
38 Ham, *Kokoda*, p. 529
39 S.E. Benson, *The Story of the 42nd Australian Infantry Battalion*, Dymocks, Sydney, 1952, p. 160.
40 Benson, *The Story of the 42nd Australian Infantry Battalion*, p. 160.
41 Benson, *The Story of the 42nd Australian Infantry Battalion*, p. 96.
42 See discussion in M. Johnston, *Fighting the Enemy: Australian Soldiers and their Adversaries in World War II*, Cambridge University Press, Melbourne, 2000, pp. 9–57.
43 M. Barter, *Far above Battle: The Experience and Memory of Australian Soldiers in War 1939–1945*, Allen & Unwin, Sydney, 1994, pp. 68–69.
44 Johnston, *Fighting the Enemy*, p. 40.
45 Johnston, *Fighting the Enemy*, p. 39
46 F.M. Cutlack, *Official History of Australia in the War of 1914–1918: The Australian Flying Corps*, vol. 8, University of Queensland Press, St. Lucia, 1984 [1923], pp. 159, 161; see also H.S. Gullett, *Official History of Australia in the War of 1914–1918: Sinai & Palestine*, vol. 7, Angus & Robertson, Sydney, 1939, p. 710.
47 Cutlack, *The Australian Flying Corps*, pp. 159 & 161.
48 D. Gillison, *Australia in the War of 1939–1945: Royal Australian Air Force 1939–1942*, Australian War Memorial, 1962, pp. 694–95.
49 'Bismarck convoy smashed!', AWM (film archive), FO1442.
50 R. Trembath, *A Different Sort of War: Australians in Korea 1950–1953*, Australian Scholarly Publishing, Melbourne, 2005, p. 134.
51 Trembath, *A Different Sort of War*, p. 129
52 P. Ham, *Vietnam: The Australian War: The Illustrated Edition*, HarperCollins, Sydney, 2010, p. 564.
53 M. Caulfield, *The Vietnam Years: From the Jungle to the Australian Suburbs*, Hachette Australia, Sydney, 2007, pp. 203–204.
54 Caulfield, *The Vietnam Years*, p. 204
55 T. Burstall, *The Soldiers' Story: The Battle of Xa Long Tan, Vietnam, 18 August 1966*, University of Queensland Press, Brisbane, 1990, p. 134.
56 Cited in B. Buick & G. McKay, *All Guts and No Glory*, Allen & Unwin, Sydney, 2000, p. 217.
57 Buick, *All Guts and No Glory*, p. 217.
58 Caulfield, *The Vietnam Years*, p. 205.

7 The unnecessary waste: Australians in the late Pacific campaigns
Karl James

1 Broadcast by the Prime Minister (Mr. Curtin), 26 January 1943, Australian War Memorial (AWM), 3DRL 6643, 2/11 (3 of 3).
2 *Commonwealth of Australia Parliamentary Debates*, Senate, vol. 181, pp. 129–30.
3 Maj. Gen. H.H. Hammer, hand-written notes on Bougainville, AWM 93, 50/2/23/440, p. 5.
4 S.E. Benson, *The Story of the 42 Aust Inf Bn*, 42nd Australian Infantry Battalion Association, Sydney, 1952, pp. 157–58.
5 P. Charlton, *The Unnecessary War: Island Campaigns of the South-West Pacific 1944–1945*, Macmillan, Melbourne, 1983; M. Hastings, *Nemesis: The Battle for Japan 1944–1945*, HarperPress, London, 2007, pp. 363–72.
6 C. Lloyd & R. Hall (eds), *Backroom Briefings: John Curtin's War*, National Library of Australia, Canberra, 1997, p. 69.
7 D. Day, *John Curtin: A Life*, HarperCollins, Sydney, 2000, p. 463.
8 See P. Edwards, 'Curtin, MacArthur and the "surrender of sovereignty": A historiographical assessment', *Australian Journal Of International Affairs*, 55(2), 1 July, 2001, pp. 175–86.
9 Extract in War Cabinet Agendum, 12 January 1944, AWM 3DRL 6643, 2/17.
10 Australian Military Forces policy directive, Summer 1943–1944, 23 December 1943, AWM 3DRL 6643, 2/17.
11 D. Horner, *High Command: Australia and Allied Strategy 1939–1945*, George Allen & Unwin/Australian War Memorial, Sydney and Canberra, 1982, p. 302.
12 *Sydney Morning Herald*, 6 March 1945.
13 D. Horner, 'Strategic policy making 1943–1945', in M. McKernan & M. Brown (eds), *Australia Two Centuries of War and Peace*, Allen & Unwin/Australian War Memorial, Sydney and Canberra, 1988, p. 279.
14 D. Horner, *Inside the War Cabinet: Directing Australia's War Effort 1939–1945*, Allen & Unwin/Australian Archives, Sydney, 1996, p. 160.
15 Meeting of Prime Ministers, London, May 1944, review by the Right Honourable John Curtin, AWM 3DRL 6643, 2/11 (3 of 3), p. 2.
16 For more information see P. Hasluck, *The Government and the People 1942–1945*, Australian War Memorial, Canberra, 1970, pp. 550–65.
17 Blamey to Lt Gen. Sir Leslie Morshead, 3 March 1944, AWM 3DRL 2632, 2/15.
18 Memorandum, MacArthur to Blamey, 12 July 1944, AWM 3DRL 6643, 2/23.
19 Japanese strength in these locations was actually far greater, with between 35 000 and 40 000 in New Guinea and about the same on Bougainville making a total of nearly 70 000 Japanese army and navy personnel plus another 20 000 civilian workers in total in these locations. There were another 12 000 Japanese on nearby New Ireland. However, these figures did not emerge until after the war: see G. Long, *The Final Campaigns*, Australian War Memorial, Canberra, 1963, pp. 22–23.

20 Long, *Final Campaigns*, p. 23.
21 Horner, *High Command*, p. 338.
22 J. Hetherington, *Blamey, Controversial Soldier: A Biography of Field Marshal Sir Thomas Blamey, GBE, KCB, CMG, DSO, ED*, Australian War Memorial/Australian Government Publishing Service, Canberra, 1973, p. 357.
23 The war establishment of an infantry division for jungle warfare was 13 118 men; the standard infantry division's establishment was around 17 000: Basic staff table of a jungle division, 21 November 1943, AWM 54, 905/25/57.
24 Lt Gen. Vernon Sturdee to Blamey, 31 October 1944, AWM 3DRL 6643, 2/35, (2 of 3).
25 Blamey to Sturdee, 7 November 1944, AWM 3DRL 6643, 2/35, (2 of 3).
26 Lt Colin Salmon, Australians at War film archive, 0388, <www.australiansatwarfilmarchive.gov.au/aawfa>, (accessed 12 August 2011).
27 See diary entries for September and October 1944 in Berryman's diary, AWM PR 84/370, 4.
28 Long, *Final Campaigns*, p. 28.
29 Berryman's diary, 7 October 1944, AWM PR 84/370, 4.
30 Berryman to Blamey, 11 January 1945 (BDO/44A), AWM PR 84/370, 12b.
31 Berryman's diary, 4 and 11 February 1945, AWM PR 84/370, 5.
32 Berryman to Shedden, 5 April 1945, AWM PR 84/370, 12b.
33 Horner, *High Command*, p 387.
34 *Sydney Morning Herald*, 28 December 1944.
35 *Canberra Times*, 10 January 1945.
36 Long, *Final Campaigns*, p. 38.
37 Blamey to Berryman, 17 February 1945, AWM 3DRL 6643, 2/49.
38 Blamey to Curtin, 13 February 1945 and Curtin to MacArthur, 15 February 1945, AWM 3DRL 6643, 2/17.
39 H. Gillan (ed.), *We had some Bother: Tales from the Infantry*, Hale and Iremonger, Sydney, 1985, pp. 116–117.
40 S. Trigellis-Smith, *The Purple Devils: A History of the 2/6 Australian Commando Squadron formerly the 2/6 Australian Independent Company 1942–1946*, 2/6 Australian Commando Squadron Association, Melbourne, 1992, p. 221.
41 MacArthur to Curtin, 5 March 1945, AWM 3DRL 6643, 2/17.
42 P.J. Dean, *The Architect of Victory: The Military Career of Lieutenant-General Sir Frank Horton Berryman*, Cambridge University Press, Melbourne, 2011, p. 289.
43 Horner, *High Command*, pp. 387–88.
44 Dean, *The Architect of Victory*, pp. 289–90.
45 Berryman to Blamey, Signal B226, AWM PR 84/370, 14.
46 Berryman's diary, 13 March 1945, AWM PR 84/370, 5.
47 Curtin to MacArthur, 27 February 1945, AWM 3DRL 6643, 2/17.
48 *Parliamentary Debates*, Senate, vol. 181, p. 128.
49 Curtin to Blamey, 17 April 1945, AWM 3DRL 6643, 2/17.
50 'Notes by Lt-Gen Sir Stanley Savige on Vol. VII, Chapt. 8, The floods and the cease fire', AWM 3DRL 2529, 128, p. 3.
51 *Parliamentary Debates*, Representatives, vol. 181, pp. 1028–30. See also Reports on matters other than equipment by the Acting Minister for the Army (Senator the Hon. J.M. Fraser) on his visit to the operational areas: War Cabinet Agendum No. 190/1945, National Archives of Australia, A5954/69,

275/3. Fraser produced a second report, 'Further Observations of Acting Minister for the Army on Operations in New Guinea, New Britain, and the Solomon Islands', that was particularly critical of the 6th Division's campaign in New Guinea and Blamey's negative reputation within the AMF, but this report was not tabled in Parliament: Further Observations of Acting Minister for the Army on Operations in New Guinea, New Britain, and the Solomon Island, AWM 3DRL 6643, 2/22.

52. G. Serle, 'Curtin, John (1885–1945)', in John Ritchie (ed.), *Australian Dictionary of Biography*, vol. 13, Melbourne University Press, Melbourne, 1993, p. 557.
53. Chifley to Blamey, 7 May 1945, AWM 3DRL 6643, 2/17.
54. 'Appreciation on Operations of the AMF in New Guinea, New Britain and the Solomon Islands, 18 May 1945', AWM 3DRL 6643, 2/17
55. MacArthur to Chifley, 20 May 1945, AWM 3DRL 6643, 2/17.
56. D. Horner, *Blamey, the Commander-in-Chief*, Allen & Unwin, Sydney, 1998, p. 535.
57. Blamey did not receive the letter approving his policy until 14 August: Long, *Final Campaigns*, p. 69.
58. Blamey to Acting Minister for the Army, 16 May 1945, AWM 3DRL 6643, 2/17; Horner, *Inside the War Cabinet*, p. 187; Horner, *High Command*, p. 405.
59. Horner, *High Command*, p. 396.
60. Shedden to Fraser and Blamey, 20 May 1945, Message 1238, AWM 3DRL 6643, 2/17.
61. Horner, *High Command*, p. 406.
62. Interview with Capt. Tom Kimber, 2/27th Battalion, AWM S00921.

8 Lost at sea: Missing out on Australia's naval history
Alastair Cooper

1. The exception is the legal case against Holocaust-denier David Irving. The subject is so fundamental to humanity, particularly North American and European public understanding of history, and the circumstances so compelling, that the dissection of Irving's historical work was and remains a subject of broad contemporary interest, and a cautionary tale for all historians about the absolute need to strive for objectivity and faithfulness to sources.
2. P. Macksey, *The War for America 1775–1783*, Harvard University Press, Cambridge, 1964, pp. xiii–xvi.
3. J. Grey, *A Military History of Australia*, Cambridge University Press, Melbourne, 1999, p. 115.
4. Grey, *A Military History of Australia*, p. 115; D. Stevens (ed.), *The Royal Australian Navy*, Oxford University Press, South Melbourne, 2001, n.1, p. 318.
5. Grey, *A Military History of Australia*, p. 149.
6. Oral History interview of Commodore A.N. Dollard, Commanding Officer of HMAS *Murchison*, Korea 1951–1952, interviewed by Lieutenant Commander T. Hughes, Australian War Memorial, item S02803.
7. The good accounts of these actions do indeed take this approach: eg. T. Frame's accounts of the loss of *Sydney* and *Voyager* both deal with the

operation of the whole ship's organisation.
8   These numbers were obtained from online catalogue searches in January 2011, using the search terms indicated, of the National Archives of Australia, the Australian War Memorial, and wikipedia.org.
9   One way many of the difficulties of naval history could be remedied is through the use of computer simulations and the combination of current and historical visual footage. Having acknowledged the potential, the limitations of the format mean this attempt will be via the written word.
10 This account of HMAS *Murchison*'s operations is based on the following sources: R. O'Neill, *Australia in the Korean War*, vol. 2, *Combat Operations*, AGPS, Canberra, 1985, pp. 450–59; W.O.C. Roberts, 'Gun battle on the Han', *Naval Historical Review*, 1(2), September 1976; V. Fazio, *River Class Frigates of the Royal Australian Navy: A Story of Ships Built in Australia*, Slipway Publications, Sydney, 2003; and HMAS *Murchison*, Reports of Proceeding, AWM series 228, item 1, AWM 228, 2 and AWM 228, 3.
11 Roberts, 'Gun battle on the Han'.
12 P. Kennedy, 'Winning war from the middle', *Journal of Military History*, 74(1), January 2010, p. 50.
13 S.G. Joyce, interviewed by T. Hughes, Australian War Memorial, Oral History Recording, item S02795.
14 Interview of Commodore Dollard.
15 Interview of S.G Joyce.

9   'Landmark' battles and the myths of Vietnam
Bob Hall and Andrew Ross

1   The term 'Viet Cong' was commonly used to describe those enemy forces recruited and trained in the Republic of Vietnam (the South). The People's Army were those recruited and trained in the Democratic Republic of Vietnam (the North) and infiltrated into the South usually down the Ho Chi Minh trail. This latter force was also commonly known as the North Vietnamese Army (or NVA). By mid-1968, many Viet Cong units were increasingly reinforced with People's Army soldiers, so the distinction between the two forces became progressively moot.
2   For example, the two volumes of the official history published to date both devote lengthy chapters to 'landmark' battles: see Ian McNeill, *To Long Tan: The Australian Army and the Vietnam War 1950–1966*, Allen & Unwin, Sydney, 1993; and Ian McNeill and Ashley Ekins, *One the Offensive: The Australian Army in the Vietnam War 1967–1968*, Allen & Unwin, Sydney, 2003.
3   Craig Stockings (ed.), *Zombie Myths of Australian Military History: The 10 Myths That Will Not Die*, UNSW Press, Sydney, 2010, p. 195.
4   McNeill, *To Long Tan*, pp. 305–75.
5   AWM 98, item 115, HQ AFV – Intelligence Phuoc Tuy – Ralliers and agents. Interrogation report, 25 August 1969, Subject: Executive Officer, 274 Regiment. This file cites a typical example of the detailed planning that went into VC/PAVN operations. In this case, 274 Regiment received orders to attack the US base at Long Binh in December 1968 and executed its orders on 21 February 1969 after nearly two months of planning, preparations and

rehearsals.
6   This and other statistical data in this chapter is drawn from the '1ATF Contact Database 1966–1971', created by Dr Andrew Ross. The database holds information on approximately 4500 combat incidents of 1ATF in Vietnam between 1966 and withdrawal of the force in 1971. The data is drawn primarily from 1ATF 'Combat After Action Reports' held in AWM series 103, HQ 1ATF (Nui Dat) records, and AWM series 95, Australian Army Commanders' diaries, and other series. We estimate that the database contains over 95% of 1ATF recorded contacts. Of the 4500 combat incidents recorded, 3909 are contacts or other battles, about 250 are mine incidents, 200 are friendly fire incidents and the remainder miscellaneous. The term 'casualties' includes both killed and wounded.
7   S. Karnow, *Vietnam: A History*, 2nd edn, Pimlico, London, 1994, p. 548. Giap was speaking about the Tet Offensive of 1968, but the point also applies to other PAVN offensives and major battles.
8   The Division in Battle, Pamphlet no. 11, *Counter Revolutionary Warfare*, Military Board, Army Headquarters, Canberra, 1966, p. 25.
9   McNeill, *To Long Tan*, pp. 366–67.
10 McNeill, *To Long Tan*, pp. 356–57.
11 *Counter Revolutionary Warfare*, p. 58. The doctrine stated prophetically that 'in this battle for the allegiance of the people the results of well directed propaganda, publicity and psychological operations (psyops) may sometimes outweigh the results achieved by successful military operations'.
12 Some debate still surrounds the enemy's military objectives. Some see the battle as an attempted annihilation ambush, while others see it as an encounter between D Company 6RAR and the enemy force as it prepared for an assault against the Nui Dat base. This debate is briefly discussed in McNeill, *To Long Tan*, but it is also addressed in B. Buick (with G. McKay), *All Guts and No Glory: The story of a Long Tan Warrior*, Allen & Unwin, Sydney, 2000; and B. Grandin, *The Battle of Long Tan as Told by the Commanders to Bob Grandin*, Allen & Unwin, Sydney, 2004. For an imagined account of the battle from the enemy perspective see Dave Sabben, *Through Enemy Eyes*, Allen & Unwin, Sydney, 2005.
13 Australian Archives A4531, item 201/2/1 part 1, Saigon – Vietnam elections – 1966, Cablegram, Australian Embassy Saigon to Department of External Affairs, Canberra, 13 September 1966.
14 H.G. Summers Jr., *On Strategy: A Critical Analysis of the Vietnam War*, Random House, New York, 1982, p. 1.
15 Analysis of the '1ATF Contact Database 1966 to 1971'.
16 '1ATF Contact Database'.
17 *Counter Revolutionary Warfare*, p. 37.
18 '1ATF Contact Database'.
19 Analysis of 1ATF Intelligence Summaries (INTSUMs) and the '1ATF Intelligence Database'.
20 1ATF Intelligence Summaries (INTSUMs); '1ATF Intelligence Database'.
21 D. Hackworth, *About Face: The Odyssey of an American Warrior*, Macmillan, Melbourne, 1989, p. 669.
22 Of the enemy weapons captured by Australian and New Zealand forces in

contacts, 748 were AK47s and 731 were other weapons including M16s, carbines and sub-machine guns, rifles, pistols, RPG launchers and machine guns: see '1ATF Contact Database'.
23 In early 1968, 2RAR, 3RAR and 7RAR were invited by HQ 1ATF to give a critical appraisal of the performance of infantry weapons in Vietnam. The results of this appraisal are found in AWM103, item R1000/1/8, HQ 1ATF Weapons – General – Review of infantry weapons.
24 HQ 1ATF Weapons – General – Review of infantry weapons. The COs of 2RAR/NZ (ANZAC), 3RAR and 7RAR each commented on the rifle's 'popularity' with 1ATF soldiers, its 'excellence', reliability, accuracy and penetrating ability. See also I. Kuring, *Red Coats to Cams: A History of Australian Infantry 1788–2001*, Army History Unit, Canberra, 2004, p. 399. The L1A1 7.62mm Self Loading Rifle (or SLR) was in service with the Australian Army for about 25 years.
25 T. Page and J. Pimlott (eds), *Nam: The Vietnam Experience 1965–1975*, Hamlyn, London,1988, p. 64.
26 AWM95, item 7/2/54, Australian Army Commander's Diaries, Vietnam – 2RAR/NZ (ANZAC) – Narrative, Annexes, 1–31 May 1970, p. 123, Routine Orders for 2 RAR/NZ, May 1970.
27 '1ATF Contact Database'. This represents the lowest figure for failure in contact. Many M60 problems were not necessarily reported in contact reports.
28 AWM95, item 7/4/53, Australian Army Commander's Diaries, Vietnam – 4RAR/NZ (ANZAC) – Map, 1–30 September 1971, Contact report, D Company 4RAR/NZ, 21 September 1971.
29 R.A. Hall, *Combat Battalion: The Eighth Battalion in Vietnam*, Allen & Unwin, Sydney, 2000, pp. 160–165.
30 G. Lockhart, *The Minefield: An Australian Tragedy in Vietnam*, Allen & Unwin, Sydney, 2007, p. 216.
31 Hall, *Combat Battalion*, pp. 110–111.

10 The myth that Australia 'punches above its weight'
Albert Palazzo

1 The views expressed in this chapter are those of the author and do not necessarily reflect the official policy or position of the Australian Army, the Department of Defence or the Australian Government.
2 P. Kelly, 'Punching above our weight,' *Policy*, 20(2), Winter 2004, pp. 29–34; M. Thomson, 'Punching above our weight: Australia as a middle power', *Strategic Insights*, 18, Australian Strategic Policy Institute, 2005, p. 2; P. Cook, 'Trade, equity and development', address to the Australian APEC Study Centre, Melbourne, 18 June 2000; G. Evans, 'The world after Wilenski: An Australian who mattered', inaugural Peter Wilenski Memorial Lecture, Canberra, 1995.
3 For examples see: P. Cosgrove, 'Year sees a versatile force punch way above its weight', *The Australian*, 12 November 2004; 'Address by the Chief of Army Lieutenant General P.F. Leahy to the Defence Management Seminar', 24 September 2004; A. Houston, 'The future of airpower: RAAF response to the

ADF NCW Roadmap', 2004 Air Power Conference CAF Keynote Speech, 16 September 2004; D. Hurley, 'Managing in crisis: The road to recovery,' 27 October 2008; & Brigadier C.W. Orme, 'Size and complexity: A soldier's perspective', address to Institute of Public Administration, 14 September 2006.

4 '1 RAR Band', *Australian Army Band Corps*, 2010; 'Punching above their weight', *Navy News*, 10 June 2010; APA-H, *Career News*, Summer 2008; *JLU(S) Newsletter*, 1(3), July 2009; 'Australian business wins more JSF contracts', *On Target*, 37, January 2004; and RAAPC, *Integrity Times*, Spring 2004.

5 'Putting the tiger in the shed: Dechaineux Rests', *Trade*, June 2005.

6 See 'Punching above our weight: Australia once again ranked 6th at Cannes; NZ placed equal 9th', *Campaign Brief*, 29 June 2010, <www.campaignbrief.com/2010/06/punching-above-our-weight-aust.html>, (accessed 18 May 2011); A. Kennedy, 'Locals on talent path', *The Morning Bulletin*, 6 June 2011, <www.themorningbulletin.com.au/story/2010/06/24/locals-on-talent-path>, (accessed 6 June 2011); Department of Industry Tourism and Resources, *Punching above its Weight: Australia's Cement Industry 2006–2012*, Commonwealth of Australia, Canberra, 2006.

7 The Anzac legend and the cult of the 'digger' have been dealt with in the previous volume: see C. Stockings (ed.), *Zombie Myths of Australian Military History*, UNSW Press, Sydney, 2010.

8 Thomson, 'Punching above our weight'.

9 P. Cosgrove, 'One mission accomplished: What's next?' *The Sydney Papers*, 12(3), Winter 2000, pp. 94–105.

10 For a brief discussion of Australia's role in East Timor see D. Horner, *Making the Australian Defence Force*, Oxford University Press, Melbourne, 2001, pp. 7–39; also, B. Breen, *Mission Accomplished: East Timor*, Allen & Unwin, Sydney, 2000.

11 For examples see Australian National Audit Office, *Management of Australian Defence Force Deployments to East Timor*, Commonwealth of Australia, Department of Defence, 2002, pp. 89–90; B. Breen and G. McCauley, *The World Looking over their Shoulders: Australian Strategic Corporals on Operations in Somalia and East Timor*, Land Warfare Studies Centre, Canberra, 2008, pp. 164–67.

12 *Defence 2000: Our Future Defence Force*, Commonwealth of Australia, Department of Defence, para 1.15.

13 J.R Ballard, *Triumph of Self-Determination: Operation Stabilise and United Nations Peacemaking in East Timor*, Praeger, Westport, 2008, pp. 67–69; Joint Standing Committee on Foreign Affairs, Defence and Trade, *East Timor: Final Report of the Senate Foreign Affairs, Defence and Trade References Committee*, Commonwealth of Australia, Canberra, 2000, pp. 49–51.

14 Ballard, *Triumph of Self-Determination*, p. 67.

15 C.A. Collier, 'A new way to wage peace: US support to Operation Stabilise', *Military Review*, January–February 2001, pp. 2–9; see also D. Stevens, *Strength through Diversity: The Combined Naval Role in Operation STABILISE*, Sea Power Centre Australia, Canberra, 2007.

16 A. Ryan, 'Primary Responsibilities and Primary Risks': Australian Defence Force Participation in the International Force East Timor, Land Warfare Studies

Centre, Canberra, 2000, pp. 75–76.
17 *East Timor: Final Report of the Senate Foreign Affairs, Defence and Trade References Committee*, p. 51.
18 Ballard, *Triumph of Self-Determination*, p. 70.
19 See Joint Standing Committee on Foreign Affairs, Defence and Trade, *From Phantom to Force: Towards a More Efficient and Effective Army*, Commonwealth of Australia, Canberra, 2000.
20 Horner, *Making the Australian Defence Force*, p. 11.
21 Horner, *Making the Australian Defence Force*, pp. 35-40.
22 T. Allard, 'Experts of stealth leave their mark', *The Age*, 25 April 2003.
23 On Iraqi military incompetence see K.M. Woods et. al., *The Iraqi Perspectives Report*, Naval Institute Press, Annapolis, 2006, pp. 39–48.
24 *The Australian Experience of Airpower*, Commonwealth of Australia, Canberra, 2007, p. 161; P. Cosgrove, 'Fighting fists forged in Falconer', *The Australian*, 20 June 2003; Allard, 'Experts of stealth leave their mark'; and 'Colonel John Mansell provides an overview of Australian Special Forces contribution to Operation Falconer', Defence Media Release, 9 May 2003.
25 Figures are for April 2003 and compiled from A. Belasco, *Troop Levels in the Afghan and Iraq Wars, FY2001-FY2012: Cost and Other Potential Issues*, Congressional Research Service, Washington DC, 2009, p. 64; *Operations in Iraq: Lessons for the Future*, [UK] Ministry for Defence, London, 2003, p. 84; *The War in Iraq: ADF Operations in the Middle East in 2003*, Department of Defence, Canberra, 2003; & United Nations Population Data Base, <unstats.un.org/unsd/demographic/products/dyb/dyb2006/Table05.pdf>, (accessed 15 June 2011).
26 D. Fickling, 'Australia criticised for troops pullout', *Guardian*, 18 April 2003; M. Wilkinson, 'Bush wants Canberra role in Iraq,' *Sydney Morning Herald*, 1 May 2003.
27 *Australian Defence Forces Deployed to Support the Rehabilitation of Iraq: Report of the Delegation 22 to 28 October 2005*, Joint Standing Committee on Foreign Affairs, Defence and Trade, Canberra, 2006, pp. 25–26. Prior to the establishment of the Training Team, Australia provided some trainers who served embedded in the US training organisation.
28 'Australia marks end of Iraq combat mission', *ABC News*, 2 June 2008, <www.abc.net.au/news/stories/2008/06/02/2262174.htm>, (accessed 16 June 2011); 'Overwatch Battle Group (West)', <www.australian-armour.com/OBG(W).html>, (accessed 16 June 2011).
29 A. Smith, *Improvised Explosives Devices in Iraq 2003–1009: A Case of Operational Surprise and Institutional Response*, Strategic Studies Institute, Carlisle, 2011, p. 40.
30 Casualty figures sourced from <icasualties.org/Iraq/ByProvince.aspx>, (accessed 16 June 2011).
31 M. Armstrong, 'Not hearts and minds: Civil-military cooperation in OBG(W)-3', *Australian Army Journal*, 8(1), Autumn 2011, pp. 64–65 and 73.
32 Casualty figures are from <icasualties.org/Iraq/Nationality.aspx>, (accessed 15 June 2011).
33 Department of Defence, 'Operation Catalyst', <www.defence.gov.au/opEx/global/opcatalyst/index.htm>, (accessed 15 June 2011).

34 J. Birmingham, 'A time for war: Australia as a military power', *Quarterly Essay*, 20, 2005, p. 19.
35 S. Naylor, *Not a Good Day to Die: The Untold Story of Operation Anaconda*, Berkley Books, New York, 2005, pp. 87 & 158.
36 G. Sheridan, 'The finest troops, but mission bound to fail', *The Australian*, 8 June 2011.
37 Department of Defence, 'Afghanistan Fact Sheet', <www.defence.gov.au/op/afghanistan/info/factsheet.htm>, (accessed 16 June 2011).
38 Figures are drawn from *The Military Balance 2011*, Routledge, London, 2011.
39 For Australian figures see Department of Defence, 'Global operations', <www.defence.gov.au/op/index.htm>, (accessed 3 June 2011); for Canadian figures see Canadian Expeditionary Force Command, 'International operations', <www.comfec-cefcom.forces.gc.ca/pa-ap/ops/index-eng.asp>, (accessed 3 June 2011). For a list of operations for both countries see *The Military Balance 2011*.
40 For Libyan figures see the operation's fact sheet, <www.comfec-cefcom.forces.gc.ca/pa-ap/ops/mobile/index-eng.asp>, (accessed 17 June 2011).
41 'Joint Task Force Afghanistan: Composition as of 30 November 2010', CEFCOM, <www.comfec-cefcom.forces.gc.ca/pa-ap/ops/fs-fr/jtfa-foia-eng.asp>, (accessed 3 June 2011).
42 Figures from <icasualties.org/OEF/Nationality.aspx>, (accessed 17 June 2011).
43 J. Molan, 'Afghanistan: The case for 6000 Australian troops', *The Interpreter*, 25 March 2009.
44 For an example see 'No Afghanistan troop boost, says Kevin Rudd', *APP*, 15 October 2009, <www.news.com.au/breaking-news/national/no-afghanistan-troop-boost-says-kevin-rudd/story-e6frfku9-1225787079953>, (accessed 17 June 2011).
45 S. Sara, 'Australia "punching above its weight" in Afghanistan', *ABC News*, 1 May 2010, <www.abc.net.au/news/stories/2010/05/012887664.htm>, (accessed 17 May 2011); K. Tranter, 'US wants us to fill the void in Afghanistan', *Sydney Morning Herald*, 24 May 2010.
46 For examples see B. West, *The Wrong War: Grit, Strategy, and the Way Out of Afghanistan*, Random House, New York, 2011, pp. 248–49; P. Bishop, *Ground Truth, 3 Para: Return to Afghanistan*, Harper Press, London, 2009, p. 36.
47 W. Mason, 'Diggers need freedom to win freedom', *The Australian*, 6 July 2010.
48 R. Shanahan, 'What did you do in the war, Australia?' *The Interpreter*, 12 March 2010.
49 'Assessing Australia's Afghan effort,' *The Australian*, 27 December 2008.
50 N. Bensahel, 'International alliances and military effectiveness: Fighting alongside allies and partners', in R.A. Brooks & E.A. Stanley 9eds), *Creating Military Power: The Sources of Military Effectiveness*, Stanford University Press, Stanford, 2007, p. 188.
51 Thomson, *Punching above our weight?*, p. 11; see also, P. Hartcher, 'Smith calls for more overseas clout', *Sydney Morning Herald*, 23 April 2008.
52 Birmingham, 'A time for war', p. 8.
53 Quoted in G. Sheridan, 'The finest troops, but mission bound to fail', *The Australian*, 8 June 2011, p. 8.
54 C. Stewart, 'Not a single submarine seaworthy', *The Australian*, 10 June 2011,

p. 5; D. Oakes, 'Neglect of amphibious fleet triggers Defence inquiry, *Sydney Morning Herald*, 16 February 2011; and J. Molan, 'Defensively speaking, Australia finds itself on dangerous ground', *The Australian*, 14 June 2011, p. 10.

55 Molan, 'Defensively speaking', p. 10; Shanahan, 'What did you do in the war, Australia?'; & Thomson, 'Punching above our weight,' pp. 10–11.

11 Critical reflections on the Australia–US alliance
Michael McKinley

1 Commonwealth of Australia, *Defending Australia in the Asia-Pacific Century: Force 2030*, Defence White Paper 2009, Australian Government, Canberra, 2009.

2 G. Evans & B. Grant, *Australia's Foreign Relations in the World of the 1990s*, Melbourne University Press, Melbourne, 1991, p. 308.

3 J. Vasquez, *The Power of Power Politics*, Rutgers University Press, New Jersey, 1983, p. 220.

4 I should like to acknowledge the benefit of long, helpful conversations with my friend and colleague, Jim George, on the ideas pertaining to this section. I have also benefited immeasurably from his writings on the meta-theory of realism and the critique it has attracted.

5 D. Day, *The Great Betrayal: Britain, Australia and the Onset of the Pacific War*, Angus & Robertson, Sydney, 1988, esp. p. 351.

6 J. Rusbridger & E. Nave, *Betrayal at Pearl Harbour: How Churchill Lured Roosevelt into WWII*, Summit, New York, 1991, pp. 99–106.

7 *Defending Australia in the Asia-Pacific Century*.

8 J.N. Rosenau, 'Peripheral international relationships in a more benign world: Reflections on American orientation towards ANZUS', paper presented to the conference on Australia, New Zealand and the United States: National Evolution and Alliance Relations, phase 1, Socio-Political Change and National Images, East-West Center, Honolulu, Hawaii, 24–26 August 1988, p. 2.

9 B. Toohey & M. Wilkinson, *The Book of Leaks: Exposes in Defence of the Public's Right to Know*, Angus & Robertson, Sydney, 1987, pp. 130-42

10 The arguments and conclusions summarised in the following reflect the findings of the writer's own survey of the recent intelligence literature which, it must be said, is voluminous. Only in the interests of brevity is the writer's unpublished but publicly presented survey (which is currently undergoing revision) cited: see M. McKinley, 'The alliance intelligence benefit and Australia: A challenge to the prevailing orthodoxy', paper presented to the 32nd Annual Convention of the International Studies Association's panel on 'Topics in Intelligence and National Security', Vancouver, British Columbia, 21 March, 1991. A broader analysis of US intelligence is to be found in M. McKinley, 'American intelligence as American knowing', *Alternatives*, 21(1), 1996, pp. 31–66.

11 The clearest expression of the defensibility of Australia is to be found in the 'Review of Australia's Defence Capabilities: Report to the Minister for Defence' by P. Dibb. See also D. Ball, 'The ANZUS connection: The

security relationship between Australia, New Zealand and the United States of America', in T.J. Hearn (ed.), *Arms, Disarmament and New Zealand: The Papers and Proceedings of the Eighteenth Foreign Policy School 1983*, University of Otago, Dunedin, 1983, pp. 79–83.
12 P. Seabury & A. Codevilla, *War: Ends and Means*, Basic Books, New York, 1989, p. 128.
13 For a full account of the works consulted in this paragraph see G. Cheesman & M. McKinley, 'Australia's regional security policies 1970–1990: Some critical reflections', Working paper No. 101, Australian National University Research School of Pacific Studies, Peace Research Centre, pp. 35–37.
14 Cheesman & McKinley, 'Australia's regional security policies 1970–1990', p. 37.
15 This argument is made at length in M. McKinley, 'The battle', in I. Bickerton et.al., *43 Days: The Gulf War*, Text/ABC Books, Melbourne, 1991.
16 A recent case in point concerned the software for the weapons systems on Australia's F/A-18 and F-111 aircraft: see J. Edwards, 'US happy to sell us weapons, but not the instructions', *Sydney Morning Herald*, 22 March 1989, p. 1.
17 R. Fox & J. Field, *The Defense Management Challenge: Weapons Acquisition*, Harvard Business School Press, Boston, 1988, p. 38.
18 D. Hedgpeth, 'GAO blasts weapons budget', *Washington Post*, 1 April 2008, p. A01.
19 As cited in D. Rasor, 'The buying and selling of the Pentagon' part 1, < www.truthout.org>, accessed 14 April 2011.
20 L. Strickler, 'Pricey Pentagon programs and the "kill fee"', CBS News, 15 February 2011, <www.cbsnews,com/8301-31727_162_20032044-10391695.html>, accessed 20 February 2011.
21 A. Davies & P. Layton, 'We'll have six of them and four of those: Off-the-shelf procurement and its strategic implications', Special Report iIssue 25, Australian Strategic Policy Institute, November 2009, p. 2.
22 POGO, 'Federal contractor misconduct database', <www.contractormisconduct.org>, accessed 22 July 2011.
23 T. Allard, '$400m lost in botched jet contract', *Sydney Morning Herald*, 13 September 2006.
24 J. Pearlman, 'Defence officials kept faults from minister', *Sydney Morning Herald*, 18 June 2009.
25 L. Besser, 'Defence tracking system loses sight of $30m', *Sydney Morning Herald*, 12 April 2010.
26 R. Baker, 'Defence bidders had inside help', *The Age*, 2 September 2010.
27 G. Perret, *A Country Made by War: From the Revolution to Vietnam ~ The Story of America's Rise to Power*, Random House, New York, 1989.
28 M. Small & J.D. Singer, *Resort to Arms: International and Civil Wars, 1816–1980*, Sage, Beverly Hills, 1982, pp. 167 & 176.
29 See B.M. Blechman & S.S. Kaplan, *Force without War: US Armed Forces as a Political Instrument*, Brookings Institution, Washington D.C., 1978.
30 M. Small, *Was War Necessary: National Security and U.S. Entry into War*, Sage, Beverly Hills, 1980, esp p. 304.
31 M.J. Glennon, *Constitutional Diplomacy*, Princeton University Press, New

Jersey, 1991; L. Henkin, *Constitutionalism, Democracy, and Foreign Affairs*, Columbia University Press, New York, 1991. See also the review article of these works: T. Draper, 'Presidential Wars', *New York Review*, 26 September 1991, pp. 64–73.

32 S.S. Malawer, 'Reagan's law and foreign policy 1981–1987: The Reagan corollary of international law', *Harvard International Law Journal*, 29, 1988, p. 85. I am most grateful to John Parker, one of my Graduate Programme in International Law students at the Australian National University, for bringing this article to my attention.

33 Among many sources detailing these categories of international legal criminality, see C. Boggs, *The Crimes of Empire: Rogue Superpower and World Domination*, Pluto, London, 2010.

34 A recent example of this is provided by the May 2011 attempt to kill Anwar Awlaki, an American-born militant suspected of involvement in terrorist plots, utilising a drone attack in Yemen: see D.S. Cloud, 'Extrajudicial executions: US tries to assassinate own citizen in Yemen; US-born cleric was target of Yemen drone attack', *Los Angeles Times*, 7 May 2011.

35 Among the works consulted in this section are J. Chace & C. Carr, *America Invulnerable: The Quest for Absolute Security from 1812 to Star Wars*, Summit, New York, 1988; R. Drinnon, *Facing West: The Metaphysics of Indian Hating and Empire Building*, Schocken Books, New York, 1990; G.P. Hastedt, *American Foreign Policy, Past, Present, Future*, 2nd edn, Prentice Hall, New Jersey, 1991; R. Hofstadter, *The American Political Tradition and the Men who Made It*, Random House, New York, 1989; M.H. Hunt, *Ideology and US Foreign Policy*, Yale University Press, New Haven, 1987; and D.M. Snow, *National Security: Enduring Problems in a Changing Defence Environment*, 2nd edn, St Martin's, New York, 1991.

12 Monumental mistake: Is war the most important thing in Australian history?
Peter Stanley

1 This account of the Henderson Smith family's troubles is taken from my *Digger Smith and Australia's Great War*, Murdoch Books/Pier 9, Sydney, 2011.

2 P. Knightly, *Australia: A Biography of a Nation*, 2000. Note Knightly is here merely reflecting a widespread belief.

3 'Houston to head Gallipoli centenary', *Channel Nine News*, 6 July 2011, <news.ninemsn.com.au/national/8269764/houston-to-head-gallipoli-centenary>, (assessed 22 July 2011); the Barr quote is from 'Anzac travellers gathering to mark a nation's pride', *The Age*, 25 April 2010.

4 M. McKenna, 'Anzac Day: How did it become Australia's national day?', in M. Lake & H. Reynolds, *What's Wrong with Anzac Day?*, UNSW Press, Sydney, 2010, p. 111.

5 M. Lake, 'How children learn about Anzac', in Lake & Reynolds, *What's Wrong with Anzac Day?*, p. 155.

6 Charles Bean, *Anzac to Amiens*, Australian War Memorial, Canberra, 1946, p. 264.

7 Australian Bureau of Statistics, 'Road fatalities and fatality rates',

Year Book Australia 2001, <www.abs.gov.au/AUSSTATS/abs@.nsf/Previousproducts/1301.0>, (accessed 22 July 2011).
8 Department of Transport and Infrastructure, 'Annual road crash casualties and rates from 1925 to 2005', <www.infrastructure.gov.au/roads/safety/publications/2008/1925_05_casulaties.aspx>, (accessed 22 July 2011); G. Long, *The Final Campaigns*, Canberra, Australian War Memorial, 1963, p. 633.
9 W. Vamplew (ed.), *Australians: A Historical Library ~ Historical Statistics*, Fairfax, Syme &Weldon, Sydney, 1987, p. 57.
10 Australian Bureau of Statistics, 'Mortality and morbidity: Suicide, 4102.0 Australian Social Trends, 2000', <www.abs.gov.au/AUSSTATS/abs@.nsf/>, (assessed 22 July 2011).
11 Australian Bureau of Statistics, 'Drug-induced deaths, Australia 1991–2001', <www.abs.gov.au/ausstats/abs@.nsf/mf/3321.0.55.001>, (accessed 22 July 2011).
12 These rounded figures are taken from the Wikipedia entry 'List of disasters in Australia by death toll', <en.wikipedia.org/wiki/List_of_disasters_in_Australia_by_death_toll>, (accessed 22 July 2011). As they include only incidents killing more than ten people, they represent a slight under-counting.
13 The exceptions are the periods when men were conscripted to serve overseas in wartime, in the Militia 1942–1945 and to a limited degree, given the choice of National Servicemen to serve in Australia or deploying to Vietnam, in south-east Asia 1963–1972. All other active service in wartime has been nominally voluntary, although regular Defence Force personnel have no choice over commitment to any given deployment, and as John Connor argues in Chapter 2, volunteers in the Great War also faced various social pressures to do so.
14 McKenna, 'Anzac Day: How did it become Australia's national day?', p. 128
15 B. Webb, 'The legend of the Anzac', *History Essays from the Keyboard of Bradley Kenneth Webb*, <www.ncs.net.au/history/essay_01.html>, (accessed 22 July 2011).
16 This idea, proposed for the Australian War Memorial's Roll of Honour, was abandoned in the 1950s when it became apparent that it was impossible to simply allocate war dead to communities. Many had either no or multiple associations with particular places. In that the same records exist, it remains impossible to associate war dead with particular communities with any reliability.
17 Memorial(s) Development Committee, 'National WWI and WW2 memorial design brochure', <www.mdc.org.au/MDC_Brochure.pdf>, (accessed 22 July 2011).
18 Lake War Memorials Forum, 'Report of 21 October stakeholder workshop', <www.lakewarmemorialsforum.org/docs/War-memorials-workshop-record.html>, (accessed 22 July 2011).
19 C. Badelow to P. Stanley, 11 February 2011, in the possession of the author.
20 Lake War Memorials Forum, 'Opinions we have already received', <www.lakewarmemorialsforum.org/forum.jsp?ShowOpinions>, (accessed 22 July 2011).
21 *Canberra Times*, 1 and 26 March 2011.
22 S. Gower, 'Reflections', *Wartime*, 53, 2011.
23 *How Australia May Commemorate the Anzac Centenary: Report of the Centenary*

of Anzac Commission, Canberra, 2011, p. 69, <www.anzaccentenary.gov.au/subs/2010/reports/anzac_centenary_report.pdf>, (assessed 22 July 2011).
24 P. Kelly, 'The next Anzac century', *The Australian*, 23 April 2011.

Epilogue

1 C.E.W. Bean, *The A.I.F. in France: May 1918–The Armistice*, vol. 7, University of Queensland Press/Australian War Memorial, Brisbane, 1983, p. 1096.

INDEX

1st Australia Corps 61, 145, 147, 150, 153
1 Corps Tactical Zone 187
1st (Anzac) Wireless Signal Squadron 61
1st Australian Division 46–7, 56
1st Australian Field Regiment 67
1st Australian Psychological Operations Unit 194
1st Australian Task Force 186
1st Battalion Royal Canadian 22e Regiment 228–9
1st South African Infantry Brigade 37–40
2nd Australia Corps 147
2/2nd Australian Battalion 131
2/11th Australian Battalion 131
2nd Australian Battalion 57–8
2nd Australian Imperial Force 75–6, 79–80, 82
2nd Battalion, Royal Australian Regiment 67–8
2nd New Zealand Division 61
3 Corps Tactical Zone 187
3rd Australian Battalion 126–8
3rd Australian Division 147
3rd Battalion, Royal Australian Regiment 65–6
4th (Anzac) Battalion 60
5th Australian Battalion 134
5th Australian Division 147, 149
5th Light Horse Brigade 60
6th Australian Division 146–7, 155
6th Battalion, Royal Australian Regiment 67, 189
6th Division, 2nd AIF 79–80, 82

7th Australian Brigade 47–8
7th Australian Division 62, 158–61
8th Australian Brigade 147
8th Battalion, Royal Australian Regiment 207–8
'9/11' attacks, failure to foresee 243–4
9th Australian Division 62, 159–60
10th British (Irish) Division 39–40
10th US Mounted Division 229
11th US Signals Brigade 217
16th British (Irish) Division 40
16th New Zealand Field Artillery Regiment 65
22nd Australian Battalion 121
26th Australian Brigade 160
27th Australian Battalion 125
27th British Commonwealth Infantry Brigade 65
36th British (Ulster) Division 40
42nd Australian Battalion 129–30
46th British (North Midland) Division 48
82nd US Airborne Division 229
161st New Zealand Field Battery 67–8
275th Viet Cong Regiment 189–90

A Military History of Australia 38
Abbott, Tony 114
ABDA Command 62
Aboriginal Australians 13–18, 31
Abrams, General Creighton 199–200
Adam-Smith, Patsy 37, 106
Afghanistan War 7, 136
  atrocities charges 113–14
  Australian involvement 96
  casualties in 226

illegality of 256–7
troops committed to 226–31
US military achievements 248
Age, The 135–6
air combat, atrocities committed in 131–2
Aitape, New Guinea 147–8, 157
AK47 rifle 187, 202–5, 208
Alamein campaign 131, 138
al-Anbar province, Iraq 219–20
al-Asad air base 221
alliances, results of 48–99, 237–9 *see also* New Zealand; United Kingdom; United States
Allied Intelligence Centre, Brisbane 108
al-Muthanna province, Iraq 224–5
Al-Qaeda 248
ambushes, in Vietnam 196–7, 199–200
'Anzac Airlines' 69
'ANZAC area' 62
'Anzac bridge' 70
Anzac Centenary Advisory Board 261
Anzac Centenary Commission 276–7, 284
Anzac Day
  Anglo-Celtic dominance of 100–1
  as national day 286
  broadening scope of 273
  commodification of 275–6
  marches during 291
  national character and 9
  symbolic value of 264
  women and 5
Anzac Force 62
Anzac Frigate project 69
'Anzac' legends 287, 290
Anzac Pact 63
'Anzacs', original *see* Australian and New Zealand Army Corps; Gallipoli landing
Anzacs, The 37
ANZUS alliance 63, 235–59 *see also* New Zealand; United States
Arming America: How the US Buys Weapons 251
armoured personnel carriers 189–90
Army of the Republic of Vietnam 196

artillery use
  by North Korean troops 182–3
  in Vietnam War 189–91
  learning in World War I 47–8
  New Zealand specialises in 65, 67
  women refused permission 108
Ashmead-Bartlett, Ellis 56–7
Asian Alternatives 93
atrocities
  by Australian troops 112–37
  'by proxy' 257
Audit Office report (US) 242
Australia *see also* Anzac Day; Australian military personnel; exceptionalist claims
  centrality of war in history of 260–86
  declares war on Italy 85
  early military activity 11–34
  economic crises in 45–6
  'fair play' in war 112–37
  gender stereotypes in 109
  industrial relations policies 108
  military alliances 73–99, 238–9
  military commitment by 7
  military relations with New Zealand 48–72
  myth of disproportionate strength 210–34
  'national pride' 265
  war in history of 8–9
  wartime economy 109–10
  wartime manpower 143–5
Australia, HMAS 151
Australia Day 138, 264–5
'Australia Remembers' year 264
Australia Station, Royal Navy 28
Australian Administrative Headquarters (UK) 121–3
Australian and New Zealand Army Corps 56, 60
Australian and New Zealand Mounted Division 60
Australian Bureau of Statistics 267, 269
Australian Feminism: A Companion 102
Australian High Commissioner in London 54

Index

Australian Imperial Force
  all-volunteer status not unique 3–4, 35–50
  casualties 265–6
  expanded to five divisions 59
  formation of 29
  in coalition with allies 231
  misbehaviour in Cairo 54–5
Australian Labor Party, defence policies 78
Australian Light Horse Brigade 54
Australian Military Board 78
Australian military personnel *see also* names of units
  as 'special force' 78–9
  assigned to 'mopping-up' campaigns 138–64
  Australian Army Training Team 224
  Australian Flying Corps casualties 61
  brought to war by alliances 238–9
  capabilities of 7–8, 213–14
  casualties 225–6, 272
  colonial troops 11–34
  early army reforms 26–8
  early navy 28–9
  exceptionalist claims 46
  in Vietnam War 196
  killed while POWs 125
  numbers by gender 105–6
  numbers by service arm 170
  Nursing Service 103–5
  withdrawn from New Guinea 142–3
Australian National Audit Office 254
Australian newspaper 87
Australian Special Operations Task Group 227
Australian Strategic Policy Institute 212–13
Australian Victories in France 36–7
Australian War Memorial
  appropriateness of focus 262
  colonial galleries 14
  disregarded by MDA 281
  genealogical information 277
  Henderson Smith letters 260
  naval records 174
  non-military casualties recorded by 272
  on colonial military actions 12
  records of atrocities 121–3
Australian Women's Army Service 107
Automedon 239
Auxiliary Territorial Service (UK) 108
awards *see* decorations and awards

BAE systems 254
Balaclava, Battle of 22
Balikpapan, Borneo 158, 160–3
Ball, Desmond 245
Ballard, John R. 218
Baria, Battle of 188, 190–1
Barr, Chris 261
Barrett, John 27
Barter, Margaret 131
Bartolomeo Colleoni 167
Bassett, Jan 105
'Battle of the Wasser' 55
Bayonet Trench attack 126–8
Bean, Charles
  Naval coverage by 169
  on Anzacs 212, 292
  on atrocities 115–18, 123–6
  on Australia-NZ cooperation 57–8
  on Cairo brawls 55
  on Gallipoli landing 264–5
  on volunteer armies 37–8
Belleau Wood, USN 217
Benson, Sergeant S.E. 140
Berlin Airlift 63
Berryman, Lieutenant General Frank 149–51
Binh Bah, Battle of 134, 189, 191, 195
Birdwood, William 59
Bismarck Sea, Battle of 132–3
Black Week 24
Blainey, Geoffrey 87
Blair, Admiral Dennis 216
Blair, Dale viii, 5
Blamey, General Sir Thomas
  in Pacific campaign 140–8, 161–2
  in World War I 47
  in World War II 61–2
  on Japanese enemy 128
  on New Zealand 62–4
  relations with Chifley 156–8

relations with Curtin 153, 155–6
relations with Menzies 146–7
Boeing 254
Boer War
   Australian involvement 14, 23–7, 86
   Breaker Morant incident 14, 25–6, 114–15
   memorial to proposed 12
   motives for participation 87
Bongiorno, Frank 87
Borneo campaigns
   in Confrontation with Indonesia 92
   in World War II 139
   motives for participation 162
   Operation OBOE One 154–5
   Operation OBOE Two 158–60
Bougainville campaign 129–30, 145–9, 156–7, 161–2
Bourke, Joanna 120
Braund, Lieutenant Colonel G.F. 57–8
Bridges, Major General William 54
Bridging Train, RAN 169–70
British Commonwealth Light Division 65
British Commonwealth Occupation Force in Japan 90
British Empire *see* imperial defence policy; United Kingdom
British Expeditionary Force 119–20
British High Commissioner in Malaya 91
British West Indies Regiment 35
British XXII Corps, New Zealanders transferred to 60
Brooke-Popham, Rupert 240
brown paper, as clothing insulation 182
Bruce, Stanley 78, 82
Brunei Bay, Borneo 154, 160
brutality *see* atrocities
Bryce, Quentin 279
Buick, Bob 136
Buick, Mike 278, 283
Buin, Bougainville 148
Bullwinkel, Vivian 280
Burnett, Captain J. 173
Burstall, Terry 135–6
Bush, George W. 247
'bush craft' 197

Butler, A.G. 106–7

cadet movement 27
Camel Corps 60
Camp David Accord 68–9
Canada 39, 66, 227–30
Canberra, HMAS 167, 175
Canberra Times 152, 280, 283
Cape Corps 41
Caribbean campaigns 41
Casey, R.G. 81
casualties of war
   Boer War 26, 31
   Bougainville campaign 149
   Canadian, in Afghanistan 229
   civilian deaths 266–7, 272–3
   East Timor 215
   frontier wars 18, 31
   importance in history 263, 265–6
   Iraq, by country 225–6
   Korean War 90
   naval collisions 167, 183
   non-military 267–9
   Pacific theatre, World War II 148
   Vietnam War 190–1, 197–8, 207–8
Caulfield, Michael 134–5
Cavell, Edith 104
Centenary of Anzac Commission 276–7, 284
Central Bureau Signals Intelligence 151
Charlton, Peter 140
Chauvel, Major General Harry 60
Chaytor, Major General Edward 60
Chifley, Ben 156–8
Chinese troops 66, 244
Christian Science Monitor 27
Churchill, Winston 81, 239
CIMIC personnel in East Timor 217
civilian casualties 266–7, 272–3
Clark, Chris viii, 4
Clark, Helen 70
claymore mines 196–7
Clinton, Bill 216
close inshore operations 181
Clothier, Sergeant Les 153
Cold War 91–2, 94, 236–7
collective security policy 90

Index

colonial troops 11–34
'coloured' troops 40–2
Commonwealth War Graves Commission Cemetery 272
Communism, perceived threat from 91–2, 94, 236–7
community resistance to conscription 44
Confrontation with Indonesia 92–3, 267
Connor, John viii–ix, 4, 16
conscription 36, 38–9
'contacts' with enemy troops in Vietnam 191–2, 198, 201
convicts, military action against 18
Cooper, Alistair ix, 6
Cosgrove, General Peter 93–4, 211, 214–15
counter revolutionary warfare 192
counter-insurgency 187–8, 192, 196
Crete campaign 131
Cullen, General Paul 128
Curtin, John
    Australia Day broadcast 138
    death of 161
    relations with Blamey 153, 155–6
    relations with MacArthur 141–4, 159
Curtin Labor government 63
Cutler, Roden 280

D445 Vietnamese Local Force Battalion 189–90
Damousi, Joy 109, 263
Dardanelles campaign *see* Gallipoli landing
Darian-Smith, Kate 109
Darwin, civilians killed at 272
Davies, Andrew 253
Day, David 76
Deakin, Alfred 86
Dean, Peter 154
death, causes of 267–8, 271 *see also* casualties of war
Dechaineux, HMAS 211
decorations and awards
    for Bayonet Trench attack 127–8
    for naval service 172

HMAS *Murchison* 172, 178
    Victoria Cross 20
Deeds That Won the Empire 29–30
Defence Contract Audit Agency (US) 253
Defence Department, procurement fraud in 254–5
Defence 'White Papers' 215, 235, 240
Defense Authorization and Appropriation Bills (US) 253
Department of Veterans' Affairs 263, 274, 279
Derrick, Lieutenant Tom 'Diver' 160
Dhi Qar province, Iraq 224–5
Dibb, Paul 245
'digger' myths 2, 275, 288 *see also* Anzac legends
'diggers', New Zealanders as 51
Director of Military Prosecutions 113–14
Dollard, Commander Allen 180–1
'Domino theory' 94
Draper, Theodore 256
dreadnought crisis 28
drug use, casualties due to 270
Duntroon training college 53
'duty' and enlistment 44–5

East African campaign 41–2
East Timor independence campaign 7, 69–70, 213–19
Eden, Anthony 80
Egypt, troop misbehaviour in 54–6
Eire 38–40, 76
el Gorah, Sinai 69
el-Alamein campaign 131, 138
Elands River Post, Battle of 14, 30
Elliott, Brigadier General 'Pompey' 123–4
Emden, sinking of 167
Empire Air Training Scheme 79, 88–9
employers, effect on enlistments 42–3
enlistments 22, 24, 42–4, 79–80
ethical exceptionalism *see* exceptionalist claims
ethnic corps in colonial Australia 23
Europe, compulsory military service in 38

Evans, Air Marshal David 284
Evans, Gareth 210, 236–7
Evatt, H.V. 'Doc' 210
exceptionalist claims
    about Australian troops 2, 5–6, 46, 112–37, 210–34
    about military nurses 106–7
    about US 257
    volunteers vs conscripts 35–6, 42
expeditionary wars 101
extrajudicial assassination 257

F/A-18 aircraft 252
family issues, effect on enlistment 43
Far East Strategic Reserve 91–3
Farrington, Petty Officer Reg 183
Federation, military involvement in 20–1
Field, James 251
Fire Support Bases in Vietnam 188–9
Firth, Dianne 284
Fischer, Tim 280
Fitchett, W.H. 29–30
Foll, Hattil 155
Forde, Frank 63
Forde, Joseph 30
Fox, Ronald 251
France, wars with 21, 36, 131
Frank E Evans, USN 167
Fraser, James 155–6
free trade deal with US 231
Freyberg, Major General Bernard 62
frontier wars, colonial 13–18

Gabriel, Richard 247
Gallipoli landing
    atrocities committed during 115–16
    attitudes to 87–8
    boxes of earth from 71
    Indian volunteers 41
    Irish volunteers 39–40
    military involvement prior to 3
    naval involvement 170
    New Zealand troops 52–3, 56–8
    symbolic value of 9, 261, 264
    tourism following 276
ganygarr (spear fight) 14–15
Gazelle peninsula 149

Gellibrand, Brigadier General John 124
gender of military personnel *see* men; women
General Accounting Office (US) 250
General Dynamics 254
German New Guinea *see* New Guinea campaigns
Germany
    as enemy, attitudes to 24, 131
    captured troops killed by Australians 117–18, 131
    Pacific threat from 88
    treatment of prisoners by 125
    workforce participation by gender 110
Gillard, Julia 237
Glebe Island Bridge 70
Glen, Frank 52
Glenn, John 242
Glennon, Michael J. 256
Gloucester Cup 178
Godley, Major General Sir Alexander 54
Government Accountability Office (US) 250
Gower, Major General Steve 284
Graves, Robert 124
Great Britain *see* United Kingdom
'Great Powers' 38
Greek campaign, World War II 61–2
Greenhalgh, Elizabeth 46, 48
grenade launchers 204, 206–7
Grey, Jeffrey 12, 38, 187
Grimshaw, Pat 109
Gulf War, Australian involvement 267
    see also Iraqi wars

Habibie, B.J. 216
Hackworth, Colonel David 202
Hall, Bob ix, 7
Halligan, Marion 283
Ham, Paul 129, 134
Hamilton, General Ian 28
Hammer, Brigadier Heathcoat 'Tack' 140
Han River, Korea 166, 179–80
Hancock, Eleanor ix, 5

Index

Handcock, Lieutenant Peter 114–15
Harris, Kirsty 104–5, 107
Hasluck, Paul 94–5
Hastings, Max 140
Hawke, Bob 264
Hele, Ivor 128
helicopters 69, 217–18, 230, 254
Henderson, Private Richard ('Dick') 59
Henderson Smith family 260–1
Henkin, Louis 256
Herald Sun 265
heroism, dominated by male exemplars 103
Hindenburg Line campaign 46, 48
History of the Military in Australia and New Zealand 11–12
HMAS... *see* names of ships, e.g. 'Canberra'
Hobbes, Thomas 237
Horner, David 146
Houston, Air Chief Marshal Angus 211, 261
Howard, John 264, 275, 279
Howse, Neville 20
Hughes, William Morris 29
'Hundred Days' offensive 39, 48
Hurley, Lieutenant General David 211
Hyland, Tom 114

imperial defence policy 81–2, 85–7, 290
imperial soldiers in Australia 11–34
Inchon Peninsula, Korea 246
Indian Army 35, 41
Indonesia 92–3, 214, 216–18
infant mortality, numbers of deaths from 268–9
influenza epidemic 266
information gathering 242–3
Inglis, Ken 12, 37
inhumanity *see* atrocities
intelligence 242–3
INTERFET force 214–15, 218
International Monetary Fund 216
International Stabilisation Force 70
Iraqi wars
 atrocities in 136
 Australian involvement 7, 96–7, 219–26
 illegality of 256–7
 US military achievements 247–50
Ireland 38–40, 76
Irving, Colonel Sybil 108
Italy, as enemy 84–5, 131

James, Karl ix, 6
Japan
 air raids on Darwin 17
 atrocities committed against 115
 atrocities committed by 130
 miniature submarine attacks 171
 nurses imprisoned by 103
 perceived threat from 28, 77, 81–2, 89–90
 racial hatred against 128–30
Jeffrey, Michael 279
Jobson, Brigadier General Alexander 124
Joyce, Stephen 178, 182
Joynt, Captain W.D. 117–18

Kaesong, Korea 179
Kandahar province, Afghanistan 228–9
Kapyong Valley, Battle of 65–7
Keating, Paul 73–4, 264
Keegan, John 117–18
Kelly, Paul 13, 286
Kelson, Brendon 284
Kennedy, Paul 177
King, Admiral 158
King, Ernest 154
King, Jonathan 37
King's African Rifles 35, 41
Kipling, Rudyard 25
Kirk, Richard 279
Kirkpatrick, John Simpson 59
Knightley, Philip 266
Kokoda Trail, Keating speech 73–4
Korean War
 as last US victory 246
 atrocities in 133
 Australian involvement 90–1, 267
 civilian deaths 267
 naval operations 166, 179–80
 New Zealand troops in 65–7
Kormoran 173

KPMG 255

Labuan Island, Borneo 160
Lake, Marilyn 74, 100, 109, 263, 273
Lake Burley Griffin, proposed memorials by 9, 262–3, 278–85
Lake War Memorials Forum 280–4
'landmark' battles 186–209
'lawful orders' 120
Layton, Peter 253
Leahy, Lieutenant General Peter 211
Leopard tanks 229–30
Leviathan 237
Leyte Gulf, Battle of 151
Libyan no-fly zone 228
Lindbergh, Charles 128
Lingayen Gulf, Battle of 151
Liverpool mutiny 28
Lockheed Martin 254
Lone Hand magazine 30
Long, Gavin 108–9, 146, 152–3
Long Dien, Battle of 188–9, 191
Long Phuoc village, Vietnam 193
Long Tan, Battle of 13, 67–8, 188, 193, 195
Loveday, Lieutenant 127
Lowe, Nathaniel 18

M16 land mine 207
M16 rifle 187, 202–5
M60 machine gun 205–6
M72 light anti-armour weapon 206–7
MacArthur, General Douglas
  Borneo plans 158–9
  Curtin and 141
  on British abandonment of the Pacific 239
  on the Mandated Territories 157–8
  Pacific campaigns 154–5
  Pacific strategy 139, 145, 149–50, 152
  role in directing Australian troops 162
Macarthur, John 21
Macksey, Piers 168
Mai Lai atrocity 134
Main Supply Route Tampa 224
Malawer, Stuart 256

Malayan Emergency 91–2, 267
Malone, Lieutenant Colonel W.G. 57–8
Mandated Territories *see* Bougainville campaign; New Britain campaign; New Guinea campaigns; Solomon Islands campaign
Mansfield, Grant 87
Manual of Military Law 119
Maori soldiers 68
marksmanship 197–8
Marshall, General George 154
Matthews, Sergeant A.E. 127–8
Mattis, General James 226
McDade, Brigadier Lyn 113–14
McKenna, Mark 263–4
McKernan, Michael 284
McKinley, Michael x, 8
McNeill, Ian 193
McQuilton, John 44
Meaker, Private 126–8
Medical Association for the Prevention of War 279–80
Mediterranean garrisons 64–5
Melbourne, HMAS 167, 173
Memorials Development Committee 278–82
men, predominance of in active service 105–6
Menzies, Robert
  brothers enlist in World War I 43
  declares war on Nazi Germany 76
  plans for Australian troops 81–2
  raises expeditionary force 78–9
  relations with Blamey 146–7
  relations with UK War Office 85
  sends troops to Vietnam 94
Merz, Lieutenant George 60–1
Mesopotamia campaign 41, 60–1
Messines, Battle for 40
Middle East theatre, World War I 60
Middle East theatre, World War II 75–6, 84
migration, effect on social history 32–3, 262
Military History of Australia 12
military nurses 102–8
militias

Index

in colonial Australia 27–9
in East Timor 219
in Vietnam War 200–1
in World War II 145
troops recruited from 79
Milne Bay, Battle of 130
mines, in Vietnam War 133–4, 196–7, 207
Minh Dam Secret Zone 207
'mini-Tet' battles 195
'missing in action' records 273
Mobile Bay, USN 217
modes of operation on board vessel 177
Molan, Major General Jim 230
Monaghan, Brigadier R.F. 129–30
Monash, General Sir John 4–5, 36–7
Moore, Captain F.L. 117
Moore-Jones, Horace 59
moral exceptionalism *see* exceptionalist claims
Morant, Lieutenant Harry 'Breaker' 14, 25–6, 114–15
Mordike, John 86
Morlancourt, Battle of 47–8
Morotai, Halmahera 155
mortar fire *see* artillery
motor vehicle accidents, deaths due to 268, 271
mounted troops in colonial Australia 23
Muir, Marnie Haig 45
Mulvaney, John 283
munitions work, women in 109
Murchison, HMAS 166, 172, 175–84
Mussolini, Benito *see* Italy, as enemy

Napoleonic Wars 21
National Archives of Australia 173–4
National Capital Authority 278–9, 281
National Capital Memorials Committee 278–9
National Constituent Assembly, Vietnam 193–4
national interest 74–6, 236
National Referendum Council 44
'native troops', volunteer status 40–2
naval history 28–9, 165–85 *see also* Royal Australian Navy; Royal Navy

naval volunteer brigades 22
Netherlands East Indies campaign 150, 154–5
New Britain campaign
5th Australian Division in 147, 149
correct approach to 162
'mopping-up' operations 139
troop numbers in reduced 157
New Guinea campaigns
Australian troops in 146–7, 157
conditions in 138
in World War I 29, 88
'mopping-up' operations 142–3, 152–3, 161–2
servicewomen sent to 107
New Guinea Infantry Battalion 157
New South Wales, enlistments from 79–80
New Zealand 48–72, 242 *see also* Anzac legend; New Zealand military personnel
New Zealand and Australian Division 56
New Zealand military personnel
attitude to Australians 4
attitude to prisoners 115–16
colonial troops from 31–2
conscription for 39
expeditionary force 54, 59, 83
in World War II 79
misbehaviour in Cairo 54–5
Staff Corps 61
New Zealand War Memorial 70–1
Newfoundland, conscription in 39
Nguyen Van Thieu 195
Nigeria Regiment 41
Nixon, Richard 195
No. 1 Dominion Squadron 64
No. 2 Dominion Squadron 64
No. 14 NZAF Squadron 64–5
No. 78 RAAF Fighter Wing 64–5
'no quarter' policy 118
nocturnal superiority in Vietnam 198
North Korean troops 90, 133, 182–3
Northrop Grumman 254
nuclear-equipped warships 69
Nui Dat, Vietnam 135
Nui Le, Battle of 189, 195

nurses, military 102–8

O'Neill, Robert 245
Operation Anaconda 226
Operation Bribie 188
Operation Catalyst 219, 223–6
Operation Desert Storm 247–8
Operation Enduring Freedom 247–8
Operation Falconer 219
Operation Iraqi Freedom 247–8
Operation OBOE One 154–5, 160
Operation OBOE Two 158–60
Operation Slipper 227
Orme, Brigadier Craig 211
Osborne, Trooper Ossie 153
Other People's Wars 73
Overwatch Battle Group – West 224
Oxford Companion to Australian Military History 38

Pacific theatre, World War II 6, 89–90, 138–64
Page, Geoff 284
Pakistan, involvement in Afghanistan War 248
Palazzo, Albert x, 7
Palestine campaigns 41
Panama invasion 256–7
Papua New Guinea *see* New Guinea campaigns
Papuan Infantry Battalion 157
Passchendaele, prisoners killed at 117–18
Paterson, Banjo 25
patriotic funds 22, 24
patrol contacts in Vietnam 191–2, 198, 201
Peleliu, USN 217
Pemberton, Gregory 96
Penang, Malaya 91
People's Army of Vietnam/Viet Cong 186, 192, 195–6 *see also* Vietnam War
Perak, Malaya 91
Perret, Geoffrey 255
Perth, HMAS 167, 172–3, 175
Petraeus, General David 230
Philippines campaign, World War II 145, 149–50

Phoney War 84
Phouc Tuy province, Vietnam 7
  atrocities in 135
  Australian troops in 187–8
  patrol contacts 198, 201
  warfare in 194–6
Pilger, John 73
Pinios Gorge, Battle of 61
politicians, reasons for going to war 75
Pooley, Grace Hendy 11–12, 15, 31–2
'populist' case 245
Power of Power Politics, The 238
Pozieres, Battle of 116, 123, 265
'pride' 265
prisoners
  killing of 112, 117–18, 120–1, 131
  rules for treatment of 120
  taken at Bayonet Trench 127
  wounded, treatment of 135–6
procurement fraud 251
Project for Government Oversight 254
Province Reconnaissance Units 200
Provincial Reconstruction Team 227
Pryor, Geoff 284
psychological warfare 194–5
'punching above her weight' myth *see* exceptionalist claims

Queen Alexandra's Imperial Military Nursing Service 108
Queensland, enlistments from 80

Rabaul, New Britain 88, 139 *see also* New Britain campaign
Rae, Ruth 104–5
Raytheon 254
Reagan administration (US) 256
'redcoats' 11–34
Reeve, John 174
Renouf, Alan 95–6
repatriation effort 274
Report on Allied Contributions to the Common Defence 213
Reveille 124
Revolutionary Development Cadre 200
Reynolds, Henry 18, 74, 263
Rhodesia 24
rifle clubs 22, 24, 31

Index

Roberts, Lieutenant Commander W.O.C. 176
Robertson, John 87
Roll of Honour 266–7, 281
Rorke's Drift, Battle of 22
Rosenau, James 242
Ross, Andrew x, 7
Rotary Wing Aviation Unit 69
Rowel, Coxswain Warwick 180–1
Royal Australian Air Force
　archive records 173–4
　atrocities committed by 131–2
　Borneo campaigns 159–60
　commitment to Iraqi War 223
　in Berlin Airlift 64
　in Vietnam War 189
　in World War II 138, 151
　Mediterranean garrisons 64–5
　number of personnel 170
　Pacific campaigns 155
　security system scrapped 254
Royal Australian Navy
　atrocities committed by 132–3
　cap on personnel 144
　first ships 29
　history of neglected 6–7, 165–85
　in Iraqi wars 223
　in World War II 138, 151, 159–60
　placed at disposal of RN 89
Royal Navy
　Australian involvement with 28–30, 77
　Pacific fleet 144
　role in colonial society 20
　transports troops from Australia 54
Royal Newfoundland Regiment 39
RPD light machine gun 205
RPG7 grenade launcher 206
Rudd, Kevin 271, 279
Russell's Top, Gallipoli 57–8
Ryan, Alan 218

Salmon, Lieutenant Colin 148
Savige, Lieutenant General Stan 156
Selective Service Act (US) 38
Self Loading Rifles 203, 205
Shedden, Frederick 151, 158
Sheffield, Gary 47

Shelton, General Henry 216
Sherick, Joseph 251
Singapore Strategy 77, 83, 239
SKS Carbine 204
Small, Melvin 256
social media, effect on atrocities 136
Soldier's Don'ts of International Law 120
Solomon Islands campaign 139, 147, 152–3
Somme, Battle of 40
South Africa 35, 37–41 *see also* Boer War
South Seas Regional Commission 63
South Vietnam *see* Vietnam War
South West Pacific Area 142
Special Air Service troops 221
Special Forces troops 219–20, 226, 232
'Special Sea Dutymen' 180
Spender, Percy 108–9
Squires, Lieutenant General E.K. 81, 84
St James's Church, Sydney, memorial plaques 18
St Quentin Canal 48
Stanley, Peter xi, 8–9
Stateline 281
Stephenson, Rob 46–7
stereotyping 288–9
Stockings, Craig xi, 5
Strategic Insights paper 212–13
Street, Geoffrey 79, 83
Sudan War 14, 23, 85
suicide, casualties due to 269
Sukarno, President of Indonesia 92–3
Summers, Colonel Harry 195
Sunday Age 114
Super Seasprite helicopters 254
surrender, killing after *see* prisoners
Sutherland, Lieutenant General Richard 150
Sydney (I), HMAS 167
Sydney (II), HMAS 167, 172, 175
Sydney, NSW 20, 171
Sydney Institute 214
Sydney Morning Herald 152

Taliban 248

tanks, in Afghanistan 229–30
Tarakan Island, Borneo 158, 160
technological change 47–8, 241, 250
termination liability cost 252–3
Tet Offensive 188, 192
Thailand 91
The Age 135–6
The Anzacs 37
The Australian Victories in France 36–7
The Oxford Companion to Australian Military History 38
The Power of Power Politics 238
The Vietnam Years 134–5
The Western Front Diaries 37
Thomas, Dylan 258
Thomson, Mark 212–13
Tientsin Crisis 77
To Long Tan 193
Tobruk campaign 131, 138, 268
Torokina, Bougainville 148
Trafalgar, Battle of 20–1
Trembath, Richard 133
trench warfare 125–6
'Tribal' class destroyers 176
Truth 30
Tu, Colonel 195

United Kingdom *see also* imperial defence policy; Royal Navy
  casualties in Iraq 225
  colonial troops from 18–19
  conscription in 38–9
  Hague Rules adopted by 119
  invasion of Australia by 16
  military alliances with 73–99, 239–40
  personnel committed to Iraqi War 222
  women's military units 108–9
United Nations 68–9, 90, 214
United States
  atrocities committed by 128–9
  attitude to Australian military aid 232–3
  Australian alliance with 8, 67, 235–59
  conscription in 38
  contribution to East Timor 215–17

Defense acquisition process 250–2
failure of intelligence services 243–4
  in Afghanistan war 248
  in Iraqi wars 219–26, 247–50
  in Korean War 90
  in Vietnam War 187, 196, 199–200
  in World War II 141–2
influence on Australian military policy 95–7
Mai Lai atrocity 134
military alliances with 73–99
military record of 246
Philippines campaign 149–50
proneness to war 255–6
Report on Allied Contributions to the Common Defence 213
servicewomen in military operations 108
'Tacoma' class frigates 179
uranium weapons 249
Uruzgan Province, Afghanistan 227, 229
USN... *see* names of ships, e.g. 'Belleau Wood'

Vasquez, John 238
Victoria colony, frontier wars in 17
Victoria Cross *see* decorations and awards
Vietnam, invasion by China 244
Vietnam War *see also* Phouc Tuy province, Vietnam
  atrocities in 133–6
  Australian involvement in 7, 67–8, 93–6
  Australians portrayed as victims of 13
  Battle of Long Tan 13, 67–8, 188, 193, 195
  'landmark' battles 186–209
  New Zealand troops in 67–8
Vietnam Years, The 134–5
Vo Nguyen Giap, General 192
volunteer armies *see also* militias
  colonial corps 14, 22–4
  in World War I 3–4, 35–50
  in World War II 79–80
von Clausewitz, Carl 98

Index

von Lettow-Vorbeck, General Paul 41–2
Voyager, HMAS 167, 173

Wady Fara attack 132
Walker, Harold 46–7
Walter Burley Griffin Society 279–80
war, as central to history 8–9, 260–86
war census cards 44
war crimes *see* atrocities
war memorials 9 *see also* Australian War Memorial
   by Lake Burley Griffin, proposed 262–3, 278–85
   for marginalised groups 100–10
   in London 275
   New Zealand War Memorial 70–1
War on Terror 258
wars of choice 74
Waterloo, Battle of 20–1, 30–1
Watson, James 30
weapons of mass destruction, failure to find 97, 221
weather, impact on naval operations 181–2
Weger, Private 126–8
Wellington, Duke of, places named after 20
Wellington Battalion 57–8
Wentworth, William Charles 21
West Australian 45
Western Front, artillery use 47–8
Western Front Diaries 37
Westmoreland, General William 200
Wewak campaign 148, 157
What's Wrong with Anzac? 74, 263

Whirlpool, Frederick 20
Whiskard, Geoffrey 80, 83
White, General C.B.B. 84
white feathers 45
Wilcox, Craig xi, 3, 114
Windschuttle, Keith 12
Wiradjuri tribe 16–17
Wiranto, General 216
women, in military history 5, 100–11, 169
Women's Auxiliary Air Force (UK) 108
Women's Auxiliary Australian Air Force 107–9
Woodard, Garry 93
Wooragee community 44
workforce participation by gender 109–10
'work-up' process for deployment 178
World Trade Center attacks, failure to foresee 243–4
World War I *see also* Gallipoli landing
   atrocities by Australian troops 115–18
   Australian involvement in 87, 290–1
   military nurses 104
   RAN size during 170
   volunteer armies 35–50
World War II 6, 89–90, 106, 138–64, 170

Yolngu People of Arnhem Land 14–15
York, Duke of 36
Yorke, Sergeant 127–8

Zombie Myths of Australian Military History 1, 46, 101

www.ingramcontent.com/pod-product-compliance
Lightning Source LLC
Chambersburg PA
CBHW031722230426
43669CB00007B/209